Digital Historical Research on Southeast Europe and the Ottoman Space

**Studies on Language and Culture
in Central and Eastern Europe**

Edited by
Christian Voß

Volume 35

Dino Mujadžević (ed.)

Digital Historical Research on Southeast Europe and the Ottoman Space

PETER LANG

Bibliographic Information published by the Deutsche Nationalbibliothek
The Deutsche Nationalbibliothek lists this publication in the Deutsche Nationalbibliografie; detailed bibliographic data is available online at http://dnb.d-nb.de.

Library of Congress Cataloging-in-Publication Data
A CIP catalog record for this book has been applied for at the Library of Congress.

This publication was enabled by funding from the
A. v. Humboldt Foundation.

ISSN 1868-2936
ISBN 978-3-631-82511-2 (Print) · E-ISBN 978-3-631-82615-7 (E-PDF)
E-ISBN 978-3-631-82616-4 (EPUB) · E-ISBN 978-3-631-82617-1 (MOBI)
DOI 10.3726/b17129

© Peter Lang GmbH
Internationaler Verlag der Wissenschaften
Berlin 2021
All rights reserved.

Peter Lang – Berlin · Bern · Bruxelles · New York · Oxford · Warszawa · Wien

All parts of this publication are protected by copyright. Any utilisation outside the strict limits of the copyright law, without the permission of the publisher, is forbidden and liable to prosecution. This applies in particular to reproductions, translations, microfilming, and storage and processing in electronic retrieval systems.

This publication has been peer reviewed.

www.peterlang.com

Table of Contents

Dino Mujadžević
Preface ... 7

Dino Mujadžević
Introduction ... 9

Historical GIS

Sotirios Dimitriadis
Mapping the Nineteenth-Century Mediterranean
Port-City: The Quay of Salonica, 1870-1911 ... 25

Elma Korić
Visualization of Ottoman Borderland in Early Modern Bosnia
(Mid-15th – Late 16th Centuries): The Ottoman *Serhat* in Bosnia and GIS ... 47

Michael Połczyński
Sovereignty and Space through GIS in the Early Modern
Polish-Lithuanian/Ottoman Frontier ... 57

Textual Analysis

Dino Mujadžević
Representations of Turkey in Bosnian Mainstream Printed
Media (2003-2014): A Corpus-Assisted Critical Discourse Analysis ... 81

Lisa Maria Teichmann / Franz-Benjamin Mocnik
A Literary Atlas of Turkey ... 113

Table of Contents

Computer-Assisted Quantitative Approaches

Siegfried Gruber
The Patriarchy Index: A Comparative Study of Power
Relations Within Southeastern Europe and Turkey — 141

Murat Güvenç and M. Erdem Kabadayı
Reading and Mapping Mid-Nineteenth Century Ottoman
Tax Registers: An Early Attempt Toward Building a Digital
Research Infrastructure for Ottoman Economic and Social History — 167

Other Approaches

Bülent Arıkan
Archaeological Perspectives for Climate Change and Human
Impacts on Environment: An Agent-Based Modeling Approach — 203

Pınar Duygulu and Damla Arifoğlu
A Keyword Search System for Historical Ottoman Documents — 211

Notes on the Contributors — 225

Preface

The papers published within this edited volume were prepared for the workshop a *Data-Driven Research in the History of Southeast Europe and Turkey* which was organized at the Center for the Mediterranean Studies of the Ruhr University Bochum in Bochum on 25-26 June 2015. The event was funded by the Alexander von Humboldt Foundation. I would like to extend my deepest gratitude to the Humboldt Foundation as well as to the Center for Mediterranean Studies and the Chair for the History of the Ottoman Empire and the Republic of Turkey at the Ruhr University Bochum, especially Prof. Markus Koller, Dr. Nedim Zahirović and Victoria Junkernheinrich.

In addition to the papers contributed by the participants, I attempted to give a general introduction to the field of digital historical studies of Southeast Europe and the Ottoman Empire, accompanied with examples from literature and projects, but I also tried to give an outline of the general developments and trends in the wider field.

The publication of this edited volume would not have been possible without the kind help of Prof. Christian Voß (Humboldt University), the editor of the series *Studies on Language and Culture in Central and Eastern Europe* (Peter Lang), who finally provided me with opportunity and encouragement to finish and publish this long-overdue project within his series. The research stay at the Institute for Slavic and Hungarian Studies at the Humboldt University in Berlin in 2019-2010, sponsored by the Humboldt Foundation, enabled me with necessary networking and impetus to finalize the edited volume. Also, many thanks to Megan Nagel for proofreading and formatting as well as to Dr. Ivana Crljenko for the help with tables.

Dino Mujadžević

Introduction

Dino Mujadžević

Digital Humanities and Digital Historical Research: General Developments

Rapidly emerging fields in the digital humanities, including prominently digital history, have profited significantly from new computing tools developed in recent decades in the context of the Information and Communication Technology (ICT) boom. Among the most interesting recent developments in computational data analysis and visualization in these fields are the following: the emergence of large, readily available "cultural data sets" (i.e., huge corpora of digitalized texts in media archives), innovative text-mining analysis software (e.g., topic modeling and keyword- and relation-extraction tools), and breakthroughs in computer graphics (e.g., interactive 3-D dynamic imagery and visualizations of complex systems and spatial data). The application of these methods in historical research is usually called digital – sometimes even data-driven – history or historical research. When they are applicable, digital historical research methods provide much more extensive empirical backing than more traditional methods, sometimes supporting inductive conclusions, and many intuitive ways of presenting results. Consequently, digital history and related fields have begun to take root in major international research.

Digital historical research emerged as an important part of the digital humanities movement which was known in the 20th century usually under the umbrella term humanities computing. This movement adopted the name under which it is currently known, digital humanities, in the early 2000s. A widely influential book, *A Companion to Digital Humanities*, appeared in 2004 influencing the adoption of digital humanities as a new umbrella term. During the early phase between the 1960s to the 1990s, various disciplines as diverse as history, electronic literature, library and archival science, media studies, and cultural studies contributed to this nascent area of scholarship.[1] Can digital humanities be defined?[2] The University College of London Centre for Digital Humanities approaches digital humanities "as the application of computational or digital methods to humanities research or, to put it another way, the application of humanities

---

[1] James Smithies, *The Digital Humanities and the Digital Modern* (London: Palgrave MacMillan, 2017), 20-21.
[2] For the theory of digital humanities see David M. Berry, *Understanding Digital Humanities*, (London: Palgrave Macmillan 2012); Matthew K. Gold, ed., *Debates in the Digital Humanities* (Minneapolis: University of Minnesota Press, 2012); James Smithies, *The Digital Humanities and the Digital Modern* (London: Palgrave MacMillan, 2017).

methods to research into digital objects or phenomena."[3] According to a useful definition found in the influential *A New Companion to Digital Humanities* "doing digital humanities involves the creation of an academic workspace where scholarly methods assume the form of computer-based techniques that can be used to create, analyze, and disseminate research and pedagogy."[4] Nevertheless, the status of digital humanities as a separate discipline ("discipline in its own right") is debated even today. For example, Jeffrey Schnapps and Todd Presner claim that digital humanities are not a single, unified field, but "an array of convergent practices." Despite this debate exceptional vibrancy and growth of research in digital humanities and neighboring fields have been noted.[5]

Over the course of years, methods ascribed to digital humanities have been standardized. According to the Taxonomy of Digital Research Activities in the Humanities, accepted by DARIAH-DE, the German arm of the European Research Infrastructure initiative DARIAH (Digital Research Infrastructure for the Arts and Humanities), following methods and their categories are used for digital research activities in humanities:[6]

Capture
conversion
data recognition
discovering
gathering imaging
recording
transcription

Creation
designing
programming web
development
writing

Enrichment
annotating
cleanup
editing

Analysis
content analysis
network analysis
relational analysis
spatial analysis
structural analysis
stylistic analysis
visualization

Interpretation
contextualizing
modeling
theorizing

Storage
archiving
identifying
organizing
preservation

Dissemination
collaboration
commenting
communicating
crowdsourcing
publishing
sharing

---

[3] Claire Warwick, Melissa Terras and Julianne Nyhan, eds., *Digital Humanities in Practice* (London: Facet Publishing, 2012), XIV-XV.
[4] Lorna Hughes, Panos Constantinopoulos, and Costis Dallas, "Digital Methods in the Humanities: Understanding and Describing Their Use Across the Disciplines," in eds. Susan Schreibman, Ray Siemens, and John Unsworth, *A New Companion to Digital Humanities* (Oxford: Wiley Blackwell, 2016), 152.
[5] Susan Schreibman, Ray Siemens, and John Unsworth, eds., *A New Companion to Digital Humanities* (Oxford: Wiley Blackwell, 2016), XVII.
[6] Hughes, Constantinopoulos and Dallas, "Digital Methods in the Humanities," 157.

As can be seen, particular methods of research activities in digital humanities include not only analysis and interpretation of data, and dissemination of scholarly results, which can be seen as most related to the work that digital historians do but also comprise activities that are focused on the digitalization of primary sources (capture, enrichment) that are associated with other disciplines (archival studies, linguistics, archaeology). The latter are, nevertheless, indispensable for historical research and sometimes also done by digital historians. For example, historians may be involved in the creation and annotation of corpora of naturally occurring language or digitally scanning, editing, and publishing of archival documents or newspapers that can be used in historical research.

The development of digital humanities is now more than seventy years old. In the early period of the collaboration between humanities and computing the field was focused on quantitative analysis and the modeling of data. The influential work of Jesuit scholar Roberto Busa (1913-2011) and English professor Josephine Miles is often seen as the starting point of computer-assisted research in the humanities. In 1949, they initiated their major work on a lemmatized concordance of the works of Thomas of Aquinas, widely known as *Index Thomisticus*, which was realized in the next thirty years with the help of the giant of computer technology, the IBM company.[7] An important moment in the development of digital humanities as a discipline took place in 1962 when an international conference on the use of computation in anthropology took place in the Austrian town of Burg Wartenstein.

Since the 1960s, much of the humanities computing focused on the implementation of computational research in literary criticism and linguistics, but history also quickly included digital research methods into its own *repertoire*. The first computer-assisted historical research appeared already in 1963.[8] It was primarily used by historians who were involved in cross-disciplinary historical social science. The economic and social history in the USA in the 1960s and 1970s became the most important propagator of computer-assisted analysis which was used for the purpose of quantitative analysis, but these approaches lost ground in the 1980s when more culturally oriented history became dominant. Similarly, in the 1960s and the 1970s, computer-

---

[7] Roberto Busa, "The Annals of Humanities Computing: The Index Thomisticus," *Computers and the Humanities* 14, no. 2 (1980) 83-90; *Digital Humanities Quarterly* 3, no. 3 (2009).
[8] For the development of the use of computers in historical research in 1960 see Robert P. Swierenga, "Clio and Computers: A Survey of Computerised Research in History," *Computers and the Humanities,* 5, no. 1 (1970): 1-21; Emmanuel Le Roy Ladurie, "L'historien et l'ordinateur", in Emmanuel Le Roy Ladurie, *Le territoire de l'historien* (Paris: Gallimard, 1973).

assisted demographic research flourished as a sub-discipline in Western Europe. The interest for computational tools among European historians led to the establishment of the London-based Association for History and Computing (AHC) in 1985.[9]

Further transformation of digital historical research occurred with the arrival of the personal computer in the mid-1980s and WWW at the beginning of the 1990s. Due to these changes, according to Gerben Zaagsma, the work in the field of computer-assisted history and related disciplines "has focused on the construction and use of historical databases and the creation of text-based digital editions."[10] As a result of this, in the next decades the European and Northern American libraries, archives, museums, and universities came into the possession of large collections of digital content. The rise of research in digital humanities and digital historical research to greater visibility, even prominence, after 2000 was driven by the availability and the increase in the size of these collections of sources for the study of history, linguistics, classics, musicology, and related disciplines. The ease of access to digital primary sources led to greater acceptance of the digital scholarship.

The fast development of ICT in the last several decades had an enormous impact on history and related humanities and social sciences disciplines. Besides providing scholars with a much faster and/or interactive way to write, communicate, disseminate their results, teach (e-learning), collect and protect sources (online digital collections) and publish their work (e-publishing), the application of new computational methods also enhanced the empirical and visual-representational side of their research. Increasingly better quantitative analysis (data/text mining, statistics, information retrieval, etc.) of a large amount of data and much more refined techniques of data visualizations have since the 1990s become popular with historians as well as other humanists and social scientists in the framework of rapidly emerging interdisciplinary fields of digital research. As previously said, the probably most interesting developments concerning computational data analysis and visualization in these fields are the creation of the so-called large cultural data sets (i.e., huge corpora of digitalized texts) and innovations in computer graphics (i.e., interactive 3-D dynamic imagery and visualizations).[11] The appearance of Web 2.0 technologies

---

[9] Gerben Zaagsma, "On digital history," *Low Countries Historical Review* 128, no. 4 (2013): 7-9.
[10] Ibid., 11.
[11] For the influence of fast technological developments on digital humanities and digital history in recent several years see Kiran Klaus Patel, "Zeitgeschichte im digitalen Zeitalter. Neue und alte Herausforderungen," *Vierteljahrshefte für Zeitgeschichte* 59, no. 3 (2011): 331-351; Hughes, Constantinopoulos and Dallas, "Digital Methods in the Humanities," 150-151; Joachim Scharloth, David Eugster, Noah Bubenhofer, "Das Wuchern der Rhizome. Linguistische Diskursanalyse und Data-driven Turn," in Dietrich Busse and Wolfgang Teubert, eds. *Linguistische Diskursanalyse. Neue*

(social networking sites and media sites, blogs, wikis, video sharing sites, etc.) in the same period also heavily impacted the way the results of historical research are disseminated and discussed in the online environment.

Some authors even claim that readily available and unprecedently large data/textual collections (e.g. Google books, digitalized media archives, on-line social networks or the internet itself) and numerous powerful interactive data visualization and exploration software tools paved a way for the next revolution in humanities and social sciences, sometimes called the digital turn or even data-driven turn. According to Scharloth, Eugster and Bubenhofer, the main feature of the data-driven approach and the difference to previous computer-assisted ("data-based") research methods is that it provides excellent empirical assistance to the research and possibly enables completely inductive conclusions ("große Datenmengen nicht nur zu befragen, sondern induktiv Strukturen in den Daten zu entdecken"). When applicable, the data-driven historical research methods and tools provide much more exhaustive factual and verifiable backing for the research and much more accessible and intuitive ways of presenting its results.[12]

The shift in the position of digital humanities was especially visible after 2006 when the United States National Endowment for the Humanities (NEH) established the Office of Digital Humanities (ODH) and began directing funding towards digital projects.[13] In the EU the European Commission's eInfrastructures program led to the emergence of digital infrastructures such as DARIAH, Common Language Resources and Technology Infrastructure (CLARIN), and European Holocaust Research Infrastructure (EHRI).[14] In 2013 a digital history working group was created within the German *Historikerverband* making it, according to Zaagma, the first national professional organization of historians to give digital history an organizational expression.[15]

Several approaches used in digital historical research and relevant neighboring disciplines have come to the foreground of this type of historical study and attracted great numbers of practitioners: GIS (Geographical Information Systems) and various approaches to text mining/text analysis. Basically, GIS, which was released commercially in 1981, is a powerful

---

Perspektiven (Wiesbaden: Springer, 2013), 345–380, http://www.scharloth.com/files/Rhizom_Zeit.pdf (accessed January 4, 2020).
[12] Scharloth, Eugster and Bubenhofer, „Das Wuchern der Rhizome," 345–380.
[13] James Smithies, *The Digital Humanities and the Digital Modern* (London: Palgrave MacMillan, 2017), 20-21.
[14] Hughes, Constantinopoulos and Dallas, "Digital Methods in the Humanities," 152.
[15] Zaagsma, "On digital history," 5.

software that uses location to enable researchers to visualize quantitative data and other sets of information on a map-like surface. Changes in time that are related to the stored geospatial data can be also tracked and visualized. Researchers "can discover relationships that make a complex world more immediately understandable by visually detecting spatial patterns that remain hidden in texts and tables."[16] After establishing itself firmly in archaeology in the 1990s,[17] GIS has seen a considerable rise in popularity since the early 2000s in various historical sub-disciplines, particularly in historical geography and economic and social history but it seems that this approach has much more possibility to spread among historians. The rising interest in the "spatial turn" in more qualitatively oriented sub-disciplines of history and other related humanities which are increasingly dealing with a rediscovery of geographical space in an interdisciplinary fashion presents an opportunity for the spreading of the use of GIS.[18] Ancient history and histories of other periods that do not dispose of a great number of written sources and rely more on archaeological records seem to be especially open to the use of GIS.

Alongside GIS, another major approach, or set of related approaches, in digital historical research is computer-assisted textual analysis. This type of computational analysis was first adopted in linguistics, especially lexicography and language teaching, and literary studies, and later also became associated with historical research. The most important research paradigm associated with computer-assisted textual analysis is corpus-assisted studies which are based on the investigation of electronically encoded texts or collections of naturally occurring language or, in other words, real language use. Computer tools enabled the analysis of relative or absolute frequencies, most important collocations of search words, and their concordances. Corpus linguistics should be seen as a methodology for linguistic or related research rather than some sort of distinct theoretical

---

[16] Alexander von Lünen and Charles Travis, eds., *History and GIS. Epistemologies. Considerations and Reflections* (Dordrecht, Heidelberg, New York, London; Springer, 2013), 3-4.
[17] K.M.S. Allen, S.W. Green, and E.B.W. Zubrow, "Interpreting space," in eds. K.M.S. Allen, S.W. Green, and E.B.W. Zubrow, *Interpreting space. GIS and archaeology* (London: CRC Press, 1998), 383–386; V. Gaffney – P. M. van Leusen, "Postscript—GIS, Environmental Determinism and Archaeology," in eds. G. R. Lock and Z. Stančič *Archaeology and Geographical Information Systems* (London: Taylor and Francis, 1995), 367–382.
[18] von Lünen and Travis, *History and GIS*, V-VI. For the uses of GIS in historiography, see T. Ott, and F. Swiaczny, *Time-integrative GIS. Management and analysis of spatio-temporal data* (Berlin, Heidelberg, New York: Springer 2001); Anne Kelly Knowles, ed., *Past Time, Past Place: GIS for History* (Redlands: ESRI Press, 2002); Ian N. Gregory, *A Place in History: a Guide to using GIS in Historical Research* (Oxford: The Arts and Humanities Data Service/Oxbow Books, 2003); Ian N. Gregory and Richard G. Healey, "Historical GIS: Structuring, Mapping and Analyzing Geographies of the Past," *Progress in Human Geography* 31, no. 5 (2007), 638-653; Ian N. Gregory – P. S. Ell, *Historical GIS. Technologies, Methodologies and Scholarship* (Cambridge: Cambridge University Press 2007); Anne Kelly Knowles and Amy Hillier, *Placing History: How Maps, Spatial Data and GIS are Changing Historical Scholarship* (Redlands: ESRI Press, 2008).

paradigm.[19] As the large collections of digitized historical sources became available in recent years (books, newspapers, documents etc.), the possibilities of the study of the use of specific concepts and associated discourses across a chosen period became apparent. The corpus-assisted approach in association with Critical Discourse Analysis for the study of the historical use of language has gained popularity in recent years. Examples of this are monographs on historical topics such as the language of New Labour, media discourses on Islam, Russian political speech, and many others[20] In addition to the corpus linguistic paradigm, another useful methodological approach used as part of textual analysis is topic modeling, which uses algorithms to discover hidden thematic structure in large collections of texts[21]

Both above mentioned computer-assisted textual analysis approaches in historical digital research are complementary with the concept of "distant reading" that was introduced by Franco Moretti in his seminal work *Conjectures on World Literature*.[22] Moretti's "distant reading" is a quantitative approach that aims at the analysis of "world literature," opposed to the study of national literatures. Additionally, Moretti also questioned the methodology of previous literary studies that were predominantly based on the analysis of a limited literary canon and were not taking other works into account. For Moretti, "distant reading" must include also these other, previously omitted, works in order to achieve more relevant research. Computational tools used for textual analysis are providing precisely what is needed to apply "distant reading" on large amounts of textual sources. This theoretical paradigm is also applicable to historical research. "Distant reading" in the context of historical research would provide more stress on the quantitative investigation based on much larger collections of historical data instead of focusing on selected smaller examples of historical information (e.g. historical documents, collection of narrative sources, newspapers, etc.).

---

[19] For the development of corpus linguistics see Michael Stubbs, *Text and Corpus Analysis. Computer-Assisted Studies of Language and Culture*. (Cambridge, Massachusetts: Blackwell, 1996); McEnery and A. Hardie, *Corpus Linguistics. Method, Theory and Practice* (Cambridge: Cambridge University Press, 2012).
[20] For the corpus-assisted discourse studies see Paul Baker, Costas Gabrielatos, Majid Khosravinik, Michal Krzyzanowski, Tony McEnery and Ruth Wodak, "A useful methodological synergy? Combining critical discourse analysis and corpus linguistics to examine discourses of refugees and asylum seekers in the UK press", *Discourse and Society* 19, no. 3 (2008), 274-276; Paul Baker, *Using Corpora in Discourse Analysis* (London - New York: Continuum, 2006); P. Baker, C. Gabrielatos and T. McEnery, *Discourse Analysis and Media Attitudes*, (Cambridge: Cambridge University Press, 2013).
[21] David M. Blei, "Topic Modelling in Digital Humanities," *Journal of Digital Humanities* 2, no. 1(2012), http://journalofdigitalhumanities.org/2-1/topic-modeling-and-digital-humanities-by-david-m-blei/, (accessed January 4, 2020).
[22] Franco Moretti, "Conjectures on World Literature," *New Left Review* 1 (2000): 54-68.

Historical Digital Research on Southeast Europe and the Ottoman Empire

This overview is an attempt to give a broad outline of the impact the digital movement had on historical Southeast Europe and Ottoman studies. The list of digital projects and researchers that will be mentioned here does not intend to be exhaustive or detailed. Its goal is to provide only a general outline and describe main developments. The number of institutions and researchers, both in the West as well as in Southeast Europe and former Ottoman territories, especially those that have been participating in the digitization of the primary sources for areas of our interest, has been huge and we cannot but name only a few of them that either stand out or are very representative for the developments in digital historical research.

The rise of digital methods in humanities and neighboring fields has affected the history of Southeast Europe from very early on. This is especially true in the case of digital collections relevant for this area that were created as early as the 1980s by Northern American or Western European research and cultural heritage centers, usually dealing with ancient history and often exceeding boundaries of Southeast Europe. A typical example of such digital research activities was the Perseus project, a digital library of humanities resources dealing with the Greco-Roman world, most prominently ancient Greek textual corpora. This project was curated by the team led by Gregory Crane at Tufts University since 1987. Initially, collected materials were kept on CD-ROMs but became accessible online in 1995.[23] Specialized digital collections related to historical Southeast Europe studies began to appear also in Western research centers: for example, Byzantine studies received a push in 2005 with the opening of the *Digitales Forschungsarchiv* based at the University of Vienna, with the task to collect visual material related to Byzantine culture.[24] Also, very importantly, the archaeology of Southeast Europe – crucial for the study of ancient and medieval periods of regional history – saw one of the first uses of GIS software in this discipline in the context of archaeological investigations on Hvar island in Croatia in the early 1990s.[25] As digital approaches became indispensable in research of the cultural heritage of Southeast Europe, the series of the Vienna-based annual *Conference on Cultural Heritage and New Technologies* (looking forward to its 25th meeting in 2020) became one of the most influential meetings for digital

---

[23] *Perseus Digital Library*, www.perseus.tufts.edu (accessed February 5, 2020).
[24] *DIFAB – Digitales Forschungsarchiv*, https://difab.univie.ac.at/en/digitales-forschungsarchiv-byzanz (accessed February 7, 2020).
[25] Vincent Gaffney and Zoran Stančič, *GIS approaches to regional archaeology analysis: a case study of the island of Hvar* (Ljubljana: Znanstveni institute Filozofske fakultete, 1991).

Introduction

researchers in humanities, archaeology and related disciplines working on topics about, among others, Southeast Europe.[26]

In Southeast Europe itself, the work on the creation of digital collections of documents, manuscripts, printed material, corpora, and visual material that could be relevant for historical research studies began mostly in the 2000s and has continued ever since. Let us take several important examples from Turkey, the country that many of the papers in this edited volume deal with. In addition to the digital catalog which is unfortunately not complete, a large part of documents kept at the Ottoman Archives of the Prime Minister's Office in Istanbul, the most important archival collection for Ottoman studies, has been already digitized and their digital copies are available for consultation to researchers who visit the archives. During the same period Istanbul's *Süleymaniye* Library digitized all of its manuscripts and most of the printed works from its collection and they can be viewed in the library.[27] The Turkish National Library in Ankara offers a full-text database of Ottoman periodicals.[28] The Centre for Islamic studies and IRCICA Farabi Digital Library from Istanbul have published parts of their collections of Ottoman resources (yearbooks, *risaleler*, articles, books, etc.) online.[29] The Hakkı Tarık Us Collection, one of the most important Turkish private collections of printed material, is stored at the Beyazıt State Library in Istanbul. This is a completely digital library consisting of books, journals, newspapers, yearbooks, almanacs for the Ottoman period. It was classified, registered, and digitized between 2003 and 2010.[30] On the other hand, the Turkish National Corpus was published online only in 2009 after several years of preparation.[31] A similar situation was observed in other Southeast European countries or former Ottoman territories.[32]

---

[26] *Conference on Cultural Heritage and New Technologies,* https://www.chnt.at/ (accessed February 7, 2020).
[27] For these and others archives from Istanbul see "Tag: Istanbul," *Hazine. Guide to Researching Middle East and Beyond,* February 7, 2019, http://hazine.info/tag/istanbul (accessed February 7, 2020).
[28] "Dijital Kutüphane," *Milli Kutüphane,* http://www.mkutup.gov.tr/tr/Sayfalar/Kutuphane-Kullanimi/SSS/Dijital-Kutuphane.aspx (accessed February 7, 2020).
[29] İSAM - İslam Araştırmaları Merkezi, http://www.isam.org.tr/; *IRCICA Farabi Digital Library,* https://e-library.ircica.org/ (accessed February 7, 2020).
[30] *Periodicals of Hakkı Tarık Us Collection,* http://www.tufs.ac.jp/common/fs/asw/tur/htu/ (accessed February 5, 2020).
[31] Yeşim Aksan, Mustafa Aksan, Ahmet Koltuksuz et.al., "Construction of the Turkish National Corpus (TNC)," *LREC Proceedings,* http://www.lrec-conf.org/proceedings/lrec2012/pdf/991_Paper.pdf, (accessed, January 28, 2020).
[32] For the digital (and other archival and library sources from Southeast Europe see *East and Southeast European Archives. A Web guide,* https://www.ese-archives.geschichte.uni-muenchen.de; "Libraries in Southeast Europe, *LibWeb,* https://www.lib-web.org/europe/southeast-europe. For the digital sources for the study of Ottoman and Turkish history in former Ottoman lands (and elsewhere) see Nicole A.N.M. van Os, "Overview of Digital Sources For [Sic] the study of the Ottoman Empire and Republic of Turkey", *Turkish Studies. Sources,* February 4, 2020,

Historical digital research focusing on the analysis, visualization, and interpretation of sources dealing with the history of Southeast Europe took an important step forward in the 2000s, especially with the growing popularity of historical GIS in ancient and Byzantine studies, often in close relation with archaeology.[33] As was the case with the creation of digital collections in Northern America and Western Europe, most of the early larger projects in the 2000s dealt with the history of Southeast Europe in larger contexts. A very illustrative example of such projects is the Harvard-based *Digital Atlas of Roman and Mediaeval Civilizations*, published online for the first time in 2007. This project provides a digital platform consisting of maps and geodatabases that enable spatio-temporal analyses of various aspects of the civilizations of western Eurasia in the first 1500 years of our era.[34]

The application of new digital approaches, primarily GIS, in Ottoman studies began to catch up with international trends around 2010 when the buzz around ICT and digital humanities worldwide started to reach its peak and historians studying Southeast Europe and the Ottoman space started to take notice. In this context, historical GIS led the way. In 2009, the noted Ottoman historian Carline Finkel in the "Afterword" to the edited volume *The Frontiers of the Ottoman World* commented on the possibilities of historical GIS *vis-à-vis* all gathered historical and archaeological data on the Ottoman frontiers by contributors:

> Each of the projects documented in this volume is tied to a specific geographic location. This simple fact opens up opportunities for virtual representation of historical and archaeological

---

https://www.universiteitleiden.nl/binaries/content/assets/geesteswetenschappen/lias/200203-digital-sources.pdf (accessed February 6, 2020).

[33] For some of the more prominent examples of early digital research in the fields of ancient and Byzantine history see: J. F. Haldon, *General Issues in the Study of Medieval Logistics: Sources, Problems and Methodologies* (Leiden, Boston: Brill, 2006); V. Gaffney – H. Gaffney, "Modelling Routes and Communications," in eds. Ewald Kislinger, Johannes Koder, and Andreas Külzer, *Handelsgüter und Verkehrswege. Aspekte der Warenversorgung im östlichen Mittelmeerraum (4. bis 15. Jahrhundert)* (Wien: Österreichische Akademie der Wissenschaften, 2010), 79–91; A. Von Lunen and W. Moschek, "Without Limits: Ancient History and GIS," in eds. M. Dear, J. Ketchum, S. Lucia and D. Richardson, *Geohumanities: Art, history, text at the edge of place* (London: Routledge, 2011), 241-250; Ph. Murgatroy, B. Craenen, G. Theodoropoulos, V. Gaffney and J. Haldon, "Modelling Medieval Military Logistics: an Agent-Based Simulation of a Byzantine Army on the March," *Journal of Computational and Mathematical Organization Theory* (2011); 1–75; M. St. Popović – M. Breier, "Tracing Byzantine Routes – Medieval Road Networks in the Historical Region of Macedonia and Their Reconstruction by Least-Cost Paths," *Proceedings of the "16th International Conference on Cultural Heritage and New Technologies* (e-book), Wien 2011, https://www.chnt.at/wp-content/uploads/eBook_CHNT16_Part4.pdf, 464–475; V. Gaffney – J. Haldon – G. Theodoropoulos – Ph. Murgatroyd, "Marching across Anatolia: Medieval Logistics and Modeling the Mantzikert Campaign," *Dumbarton Oaks Papers* 65–66 (2011–2012): 209–235.

[34] *Digital Atlas of Roman and Mediaeval Civilizations*, https://darmc.harvard.edu/ (accessed February 5, 2020).

findings using GIS (Geographical Information Systems) software. GIS provides a means of digitally storing and analysing large amounts of data relating to defined locations.[35]

The 2014 paper with the title "Digital Frontiers of Ottoman Studies" by Chris Gratien, Michael Połczyński, and Nir Shafir can be seen as a programmatic manifesto for digital historical research in Ottoman studies.[36] In this paper Nir Shafir stressed that digital approaches provide many new perspectives in Ottoman Studies, especially the digitization of the large collections of manuscripts, where abundance and dispersion constitutes a research problem:

> … digitization allows us to address that most elusive question of readership and reception in the early modern period. Only when we can quickly go through twenty or thirty manuscripts in a few hours, looking at comments, ownership marks and little treatises grouped alongside them can we start making sense of the circulation and reception of these texts.[37]

Two workshops in 2015 tried to make sense of the already fast-developing field of digital historical research of Southeast Europe and the Ottoman Empire. The Digital Ottoman Platform workshop convened at the Institute for Advanced Study at Princeton on June 8–12, 2015. It was organized by professors Sabine Schmidtke and Amy Elizabeth Singer as well as by Chris Gratien, Michael Połczyński, and Nir Shafir. The conference was attended by an additional 19 participants. The collective conclusion of the workshop was that a gazetteer of the Ottoman lands, a geo-referenced catalog of places, is very much needed and would constitute the greatest contribution to scholarship.[38] The team around Amy Singer established a web portal *OpenOttoman*, the major goal of which to provide access to already existing digital tools and digitized resources on the

---

[35] Caroline Finkel, "Afterword," in *The Frontiers of the Ottoman World*, ed. A.S. Peacock (British Academy, 2009). For early examples of digital historical research on Ottoman Empire see Mihailo. St. Popović, "Die fünf vorzüglichsten Städte Macedoniens auf Plänen des k. k. Konsuls Wilhelm von Chabert aus dem Jahre 1832," *Thetis. Mannheimer Beiträge zur Klassischen Archäologie und Geschichte Griechenlands und Zyperns* 18 (2011) 187–196; Mihailo St. Popović, "The Dynamics of Borders, Transportation Networks and Migration in the Historical Region of Macedonia (14th-16th Centuries)," in Michael Borgolte, Julia Dücker, Marcel Müllerburg, Paul Predatsch and Bern Schneidmüller, eds., *Europa im Geflecht der Welt. Mittelalterliche Migrationen in globalen Bezügen* (Berlin: De Greuyter, 2012), 155–172; Amy Singer, "The Ottoman Balkans and the Middle East Compared: How Might This Be Accomplished?" in Eyal Ginio and Karl Kaser, eds., *Ottoman Legacies in the Contemporary Mediterranean: the Balkans and the Middle East Compared*, (Jerusalem: The Forum for European Studies, 2013), 23-40; Michael Polczynski and Mark Polczynski, "A Microsoft Excel Application for Automatically Building Historical Geography GIS Maps", *Transactions in GIS* 17, no. 1 (2013): 148–157; Emrah Safa Gürkan, "50 günde devr-i Bahr-ı Sefid: Königsbergli Lubenau'nun kadırgayla imtihanı/ Around the Mediterranean in Fifty Days: Reinhold Lubenau's struggle with the galley", *Journal of Ottoman Studies* 43 (2014): 273-300.
[36] Chris Gratien, Michael Polczynski and Nir Shafir "Digital Frontiers of Ottoman Studies" by *Journal of the Ottoman and Turkish Studies Association*, 1, no. 1-2 (2014), 37-51.
[37] Ibid., 41.
[38] Amy Singer, "Designing the Digital Ottoman Project", www.ias.edu, https://www.ias.edu/ideas/2015/singer-digital-ottoman (accessed, February 5, 2020).

Ottoman history, especially gazetteers.[39] The second event, the workshop *Data-driven Research in the History of Southeast Europe and Turkey*, convened in Bochum, Germany, on 25-26 June 2015 (more about this conference in the third part of the *Introduction*).

During the 2010s, a plethora of noted major digital historical projects with online presence contributing to the research of Southeast Europe emerged. Spatio-temporal historical data on the region is available from sites of projects such as *ORBIS: The Stanford Geospatial Network Model of the Roman World*,[40] community-built gazetteer *Pleiades* (Greek and Roman world, Byzantine and Early Medieval geography).[41] Several projects' online interfaces display geographical data from textual sources: *Hestia* brings a geospatial analysis of Herodotus' *Histories*;[42] the site of the project *ToposText*[43] displays an indexed collection of ancient texts and mapped places relevant for the history of the ancient Greeks. The platform *Topographies of Entanglements. Mapping Medieval Networks* established by the Austrian Academy of Science aims to employ tools of network visualization as well as network and complexity theory to analyze the medieval world, with special attention to the Byzantine world.[44] The digital historical cartography of the Byzantine Empire is the focus of a sub-project of the *Tabula Imperii Byzantini*, a project of the Austrian Academy of Science.[45] The online platform *Visual Archive Southeastern Europe*, hosted by Graz and Basel Universities, aims at collecting visual sources for the history of Southeast Europe.[46] The collection *GeoPortOst* established by the Leibniz Institute for East and Southeast European Studies at Regensburg offers online access to more than 3.000 maps of East and Southeast Europe, with a focus on the historical, ethnographical and socio-economical maps.[47]

In the post-2010 period, several major Ottoman-themed digital research projects also appeared. The *IslamAnatolia* funded by the European Research Council (ERC) and based at the University of St Andrews explored the transformation of Anatolia from a Christian to a

---

[39] *OpenOttoman*, https://openottoman.org (accessed, February 5, 2020).
[40] *ORBIS: The Stanford Geospatial Network Model of the Roman World*, http://orbis.stanford.edu/ (accessed, February 6, 2020).
[41] *Pleiades*, https://pleiades.stoa.org/home (accessed February 6, 2020).
[42] Hestia, https://hestia.open.ac.uk/ (accessed February 6, 2020).
[43] *ToposText*, https://topostext.org/ (accessed February 6, 2020).
[44] *Topographies of Entanglements. Mapping Medieval Networks*, https://oeaw.academia.edu/TopographiesofEntanglements/Mapping-Medieval-Networks (accessed February 6, 2020).
[45] „Die digitale Tabula Imperii Byzantini (Dig-TIB) als Beitrag zum Weltkulturerbe", *TIB - Tabula Imperii Byzantini*, https://tib.oeaw.ac.at/index.php?seite=sub&submenu=digtib (accessed February 6, 2020).
[46] *Topographies of Entanglements. Mapping Medieval Networks Visual Archive Southeast Europe*, https://gams.uni-graz.at/context:vase (accessed February 6, 2020).
[47] *GeoPortOst*, http://geoportost.ios-regensburg.de/ (accessed February 10, 2020).

predominantly Muslim society over the period from c. 1100 to 1500 AD by creating a publicly accessible database of information about the extant manuscripts produced and circulated in Anatolia during the formative period of Islamisation.[48] *Industrialisation and Urban Growth from the mid-nineteenth century Ottoman Empire to Contemporary Turkey in a Comparative Perspective, 1850-2000*, an ERC project based at Koç University, aims at building digital research infrastructure for the social and economic history of the Ottoman Empire and the Republic of Turkey. It uses geospatial data and correspondence analysis to contextualize and compare changes in occupational structure and urban growth trajectories across the Ottoman Empire in the 19th century and for Turkey in the 20th century.[49] The project *Hermeneutic and Computer-based Analysis of Reliability, Consistency and Vagueness in Historical Texts* at the University of Hamburg investigates how annotation, ontological modeling and inference rules, and similarity measurement can be used to perform hermeneutic investigations on historical texts. The research corpus consists of two works by the 18th-century historian of the Ottoman Empire Dimitrie Cantemir.[50]

Contributions to the Edited Volume

The papers published within this edited volume (*Digital Historical Research of Southeast Europe and Ottoman Space*) were among those that were prepared for the workshop *Data-driven Research in the History of Southeast Europe and Turkey*. The workshop was organized and convened by the author at the Center for Mediterranean Studies of the Ruhr University Bochum (25-26 June 2015). The event was funded by the Alexander von Humboldt Foundation. As data-driven history and related fields have been in recent years taking roots in major international research centers, this workshop sought to examine the current state of the digital/data-driven research in history and neighboring disciplines studying Southeast Europe and the Ottoman Empire and to give impetus to it by bringing together scholars working on these topics with various digital approaches. In addition to presenting personal research projects of the participants, the discussion at the workshop focused on two main groups of issues. Firstly, it looked into the capabilities of data-driven methods and

---

[48] *IslamAnatolia*, https://www.islam-anatolia.ac.uk (accessed February 10, 2020).
[49] *Urban occupations OETR*, https://urbanoccupations.ku.edu.tr/ (accessed February 10, 2020).
[50] *HERCORE*, www.inf.uni-hamburg.de/inst/dmp/hercore/projects.html?fbclid=IwAR2YJXeF8tPkqN4C2i9lxVYcpZHGKVKDa5R9nOFy2eMvYuoUSY9RrM6fyMA (accessed February 10, 2020).

tools to improve regional-specific problems of historical research (e.g. lack of written sources for certain periods, their multilingual nature, internationally dispersed archival records, diverging ethno-nationalist historiography traditions, lack of regional reference corpora, etc.). Secondly, the workshop considered common problems facing data-driven research of history everywhere (e.g. un/availability of data and digitized textual collections, copy-right issues, censorship etc.).

The papers included in this edited volume incorporate the application of various digital approaches such as corpus-assisted critical discourse analysis, GIS, agent-based modeling, computational statistics, etc. The approach that is the most common among the authors is GIS (Sotirios Dimitriadis, Elma Korić, and Michael Połczyński). All three papers display the successful use of geospatial technology as the main assisting method in the investigation of the history of the Ottoman realms in the Balkans and the Black Sea region. Some of the papers discussed later (Lisa Maria Teichmann and Franz-Benjamin Mocnik; Murat Güvenç and M. Erdem Kabadayı) also use geospatial mapping.

The paper by Sotirios Dimitriadis *Mapping the Nineteenth-Century Mediterranean Port-City: The Quay of Salonica, 1870-1911* traces building blocks and individual properties along the waterfront of Salonica, tracks changes in ownership and land use over the period, and connects them to the context of Salonica's economic and social transformation during the period in question. For that purpose, he organizes the archival data with the assistance of an open-source geographical information system (QGIS) and compares them with available maps from the period.

In his paper *Sovereignty and Space through GIS in the Early Modern Polish-Lithuanian/Ottoman Frontier* Michael Połczyński studies processes of conflict, mediation, reconciliation, and disparate notions of sovereignty and legitimacy of rule in the areas along the Polish-Lithuanian/Ottoman border in the 16-17th century. To assist this research, he built a gazetteer for the region using Ottoman, Polish, and other local sources employing GIS and related technologies in order to better envision and study these concepts *in situ*.

The paper by Elma Korić *Visualization of Ottoman Borderland in Early Modern Bosnia (Mid-15th – Late 16th Centuries): The Ottoman Serhat in Bosnia and GIS* aims to practically demonstrate the use of new technologies (GIS) to create a visualization of the Ottoman borderland in Early Modern Bosnia based on sources of Ottoman origin (*tapu tahrir defterleri, maliyeden müdevver defterleri*) from the period 1468-1587 and Bosnian-Herzegovinian scholarly works based upon them in the period since 1950. According to her research, the borderland of the Bosnian *eyalet* represented one of the most turbulent Ottoman borders to the lands of Early Modern Christian Europe. GIS software is used to visualize the information about fortresses and soldiers stationed at in the Ottoman border.

Corpus-assisted analysis of textual material is represented in this edited volume with two papers. Both research works are based on the extraction of data from the texts with the aim to complement the research in history or neighboring disciplines. Lisa Maria Teichmann and Franz-Benjamin Mocnik in their paper *A Literary Atlas of Turkey* offer an approach based on the extraction of spatial elements (toponyms) from a large collection of Turkish literary texts (the METU Turkish Corpus) through an automated search and filtering. On the basis of this, a digital, interactive map displaying a spatial representation of the Turkish literary world is created.

The paper *Representations of Turkey in Bosnian Mainstream Printed Media (2003-2014): A Corpus-Assisted Critical Discourse Analysis* by this author uses the theoretical framework of Critical Discourse Analysis and corpus-linguistic methodology to analyze how the representation of Turkey in Bosnian printed media was used to shape public opinion on Turkish foreign policy towards Bosnia and Herzegovina between 2003 and 2014. For this purpose, a large corpus from major Bosnian media was created and investigated through collocation and concordance analysis. The results were qualitatively interpreted to establish which words were used as part of discourses supporting or criticizing Turkish foreign policy in Bosnia and Herzegovina.

A further two papers apply a computer-assisted quantitative methodology to analyze the demographic and social history of the region. Siegfried Gruber's paper *The Patriarchy Index: A Comparative Study of Power Relations Within Southeastern Europe and Turkey* proposes a data-based measurement for patriarchy in comparative studies of power relations in historical families, the Patriarchy Index. In this paper, approaches for measuring this index are suggested. A list of numerical variables that are easily derived from census microdata and can be used for measurement purposes is provided.

The paper by Murat Güvenç and M. Erdem Kabadayı named *Reading and Mapping Mid-Nineteenth Century Ottoman Tax Registers: An Early Attempt Toward Building a Digital Research Infrastructure for Ottoman Economic and Social History* uses methods of cluster analysis and multiple correspondence analysis as well as geospatial mapping to approach the 1845 Ottoman tax registers (*temettuat*) from the city of Bursa. After the sources were collected, they were manually read, entered, and coded. After this preparation, the data was interpreted by using the above mentioned digitally assisted approaches and mapped.

Bülent Arıkan's paper *Archaeological Perspectives for Climate Change and Human Impacts on Environment: An Agent-Based Modeling Approach* presents computational modeling methods as a way to simulate complex, dynamic, and non-linear processes in a given environment at a given time that occur naturally or due to anthropogenic influence in the context of archaeological researches. He introduces stochastic models that focus on one variable and agent-based models that are capable of estimating changes in a multitude of social, economic, and environmental variables across time and space.

Finally, the study by Pınar Duygulu and Damla Arifoğlu titled *A Keyword Search System for Historical Ottoman Documents* presents a keyword search system for the easy indexing and retrieval of historical Ottoman documents by matching the visual shapes of words. With the help of this search system, one would be able to search any keyword through thousands of documents in a fully automatic manner and the retrieving of digitized Ottoman documents would be made much easier for students of this period.

Mapping the Nineteenth-Century Mediterranean Port-City: The Quay of Salonica, 1870-1912

Sotirios Dimitriadis

Abstract

Developments in data-research, and their applications in the realm of humanities, promise to fully overhaul the way historians conduct their research. From data sampling and processing to geo-spatial imaging, scholars acquire access to powerful tools that may revolutionize the relationship between the historian, their material and the public. My doctoral dissertation on the transformation of nineteenth-century Salonica into a typical fin-de-siècle Mediterranean port-city was heavily informed by the "spatial turn" of contemporary historiography. Though inspired by recent scholarly works, such as Jens Hanssen's book on Beirut, and Sibel Zandi-Sayek's work on Izmir, I nonetheless noticed the difficulty in obtaining enough data to perform both quantitative and qualitative observations. In my own research, I made extensive use of a unique source: the cadastral registries of Salonica and its environs that were compiled by local Ottoman authorities between the mid-1870s and 1911. The registries, kept today in the Historical Archive of Macedonia, give a thorough account of property ownership, uses of space, and real-estate values in Salonica in the final years of Ottoman rule in the region. Employing contemporary data-sampling and imaging techniques on this material provides us with the possibility of completely mapping a Mediterranean city over a forty-year period: neighborhood by neighborhood, block by block, individual property by individual property. For the purpose of this proposal, I intend to use that archive, organize its contents through the use of an open-source geographical information system (QGIS), and juxtapose them with available maps of Late Ottoman Salonica to reconstruct a single street of the city: Its quay. The quay of Salonica was built between 1870 and the early 1880s on the initiative of the local Ottoman authorities. After the demolition of the coastal wall of the city, a surface of about 90,000 m² was claimed from the sea, arranged between two boulevards. My paper will trace building blocks and individual properties along the waterfront, track changes in ownership and land use over the period, and connect them to the context of Salonica's economic and social transformation during the period in question. Providing the city with a modern waterfront was meant as a testament to the emergence of the city as one of the major ports in the Eastern Mediterranean, and it was representative of the alliance between the Ottoman administration and the local commercial elites that spearheaded that development. Both groups were invested in modernizing Salonica's cityscape as proof of their modernist credentials. Beyond the symbolic level, urban real-estate emerged as a very profitable investment, closely tied to the commercial and money-lending sectors of the local economy, and property tax comprised a substantial part of state revenues in the city. The application of this process to other, comparable port-cities of the region requires a thorough analysis of a sample of significant size. Analyzing and visualizing such numbers through the use of contemporary geographical information software will hopefully be a step in that direction and offer new possibilities to urban historians and scholars working on the same period.

One day in May 1870, thousands of citizens of the Ottoman port of Salonica gathered by the city's coastal walls; some crowded its ramparts, while others approached the scene from the sea on boats. At the head of the crowd was Sabri Paşa, the governor-general of the province, accompanied by the heads of all three of the city's religious communities, the consular corps, the military and civil officials, and all local citizens of note. Even though the walls had been last repaired as recently as the 1830s, they were now thought to be a detriment to the city's development. Their rubble would be used to straighten the shoreline and extend it into the sea, thus making space for a line of waterfront apartment blocks and a promenade that would run parallel to the water. The Ottoman authorities advertised the construction of the quay as a first step to the modernisation of urban space in the city, and the project attracted great interest from the local population and foreign investors both. At the height of the ceremony, when the sultan's orders that authorised the project were read, Sabri Paşa was presented with a silver hammer and started chipping away at the wall, to the jubilant applause from all those present.[1]

This paper will follow the development of Salonica's waterfront district from the time of its construction to the end of the period of Ottoman rule in the city in the course of the Balkan Wars. I will use a rich set of data provided by the local cadastral registries to identify individual properties along the waterfront, track the evolution of land values and the use of space, and trace patterns in property ownership and investment in real-estate. In this task, I will employ an open-source geospatial referencing system (QGIS) to organise, understand and visualise data, and juxtapose them with available visual representations of the Ottoman city. By using a unique source of quantitative data in conjunction with the opportunities offered by new information technologies, I want to contribute to the historical debate on the emergence of the late Ottoman port-city, and with urban space in the modern world in general.

The concept of space is a key concept in this project, and its importance in the history of late Ottoman Salonica and other urban centres of the empire was both symbolic and economic. Providing the city with a modern waterfront was meant as a testament to the emergence of the city as one of the major ports in the Eastern Mediterranean, and it was representative of the alliance between the Ottoman administration and the local commercial elites that spearheaded that development. Both groups were invested in modernizing Salonica's cityscape as proof of their modernist credentials. Beyond the symbolic level, urban real estate emerged as a very profitable investment, closely tied to the commercial and money-lending sectors of the local economy, and property tax comprised a substantial part of state revenues in the city.

My work is strongly informed by the growing literature on space and its transformations in modern history. The growing interest in social and cultural geography among historians has

---

[1] Alexandra Yerolympos, *Urban Transformations in the Balkans* (1820-1920) (Thessaloniki: University Studio Press, 1996), 63-64, citing French diplomatic sources.

contributed to a "spatial turn" in the discipline in the last decade or so.[2] Scholars active in a variety of fields, from the emergence of industrial society in Western Europe to the imposition of colonial rule in Asia and Africa, have made aware the importance of space in the study of cultural, social and economic changes that make up what we generally refer to as "modernity."[3] The study of port-cities in the Ottoman Empire and the Mediterranean has greatly benefitted from approaches that analytically prioritise space over other categories previously used, such as the state/non-state, or community.[4]

The emergence and evolution of information technology is proving highly complementary to the historians' growing preoccupation with space. The application of a variety of geo-spatial software programs in historical research make up a substantial part of the nascent field of digital historiography. Geographical information systems (GIS) allows researchers to inscribe large amounts of quantitative data on a visual surface – a "map," which can be triangulated and geo-referenced, self-generated or rector maps, two- or three-dimensional. GIS software provides researchers with options for the visualisation of diverse sets of information; they can be used to track the change over time and the spatial distribution of specific data sets, or to ascribe vectors (that themselves can represent everything from transportation networks to trade routes to troop movement) onto historic maps. This process of visualisation, in turn, allows for an understanding of trends and patterns that is difficult with previous methods of organising and presenting data, and may lead to its own research questions.[5]

---

[2] A genealogy of contemporary social geography arguably starts with Henri Lefebvre's seminal *The production of space* (Oxford: Blackwell, 1991); also see David Harvey, *The limits to capital* (Oxford: Blackwell, 1982) and Manuel Castells, *The city and the grassroots: a cross-cultural theory of urban social movements* (Berkeley: California University Press, 1983).

[3] A highly selective bibliography includes Brenda S.A. Yeoh, *Contesting Space: Power Relations and the Urban Built Environment in Colonial Singapore* (Kuala Lumpur and Oxford: Oxford University Press, 1996); Jyoti Hosagrahar, *Indigenous Modernities: Negotiating Architecture and Urbanism* (London: Routledge, 2005); Peter Scriver and Vikramaditya Prakash, eds., *Colonial Modernities: Building, Dwelling and Architecture in British India and Ceylon* (London: Routledge, 2007); William J. Glover, *Making Lahore Modern: Constructing and Imagining a Colonial City* (Minneapolis: Minnesota University Press, 2008).

[4] See for example Paul Rabinow, *French Modern: Norms and Forms of Social Environment* (Cambridge, Massachusetts and London: MIT Press, 1989); Jens Hanssen, *Fin de Siècle Beirut: The Making of an Ottoman Provincial Capital* (Oxford: Oxford University Press, 2005) and Sibel Zandi-Sayek, *Ottoman Izmir: The Rise of a Cosmopolitan Port, 1840-1880* (Minneapolis and London: Minnesota University Press, 2012). For an overview of the literature on nineteenth-century Ottoman and Mediterranean port-cities, see Sakis (Athanasios) Gekas, "Class and cosmopolitanism: the historiographical fortunes of merchants in Eastern Mediterranean ports," *Mediterranean Historical Review* 24, no. 2 (December 2009): 95-114.

[5] For the uses of GIS in historiography, see Anne Kelly Knowles and Amy Hillier, *Placing History: How Maps, Spatial Data and GIS are Changing Historical Scholarship* (Redlands: ESRI Press, 2008) and Ian N. Gregory and Richard G. Healey, "Historical GIS: Structuring. Mapping and Analyzing Geographies of the Past," *Progress in Human Geography* 31 (5) (2007), 638-653. For applications in the specific sub-field of Ottoman and Middle East Studies, see Chris Gratien, Michael Polczynski and Nir Shafir, "Digital Frontiers of Ottoman Studies," *Journal of the Ottoman and Turkish Studies Association* 1, no. 1-2 (2014): 37-51.

I have collected the data sets for this paper through extensive work on unique source material: The cadastral registers of late Ottoman Salonica, which are still kept in the city, at the Historical Archive of Macedonia. Starting from the early 1870s, the Ottoman administration in the city embarked on a project to record all existing properties in the city, as well as all future property transfers. Ottoman civil servants recorded a dearth of information on each property, including its owner, its address, down to the street number, its size, its function, its market value and the value estimated for taxation purposes. This process, in lieu of the Ottoman Land Law of 1858, aimed at normalising the collection of property taxes through the award of title deeds (*tapu*) for each property and the guarantee of individual owners' rights.[6] The resulting archive of about two hundred roll-call registers (*yoklama* and *defter-i hakkanî*) and property tax registers (*esas* and *hulasa defteri*) of Salonica and the surrounding countryside can be used to reconstruct its cityscape over a period of forty years neighbourhood by neighbourhood, street by street, down to the level of the individual property.

In this paper, I intend to use this archive along with a geo-spatial information software, Quantum GIS, in order to reconstruct a specific and representative district of late Ottoman Salonica – that of its quay, from its construction in 1870 to the end of Ottoman rule in the city in 1912. I will draw data from about fifteen registers, so as to distinguish individual properties in the district, and trace their development over this forty-year period. I will project that information onto a historical map, the 1880 map prepared by the head municipal engineer Antoine Wernieski, which will function as the raster for my QGIS project.[7] Having inscribed the individual properties on the map as features, I will insert values for different attributes following the categories already present in the cadastral registries: street number, function, owner's name, and property value. I will organise this data in two distinct layers to correspond to the three stages in the district's history and its transformation over time: The long period of construction, which lasted until the early 1880s; and the thirty years that followed, which established the quay as the prime venue of leisure and entertainment in Salonica.

---

[6] For the historiographical surrounding the Land Law of 1858, see Huri İslamoğlu, "Property as contested domain: A revaluation of the Ottoman Land Code of 1858", in *New perspectives on property and land in the Middle East*, ed. Roger Owen (Cambridge, Massachusetts: Harvard University Press, 2000), 3-61.
[7] The map is available as Map I, in the Appendix section. Başbakanlı Osmanlı Arşivi (BOA), Y.EE 64/4.

I. Constructing the Quay

The planning and construction of the quay of Salonica was the first major transformation of the city's urban fabric. Though there had been debates on such a project already since 1863, construction had to wait until Sabri Paşa's appointment to the post of provincial governor (*vali*) in 1869. The paşa had already made a name for himself while serving in the model province of Danube as a deputy governor under Midhat Paşa. After his appointment to Salonica, Sabri Paşa immediately put forward a plan for the construction of the quay. The plan called for the demolition of the coastal walls and towers of the city, and the use of the debris to straighten the waterfront and gain land from the sea. Sabri Paşa successfully petitioned Istanbul to award the construction contract to the provincial public works bureau under the supervision of the Italian engineer Paolo Vitalli, who had apparently assisted Sabri Paşa in Izmir. The project would result in roughly 90,000 m^2 of freed land, one third of which would be reserved for public uses and the rest auctioned off to private bidders. The projected boulevard would also be used as a mooring station for incoming ships - and the lighters that served those too large to dock. Since the state seemed unable to contribute financially, the auctions would have to cover the cost, calculated at about 100,000 *lira*s. The sale of new property met with great interest. Almost immediately all but a very few of the offered plots were auctioned off at a total price of about 85,000 *lira*s.[8]

That sense of euphoria did not last for long. By 1871 half of the collected sum of money had already been spent, but the project had little progress to show for it. Investors began asking for the return of their money and they contemplated the additional sell-off of the land which the original plan had reserved for public use. An official investigation addressed rumours of corruption. Though the locals suspected it would end in exoneration, the final report accused Sabri Paşa of having embezzled 12,000 *lira*s along with Vitalli, in order to buy agricultural land in the area; a total of about 20,000 were left unaccounted for after the audit. Embarrassed by the result and fearful of the possibility of compensating the buyers, the Ottoman government refused to endorse the results of the investigation and, although the *paşa* was recalled from his post, he continued his career in the upper echelons of the Ottoman bureaucracy and retained his popularity with the local population.[9] The engineer Vitalli was the only one officially condemned, and was

---

[8] Yerolympos, *Metaxy Anatolis kai Dysis: Boreioelladikes poleis stin periodo ton othomanikon metarrythmiseon [Between East and West: Northern Greek cities in the period of Ottoman reforms]* (Athens: Trohalia, 1997), 135-139. Compare the history of the construction of the Izmir quay as presented in Zandi-Sayek, "Struggles over the shore: building the quay of Izmir," *City & Society* 12, no. 1 (2000): 55-78.
[9] Yerolympos, *Metaxy Anatolis kai Dysis*, 131-132.

subsequently fired from his position. Work on the quay continued, but at an extremely slow pace, until the project's final conclusion in the early 1880s.[10]

As foreseen in the plan, the quay district evolved between two parallel boulevards. One followed the course of the old walls, while the other hugged the newly reclaimed and straightened waterfront. The two boulevards were simply named the Second and First Quay Boulevards (*İkinci* and *Birinci Rıhtım Caddesi*) respectively. The district was bordered to the northwest by Pier Boulevard (*İskele Caddesi*), a street that ran parallel to the waterfront and connected the quay to the city's commercial and administrative centre; to the southeast, the quay ended at the building of the local Military Command (*İdare-i Askeriye*) and the so-called "Bloody Tower" (*Kanlı Kule*), the old prison that was later removed and rebranded as the White Tower (*Beyaz Kule*).[11] Within that oblong area, the plan delineated sixteen city blocks of various surface sizes, separated by streets that extended vertically from the core of the city. The sixteenth block was reserved for the Ottoman military and eventually housed the Military Inspectorate and the Military Command; the other fifteen were parcelled and auctioned off.

Neither the long delays in the completion of the project or Sabri Paşa's implication in the embezzlement scandal seem to have affected investors' interest in the project. Though no record of the auction process itself seems to have survived, the new owners were required to register their properties with the authorities. The initial series of roll-call registers record a significant number of transactions in the quay (*rıhtım*). There are hundreds of entries detailing the registration and transfer of property in the district; by comparing the entries from the earliest registers to each other, to later registers and to the Ottoman maps of the city, I can place just over twenty-five individual plots as features in the QGIS map. These features represent a fraction of the district in terms of size and value – between a fifth and a fourth; nonetheless, in combination with other entries in the registers, which I could not locate with precision, they offer a representative image of the initial stage in the development of the quay. The assorted data are presented in Table I, in the appendix section. Map II is a result of processing this data through QGIS.

This list contains a representative cross-section of Salonica's commercial and banking elites, which cuts across confessional lines. Saul Modiano probably emerged as the largest investor

---

[10] Yerolympos, *Urban Transformations*, 66-67. See also the local newspaper *Faros* 603, September 19 [October 1], 1881; 678, June 16 [28], 1882.
[11] These two buildings eventually gave the two boulevards their official names. The First Quay Boulevard became White Tower Boulevard, and the Second Quay Boulevard the Military Command Boulevard.

in property in the district in this initial period; other members of the Modiano clan are also present in this list.[12] Other smaller local Jewish commercial houses were also involved in property acquisition: The plots of Sa'iaz, Hassid, Fransez, Florentin and other Salonican Jewish entrepreneurs were often seen as extensions of these families' original properties, which had been neighbouring the coastal wall of the city before its demolition. The other great Jewish family of the city, the Allatinis, had a more modest presence in the district compared to the Modianos.[13] The prospects of the new district, however, attracted the interest of all communities. The Kapancı, a notable family of the heterodox *mu'amin* sect of Islam, also enjoyed extensive properties on the quay.[14] The list of Muslim owners included the money-lenders Şevki Efendi and Halil Efendi, the timber merchant İbrahim Ağa, and admiral Mehmed Paşa.[15] Greek Orthodox elite families like the Hatzilazarou were also buying land in the quay, their properties concentrated to the two extremes of the stretch – towards the Custom House to the northwest, and near the Christian quarters of the city in the southeast.

The preoccupation of the local elites with the city's real-estate market predated the construction of the quay. Investment in urban properties functioned as an integral part of the commercial and money-lending operations that sustained Salonica's economy. With the city's commercial importance increasing rapidly in the second half of the nineteenth century, the need to address chronic shortages strengthened the ties between the smaller merchants to the bigger commercial houses of the city, the Allatinis, the Modianos, and their partner firms. The latter employed their good reputation and personal connections with the local banking branches to issue bonds at a relatively low interest rate, then invested the money in bonds issued by smaller players at a higher interest.[16] Debtors were usually obliged to put up their properties for security. Formal mortgages were not very frequent, as the creditors put little faith in the Ottoman legislation on bankruptcy and the Ottoman court system. They preferred that the debtor temporarily transfer

---

[12] For this prominent Italian Jewish family, reputed to be one of the largest property owners in the empire, see Evangelos Chekimoglou and Kirki Georgiadou-Tsimino, *Istoria tis Epixeirimatikotitas sti Thessaloniki, t. B₁: I Othomaniki periodos* [The history of entrepreneurship in Thessaloniki], vol. B₁: The Ottoman period] (Thessaloniki: Politistiki Etairia Epiheirimation Boreiou Ellados, 2004), 274-275.
[13] In 1883, Carlo Allatini was recorded purchasing a whole block, which contained a house and 3 stores, from merchant Bohor Russo for 225,000 *kuruş*. IAM, *Yoklama* 60, July 1299 [1883], entry 20.
[14] Mark Baer, "Globalization, cosmopolitanism and the Dönme," *Journal of World History* 18, no. 2(2007): 150-151; *Salname-i vilayet-i Selânik* XV [XIV], 1315 [1897], 298-301. Not incidentally, the business leader among the *dönme* coincided with the leading families within the three different subgroups of the sect.
[15] IAM, *Yoklama* 30A, February 1295 [1880], entry 169; *Yoklama* 60, March 1299 [1883], entry 27.
[16] Evangelos Chekimoglou, *Ypothesi Modiano: Trapeziko Krach sti Thessaloniki tou 1911* [The Modiano affair: Banking crash in 1911 Thessaloniki] (Thessaloniki: n.p., 1991), 17-23.

ownership of their property to the creditor, until the terms of the loan were fulfilled.[17] This practice was sanctioned in Ottoman law as *ferağ bilvefa* and was applicable not only for freehold properties (*mülk*), but also for the usufruct rights to *miri* and *vakıf* properties.[18]

Naturally, the sustainability of such ventures depended on the quick recuperation of the invested capital,[19] as well as the constant increase in property prices. At the same time, the complexity of the legal provisions that governed property rights proved detrimental to the profitability of urban real-estate. Issues of acquisition, inheritance or the payment of taxes were resolved by Islamic judges (*kadıs*) through the application of Islamic law (*şeriat*), administrative ordinances issued from Istanbul (*kanun*), which were by the mid-19th century represented in the city by the secular courts (*nizamiye*), by Greek Orthodox and Jewish canonical law – and even European courts, that operated in the respective foreign consulates and adjudicated cases that arose between foreign subjects.[20] The recognition of the validity of parallel legal systems went hand in hand with the recognition of parallel ownership rights for the same properties. A substantial part of commercial and residential properties in Salonica was attached to a number of Muslim religious foundations (*evkâf*).[21] While owners of usufruct rights on such properties could operate, rent, sell or bequeath them, such actions were still subject to a number of restrictions.[22]

For Salonica's main merchants and money-lenders, buying property along the waterfront represented a profitable investment in real-estate without the need to navigate through the legal complexities of the local property market. All properties in the new district were designated as *mülk*, which means they came with full rights to their owners. By initiating the demolition of the walls and by planning the new district, the Ottoman authorities presented the local elites with an opportunity to profit, while at the same time providing the city with modern spaces and broadening their own tax base. The construction of the quay proved to be the first in a series of spatial interventions by the local authorities, which became the basis of the consensual relationship between the Ottoman state and urban elites. As for the district itself, with construction slowly

---

[17] Ibid., 23-24.
[18] Martha Mundy and Richard Saumarez Smith, *Governing property, making the modern state: Law, administration, and production in Ottoman Syria* (London: I.B. Tauris, 2007), 38, 46.
[19] By the beginning of the 20th century, local bankers estimated that each property in the city brought in revenues up to 8% of its total worth. Since properties acquired as mortgage had probably cost their current owners a lot less than their market value, the investment could be recouped in as little as five years. Chekimoglou, *Ypothesi Modiano*, 26-27.
[20] Zandi-Sayek, *Ottoman Izmir*, 47-48, 52-53, 57-58.
[21] Eyal Ginio, "The shaping of a sacred space: The *tekke* of Zühuri Şeyh Ahmet Efendi in eighteenth-century Salonica," *The Medieval History Journal* 9, 2 (2006), 271-296.
[22] İslamoğlu, *passim*.

reaching an end in the early 1880s, it would soon emerge as Salonica's main promenade, the heart of the city's social and cultural life, and a façade of modernity to greet those travellers approaching the city by sea.

II. Developing the Waterfront District

When the first properties along the waterfront were auctioned off, construction had just begun and the quay existed only in the maps drawn by the engineers of the provincial technical bureau. Twenty years later, it had been transformed into a densely built district frequented by thousands of Salonica's residents. The locals took advantage of the spaces opened up by the construction of the quay, and First Quay Boulevard quickly became the main promenade of the city. The city's social life was completely transformed, as the idleness and informality of domestic life moved out of the houses, with families strolling down the quay towards the White Tower and its public gardens. This trend was only reinforced by the concentration of several hotels, clubs (*kulüp*), cafés (*kahvehane*), beer-houses (*birahane*) and, at the end of the period, cinemas. The presence of several department stores gave the district a strong commercial dimension, while residential buildings were largely confined to the back of each block, along Second Quay Boulevard.

In 1906 the Ottoman authorities performed a cadastral survey of the city for the purposes of updating their property tax registers. The properties along the waterfront were recorded in the seventh *Esas* register, which will be the main source for tracing the development of the district during this stage (*Table II*).[23] There were ninety-three addresses recorded for First Quay Boulevard; these included 31 (mostly described as *hâne*, houses, but there were a few dubbed as *apartmans* and *konaks*, i.e. mansions, as well). There also were 53 shops (*dükkân* and *mağaza*), a department store (*dükkânhâne*), and a covered fish market (*balıkhâne*) containing 20 stores. At the same time, a large number of venues pertaining to the entertainment and leisure of locals and visitors appeared along the waterfront. The 1906 register records about fifteen cafés, five beerhalls, two hotels, and two restaurants (*lokanta*).[24] Second Quay Boulevard was somewhat more residential. Residential buildings comprised almost half of the properties surveyed there (68 out of 147). These were generally larger and higher than the ones on the waterfront itself: Buildings of two or three storeys

---
[23] IAM, *Esas Defteri* 7, 111-114.
[24] Ibid., 116.

were frequent, and more than ten of the buildings surveyed were classified as mansions. There was an equally strong presence of commercial buildings here (54 mağazas and dükkâns), while entertainment venues were comparably fewer in number (four cafés, five taverns and beerhalls, four restaurants).[25]

The great commercial and financial houses of the city, and especially the Modiano clan, were well represented among the property owners of the quay (*Map III*). In 1906, more than 35 properties were listed as owned by "the sons of merchant Saul" (*Saul pazargânzâdeler*) or "the heirs of Saul Modiano" (*Saul Modiano veresesi*), and another ten by the lawyer Liyaci, son of Davi Modiano. While almost three quarters of the Modiano holdings were shops, there were also two cafés, two hotels, some pharmacies, and a number of residential buildings that included a three-storey *konak* with twenty rooms.[26] These either represented purchases that Saul Modiano had completed during his lifetime and bequeathed to his sons, or individual purchases the latter made over the years. One must bear in mind that the map based on the 1906 registers transmit a static image that does not necessarily correspond to the reality of the real estate market in Salonica. Conversely, the study of the registers of property transfers (the *yoklama defter*s and the *defter-i hakkanî*s) reveal that, rather than slowly accumulating real-estate titles over time, the Modiano properties constantly changed hands, with the family buying, when the price was deemed advantageous, or selling, when cash was required for their commercial and financial holdings.[27]

The three sons of İbrahim Kapancı, Yusuf, Mehmed and Ahmed, also owned a significant number of properties on the waterfront. Most of them were concentrated on the north-western end of the quay, around the little square formed where Sabri Paşa Boulevard reached the sea. Ahmed Kapancı owned a hotel at that location, as well as the three shops and the café that were located at the ground floor of the building.[28] Right next to the hotel, Mehmed Kapancı owned the

---

[25] Ibid., 117-120.
[26] Ibid., 111-124.
[27] Thus in June 1892, Yako Modiano bought 6 shops on the quay from Fakima, wife of Levi Isaac Kazaz, for a total sum of 90,000 *kuruş*. Sixteen months later, he sold them to the monk Haritos, son of Anagnostis, for a profit of 10,000 *kuruş*. What is interesting is that the estimated value of the sold properties had dropped in the meantime from 95,000 to 80,000 *kuruş*. See IAM, *Defter-i Hakkanî* 9, March-August 1308, 54; *Defter-i Hakkanî* 11, 1309, 48.
[28] The ownership of this particular building is a testimony to the complexity of Ottoman property law, and strategies applied by property owners, to operate within that context. Originally, that property, was divided in 19 shares between Ahmed and Yusuf Kapancı, and İsma'il Rağıb Efendi, each with 5.5 shares, and Galib and Refik Efendis, who held the remaining 2.5 shares. The latter split their share into three thirds and sold it to the other owners in July 1893 for 20,820 *kuruş* each, and Yusuf sold his share to his brother in November of the same year for 83.300 *kuruş*. IAM, *Defter-i Hakkanî* 11, 39, 83. By 1906, the property was attributed to Ahmed Kapancı and company (*şürekâsı*). IAM, *Esas Defteri* 7, 115.

Café Bellevue, which he rented out to interested parties.[29] To Mehmed belonged another five shops, a café, a restaurant, and a house in the vicinity as well, while Yusuf and Ahmed owned some property, including the Sporting Club and the beer-hall "America", at the other end of the quay.[30]

A number of other prominent locals had stakes in the waterfront district. The Hatzilazarou family owned a significant number of properties, including four cafés, a casino, a garden restaurant, a distillery for alcoholic beverages, and two large empty lots that awaited construction.[31] Other Greek Orthodox investors, especially the entrepreneurs from Ağustos [Naoussa], men like Giorgos Kirtsis or Hatzidimitrios Goutas, appear in the sources as owners of a small number of properties, including a café and a hotel.[32] Hacı Yusuf Agâh owned three large cafés near the docks, as well as the houses above them.[33] Yusuf Paşa, in his capacity as financier [*kontratçı*], maintained a row of cafés and shops near the White Tower.[34] Joseph Elion and Jacob Florentin each owned two large *konak*s on the streets behind the waterfront.[35] While not holding a significant stake in the area by 1906, important notables of the city, like the Allatini family, Alfred Abbott, the future mayor Hulusi Beyefendi, or Mehmed Karakaş Efendi still owned some minor property.

Although all prominent inhabitants of Salonica appear to have been interested in the waterfront area real estate, not all properties there belonged to locals. Many owners were absentee landlords, cashing in on the revenue their properties brought them from outside the city. The heirs of Cevâd Şakir Paşa, all residing in Istanbul, owned almost forty distinct properties on the quay, and as many in the nearby streets.[36] The steamer companies that serviced the port of the city had also invested heavily in the development on the quay. The Austrian Lloyd company's directors owned a large warehouse complex just beyond the port end of the quay.[37] The headquarters of the *Messageries Maritimes* were located nearby, at the beginning of the Quay Boulevard; a number of shops and a café at the adjacent alley, aptly named *Mesajeri Aralığı*, also belonged to the French company.[38]

---

[29] Ibid. See also Marc Baer, *The Dönme: Jewish converts, Muslim revolutionaries, and secular Turks* (Stanford, California: Stanford University Press, 2010), 46; *Faros* 1641, October 14 [26], 1892.
[30] IAM, *Esas Defteri* 7, 121-123 and 113, 120, respectively.
[31] Ibid., 113-122.
[32] IAM, *Defter-i Hakkanî* 11, 60; *Esas Defteri* 7, 114-115, 124.
[33] IAM, *Defter-i Hakkanî* 11, 44. His heirs apparently sold off their share in the family property, as they are not recorded in the 1906 registry.
[34] IAM, *Esas Defteri* 7, 115.
[35] Ibid., 119-120.
[36] Ibid., 11-121. The figure included the 19 stores at the fish market, and the department store on the water.
[37] The Ottoman authorities estimated its value at 667,000 *kuruş*. IAM, *Defter-i Hakkanî* 10, 11.
[38] IAM, *Esas Defteri* 7, 111, 117, 121.

Investment in the properties along the waterfront was from the onset focused on sites of retail shopping, leisure and entertainment. Property owners rented out their cafés and could expect a high return.[39] The numerous cafés, beer-halls, restaurants and cinemas of the district provided residents with forms of entertainment markedly different than those that had been offered by the coffee-houses and taverns (*meyhane*) of the city. These had been almost exclusively male spaces, usually catered for regular clients that lived in the same neighbourhood, and served local beverages like *rakı*.[40] The new cafés that spread from the quay to the rest of the city were modelled after the Viennese cafés in terms of design and services provided.[41] They allowed entrance to women and children, gradually evolving into venues where young men and women could socialise, under the (gentler or stricter) supervision of their parents.[42] The cafés and beer-halls of the quay would frequently invite musicians, actors, and all kinds of performers to entertain their clients.[43] The first regular cinema shows in Salonica started in 1903 in the beer-hall brasserie *Olympia*, organised by actor and impresario Plutarch Imrahoris and photographer Leitmer, who imported the equipment from Germany.[44]

Leisure and entertainment were not the only functions of Salonica's quay. Throughout the period in question, the quay also doubled as the city harbour. The main passenger pier stood at its northwestern end at the junction to Pier Boulevard, and there were mooring points for the use of the numerous rowboats that ferried people and cargo between the incoming ships and the city. This situation continued even after the construction of Salonica's modern port facilities at the beginning of the twentieth century. The two boulevards of the quay were often congested, and the situation was exacerbated with the construction of a horse-drawn tram line in 1893. Strolling pedestrians needed to carefully navigate between the tables of the cafés, carts and carriages, porters

---

[39] For Mehmed Kapancı and his *Bellevue* café, see Baer, *The Dönme*, 46.
[40] Meropi Anastassiadou, "Les cafés à Salonique sous les derniers Ottomans", in *Cafés d'Orient revisités*, eds. Hélène Desmet-Grégoire and François Georgeon (Paris: CNRS Editions, 1997), 79-82.
[41] Kostas Tomanas, *Ta kafeneia tis palias Thessalonikis* [The coffee-houses of old Thessaloniki] (Thessaloniki: Pitsilia sto Chaki, 1997), 20-22. For the Viennese café as a type, see Tag Gronberg, "Coffeehouse Orientalism", in *The Viennese café and fin-de-siècle culture*, eds. Charlotte Ashby et al. (London and Oxford: Berghahn, 2013), 59-77. One should note that the Viennese café initially carried strong Oriental connotations, which were reinvented during the nineteenth century in the form of advertisements or nostalgia. Conversely, the café in Salonica was a venue oriented consciously towards Europe.
[42] The café *America* was reported to be the preferred venue of matchmakers, and the two families would often meet there for the first time. Tomanas, 31.
[43] Dionysios Lappos, owner of three cafés of the quay, invited travelling performers, such as Miss Mavons with her eight trained dogs, or Miss Evelyn and her "electric orchestra," and staged novelty shows in his premises. Anastassiadou, 84-85.
[44] Tomanas, *Oi kinimatografoi tis palias Thessalonikis* [The cinemas of old Thessaloniki] (Thessaloniki: Nisides, 1993), 8-9; Anastassiadou, 85-86.

loading and unloading cargo, and passing trams; accidents were frequent. In even starker contrast to the rest of the district, in 1879 the Sa'iaz factory built a silk reeling factory in the middle of the quay – the only major industrial unit within the historical core of the city. Despite constant complaints about the soot that came from the factory's tall chimney or the loud siren that signalled the beginning and end of each shift, the filature continued its operation until 1917.[45]

III. Appendix

A) Tables

Table I: Initial purchases of waterfront plots

id	size[46]	Owner	Seller	Value (est.)[47]	purchase price	year	Source
1	1135	Liyaci Modiano and Enriko Errera	Quay Commission	235,000		Feb 1891	d.h. 3
2	800	Şevki Efendi	Quay Commission	109,616		Feb 1880	yok. 30A
3	2280	Fakima, wife of Saul Modiano		270,500		Feb 1880	yok. 30A
4	570	Celaleddin Efendi and Abdü'l-Kerim Efendi	Quay Commission	86,438		Feb 1880	yok. 30A
5	570	Mordehai Abastado		78,419		Feb 1880	yok. 30A
6	150	Kıraç İnayet Ağa		21,310		Feb 1880	yok. 30A
7	103	Samuel Varsano		9,000		Sep 1884	yok. 30A
8		Samuel and Mişon Varsano		50,000		Sep 1875	yok. 30
9	1,003	Mehmed Eşref Paşa		107,390		Feb 1880	yok. 30A
10	894	Saul Modiano	Mario Fernandez	190,000	175,000	Jan 1884	yok. 30
11	375	Şalom Sa'iaz		26,320		Jun 1875	yok. 30

---

[45] Anastassiadou, *Salonique, une ville Ottoman a l'âge des réformes* (Leiden, Brill, 1997), 198-199. Ironically, by 1906 the Saiaz family had largely moved away from their factory, and were listed as inhabitants of the Hamidiye neighbourhood. IAM, *Esas Defteri* 7, 120.
[46] The cadastral authorities measured properties in sq. *zira* (also known as sq. pic, or *arşın*), which corresponds to 0.57417 sq. metres. The values here have been converted to sq. metres.
[47] The values are in *kuruş*, the silver coins worth one hundredth of the golden *lira*.

12	548	Samuel Sa'iaz		108,900		Apr 1874	yok. 30
13	259	Yuda Boton		20,318		Mar 1876	yok. 30
14	259	Yako Fransez		20,318		Mar 1876	yok. 30
15	312	Isac Modiano		32,760		Feb 1876	yok. 30
16	570	Reina, wife of İsac Navarro		40,290		Feb 1880	yok. 30A
17	510	İsac Tiano		36,748		Feb 1880	yok. 30A
18	225	Yako, Samuel and Levi Modiano		19,750		Oct 1878	yok. 30
19	225	Mehmed and Celil Kapancı		19,750		Oct 1878	yok. 30
20	205	Yozef Hassid		16,000		Oct 1878	yok. 30
21	205	Mişon Hassid		18,000		Oct 1878	yok. 30
22	874	Yako Sidis					d.h. 24
23	144	Yako Florentin		27,000	18,900	Jan 1900	d.h. 24
24	550	Kostakis Megavouli		50,907		Jun 1874	yok. 30
25	550	Periklis, Evripidis and Nikolas Hatzilazarou		50,907		Mar 1890	yok. 30
26	171	Aristidis Hatziarapis	İbrahim Ağa		11,500	Mar 1884	yok. 60

Table II: A full list properties in the quay in 1906

Id	Street	Number	Function	Owner	Value
1	First Quay Blvd	1-3	beer-hall	Hulusi Beyefendi	100,000
2	First Quay Blvd	4	shipping agency	Messageries Maritimes	450,000
3	Second Quay Blvd	1	Bakery	Hulusi Beyefendi	80,000
4	Second Quay Blvd	3	Shop	Hulusi Beyefendi	18,000
5	Second Quay Blvd	5	Shop	Hulusi Beyefendi	18,000
6	Second Quay Blvd	7	Store	Messageries Maritimes	30,000
7	Second Quay Blvd	9, 11, 13	Store	Messageries Maritimes	82,500
8	Second Quay Blvd	15	Store	Messageries Maritimes	35,000
9	First Quay Blvd	5	beer-hall	Fresnes Agency	60,000

10	First Quay Blvd	6	Café	Şevki Efendi	140,000
11	First Quay Blvd	7	Imperial Hotel	Şevki Efendi	150,000
12	First Quay Blvd	8, 9	Shop	Liyaci Modiano and Karlo Allatini	30,000
13	First Quay Blvd	10	Café	Liyaci Modiano and Karlo Allatini	100,000
14	Second Quay Blvd	17	Store	Fresnes Agency	13,000
15	Second Quay Blvd	19	Mansion	Fresnes Agency	300,000
16	Second Quay Blvd	21	Store	Fresnes Agency	15,000
17	Second Quay Blvd	23	Store	Fresnes Agency	15,000
18	Second Quay Blvd	25	beer-hall	Şevki Efendi	25,000
19	Second Quay Blvd	27	House	Şevki Efendi	15,000
20	Second Quay Blvd	29, 31	Shops	Şevki Efendi	23,000
21	Second Quay Blvd	33	Shop	Şevki Efendi	15,000
22	Second Quay Blvd	35	Store	Liyaci Modiano	40,000
23	Second Quay Blvd	37	Store	Liyaci Modiano	40,000
24	Second Quay Blvd	39	Bakery	Liyaci Modiano	60,000
25	First Quay Blvd	11	Café	Cevad Paşa and Şakir Ferik Paşa	75,000
26	First Quay Blvd	12-18	station house, 3 cafés, 2 shops, club	Cevad Paşa and Şakir Ferik Paşa	243,500
27	First Quay Blvd	19	fish market	Cevad Paşa and Şakir Ferik Paşa	271,500
28	First Quay Blvd	20-24	room, club, café with garden, shop	Cevad Paşa and Şakir Ferik Paşa	217,500
29	First Quay Blvd	25	Water Company	Cevad Paşa and Şakir Ferik Paşa	360,000
30	First Quay Blvd	26-29	restaurant with court, room, 2 houses	Cevad Paşa and Şakir Ferik Paşa	82,000

31	First Quay Blvd	30		Cevad Paşa and Şakir Ferik Paşa	85,000
32	Second Quay Blvd	41	Shop	Cevad Paşa and Şakir Ferik Paşa	12,000
33	Second Quay Blvd	43-55	tavern, store, 5 shops	Cevad Paşa and Şakir Ferik Paşa	144,000
34	Second Quay Blvd	57	Store	Cevad Paşa and Şakir Ferik Paşa	25,000
35	Second Quay Blvd	59-61	2 houses	Cevad Paşa and Şakir Ferik Paşa	60,000
36	Second Quay Blvd	63	Store	Cevad Paşa and Şakir Ferik Paşa	10,000
37	Second Quay Blvd	65-83	5 shops, 2 stores, 2 houses, 1 bakery	Cevad Paşa and Şakir Ferik Paşa	155,500
38	Second Quay Blvd	85	Shop	Cevad Paşa and Şakir Ferik Paşa	25,000
39	First Quay Blvd	31	Shop	monk Papaiosif	15,000
40	First Quay Blvd	32-33	shop, store	monk Papaiosif	30,000
41	First Quay Blvd	34	Store	monk Papaiosif	15,000
42	First Quay Blvd	35	Garden	Liyaci Elyon	
43	First Quay Blvd	36	house with court	Celal Efendi	115,000
44	First Quay Blvd	37	house with court	Celal Efendi	125,000
45	Second Quay Blvd	87	mansion with garden	monk Papaiosif	300,000
46	Second Quay Blvd	89	Shop	Liyaci Elyon	15,000
47	Second Quay Blvd	81	mansion with garden	Liyaci Elyon	235,000
48	Second Quay Blvd	93	Shop	Liyaci Elyon	15,000
49	Second Quay Blvd	95	Mansion	Avram Abastado	160,000
50	First Quay Blvd	38	House	Liyaho Hamil	90,000
51	First Quay Blvd	39	House	Yozef Benrubi	130,000

52	First Quay Blvd	40	house with court	Haccar Hanım, wife of Mehmed Paşa	70,000
53	First Quay Blvd	41	house with court	Haccar Hanım, wife of Mehmed Paşa	70,000
54	First Quay Blvd	42-43	2 pharmacies	heirs of Saul Modiano	30,000
55	First Quay Blvd	44	Shop	heirs of Saul Modiano	70,000
56	First Quay Blvd	45	empty lot	Beniko Saltiel	80,000
57	First Quay Blvd	46	Store	Beniko Saltiel	30,000
58	Factory Str	4	silk factory	Şalom Sa'iaz	1,500,000
59	Aragon Synagogue Str	1	house with court	Leon Karaso	75,000
60	Second Quay Blvd	97	Shop	Leon Karaso	17,500
61	Second Quay Blvd	99	Store	Leon Karaso	12,500
62	Second Quay Blvd	101	Store	Leon Karaso	12,500
63	Second Quay Blvd	103	Store	Rahil, wife of Benjamin Alhassid	12,000
64	Second Quay Blvd	105	Mansion	Rahil, wife of Benjamin Alhassid	80,000
65	Second Quay Blvd	107	Store	Rahil, wife of Benjamin Alhassid	12,000
66	Second Quay Blvd	109	mansion with court	heirs of Mehmed Paşa	90,000
67	Second Quay Blvd	111	Store	heirs of Saul Modiano	20,000
68	Second Quay Blvd	113	Store	heirs of Saul Modiano	20,000
69	Second Quay Blvd	115	Store	heirs of Saul Modiano	20,000
70	First Quay Blvd	47	Apartment	Daniel Gatenyo	200,000
71	First Quay Blvd	48	Apartment	Mişon, son of Yuda Asseo	170,000
72	First Quay Blvd	49	House	Davi Elyon	175,000
73	First Quay Blvd	50	House	Davi Elyon	42,500

74	First Quay Blvd	51	House	Yako Yakovil	80,000
75	First Quay Blvd	52	Store	Yako Yakovil	10,000
76	First Quay Blvd	53	Store	Yako Yakovil	10,000
77	First Quay Blvd	54	House	Flor, wife of Isac Alhassid	150,000
78	First Quay Blvd	55	House	Mişon Alhassid	160,000
79	First Quay Blvd	56	House	Nassim Kapovano	225,000
80	Ayasofya Blvd	1	Mansion	Yozef Elyon	165,000
81	Second Quay Blvd	117	mansion with garden	Yozef Elyon	175,000
82	Second Quay Blvd	119	mansion with garden	Isac Boton	250,000
83	Second Quay Blvd	121	mansion with garden	Mişon Şalom	200,000
84	Second Quay Blvd	123	mansion with court	Yako Florentin	80,000
85	Second Quay Blvd	125	mansion with court	Yako Florentin	190,000
86	Second Quay Blvd	127	empty lot	Yako Sidis	47,000
87	Second Quay Blvd	129	House	Yuda Alkalabi	150,000
88	First Quay Blvd	57	empty lot	Yako Sidis	100,000
89	First Quay Blvd	58	House	İsac Florentin	
90	First Quay Blvd	59	House	Haim Salem	175,000
91	First Quay Blvd	60	empty lot	Periklis and Nicolas Hatzilazarou	80,000
92	Second Quay Blvd	131	Shed	Yako Sidis	29,000
93	Second Quay Blvd	133	lot with shed	İsac Florentin	25,000
94	Second Quay Blvd	135	Shed	İsac Florentin	5,000
95	Second Quay Blvd	137	Store	İsac Florentin	52,000
96	Second Quay Blvd	139	empty lot	Haim Salem	38,500
97	First Quay Blvd	61	Apartment	Osman Bey	110,000
98	First Quay Blvd	62	Apartment	Osman Bey	100,000

99	First Quay Blvd	63	empty lot	Mihalaki Bey	60,000
100	First Quay Blvd	64	Shop	Mihalaki Bey	6,000
101	First Quay Blvd	65	empty lot		27,500
102	First Quay Blvd	66	Shed		17,500
103	First Quay Blvd	67	House	Salomon Sapporta and Yuda Nar	80,000
104	First Quay Blvd	68	House	Salomon Sapporta and Yuda Nar	60,000
105	Second Quay Blvd	141	Mansion	Nehama Mallah	120,000
106	First Quay Blvd	69	Shop	Mişon Benyamin	60,000
107	First Quay Blvd	70	Café	Mişon Benyamin	6,000
108	First Quay Blvd	71	Café	Periklis Hatzilazarou	5,000
109	First Quay Blvd	72	Shop	Periklis Hatzilazarou	30,000
110	Second Quay Blvd	143	Shop	Mişon Benyamin	8,000
111	Second Quay Blvd	145-149	3 shops	Mişon Benyamin	24,000
112	Second Quay Blvd	151	Shop	Mişon Benyamin	6,000
113	Second Quay Blvd	153	lot with shed	Periklis Hatzilazarou	40,000
114	First Quay Blvd	73	casino with garden	Achilles Tungaris	105,000
115	First Quay Blvd	74-74/1	empty lot, shop	Yorgos Kirtsis	93,000
116	First Quay Blvd	75-76	beer-hall on top of a shop	Şevki Efendi	105,000
117	First Quay Blvd	77	Shop	Şevki Efendi	15,000
118	First Quay Blvd	78	Sporting Club	Yusuf Kapancı Efendi	87,500
119	First Quay Blvd	79-80	house on top of Club Italia	Dimitris Şerefi	205,000
120	First Quay Blvd	81	America Beer-Hall	Yusuf and Ahmed Kapancı	50,000
121	First Quay Blvd	82	Casino	Fazil and Cemil Bey	50,000

122	First Quay Blvd	83	Alhambra Theatre with garden	Kapovich	125,000
123	First Quay Blvd	84	beer-hall with garden	Stella, wife of Dr Panayotis Rokas	55,000
124	First Quay Blvd	85	House	Hafez İbrahim Efendi	70,000
125	First Quay Blvd	86	House	the sons of Saul Modiano	200,000

B) Maps

Map I: Antoine Wernieski, *Plan de Salonique*, detail (c. 1884-1885).

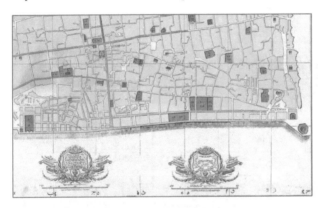

Map II: Properties in the quay, c. 1875-1885.

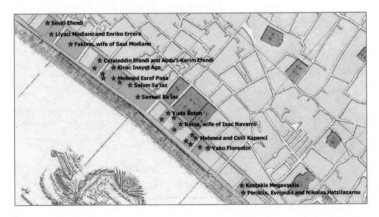

Map III: Distribution of spatial functions, 1906

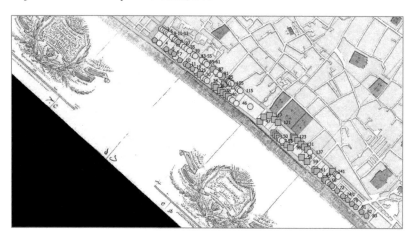

Key: Circles-commercial; squares-residential; pentagons-entertainment venues.

Map IV: Properties in the quay 1906

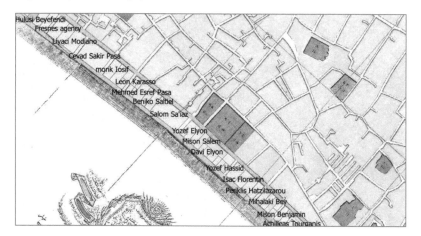

Visualization of Ottoman Borderland in Early Modern Bosnia (Mid-15th – Late 16th Centuries): The Ottoman *Serhat* in Bosnia and GIS

Elma Korić

Abstract

Throughout the early modern period, Bosnia was administratively part of a large global empire, the Ottoman state. Various manifestations of Ottoman rule in the territory of the Bosnian eyalet, an administrative unit that for a long time encompassed areas outside the borders of today's Bosnia and Herzegovina, have often been the subject of both Bosnian-Herzegovinian, regional and world historiography. The Ottoman borderland (serhat) in Bosnia was the subject of many earlier studies by Bosnian-Herzegovinian Ottoman period scholars. These studies were based on different kinds of Ottoman censuses and other documents from the offices of the Ottoman administration, and due to the nature of the documents, their focus was mostly on the military aspect of the serhat. This presentation aims to practically demonstrate the use of new technologies (GIS) to create a visualisation of the Ottoman borderland in Early Modern Bosnia based on sources of Ottoman origin (tapu tahrir defterleri, maliyeden müdevver defterleri) from the period 1468-1587 and Bosnian-Herzegovinian scholarly works based upon them in the period 1950-2014.

Throughout the early modern era, Bosnia was administratively part of a large global empire, the Ottoman state. Various manifestations of Ottoman rule in the territory of the Bosnian *eyalet*, an administrative unit that for a long time encompassed areas outside the borders of today's Bosnia and Herzegovina, have often been the subject of both Bosnian-Herzegovinian, regional and world historiography. Due to its specific geopolitical position, Bosnia in the early modern era was an extremely turbulent border area and interest zone, as well as the site of struggle for dominance between the greatest powers of the time: the Venetian Republic, the Habsburg Monarchy and the Ottoman Empire. It is precisely at the point of collision and encounter of the world's most significant empires that borders often changed their course. An increased interest in the study of Bosnia and Herzegovina's Ottoman past in the past two decades or so within world historiography was inspired by the formation of new borders in Southeast Europe, and especially in the Balkans following the dissolution of Yugoslavia. The aim of such inquiries into the past was mostly to determine whether the conflicts and violence of the 1990s had their roots in the early modern period when the Western Balkans was a borderland characterised by intensive inter-cultural exchange as well as daily violence and reprisals.

The necessary new approaches to the study of early modern history of Bosnia as a borderland, informed by contemporary methodological approaches promoted by relatively new sub-disciplines in the study of history such as borderland studies, were conditioned precisely by its specific geopolitical position at the age-old crossroads between different cultures and civilisations. Given that the Ottoman borderland in Bosnia encompassed an area whose large part still represents the official border between Bosnia and Herzegovina and the Republic of Croatia today, Croatian historiography has produced a multitude of scholarly works devoted to various aspects of the history of this borderland, i.e. the emergence and development of the Habsburg military frontiers of Croatia and Slavonia.[1] A significant contribution to the study of this three-way borderland was provided by Ottoman history scholars and numerous others within the *Triplex Confinium* international project.[2]

The Ottoman borderland (*serhat*) in Bosnia was the subject of all earlier studies by Bosnian-Herzegovinian scholars of the Ottoman period. These studies were based on different kinds of Ottoman censuses and other documents from the offices of the Ottoman administration, and due to the nature of the documents, the focus was mostly on the military aspect of the area. It is noteworthy that these scholars devoted more attention to studying the *serhat* at the north-western end of the Bosnian sanjak, which up until the fall of the medieval Kingdom of Hungary bordered with the Hungarian duchies of Jajce and Srebrenica, and then the Habsburg military frontiers of Croatia and Slavonia.[3] Compared to this, the Ottoman-Venetian borderland to the south-west of the Bosnian *eyalet* received relatively little scholarly attention.[4] Apart from a few lonely examples,

---

[1] As a result of an analysis of relevant monographs, anthologies, source editions and articles in magazines printed in the Republic of Croatia between 1959 and 2013, performed in search of the characteristics of historiography about Military Frontier in Croatia, Buczynski provided a list of a total of 48 books, 353 articles by 168 authors. Alexander Buczynski, „Trendovi u vojnokrajiškoj historiografiji na području Republike Hrvatske poslije 1959. godine", in *Zbornik radova Franz Vaniček i vojnokrajiška historiografija*, eds. Robert Skenderović and Stanko Andrić (Slavonski Brod: Hrvatski institut za povijest - Podružnica za povijest Slavonije, Srijema i Baranje, 2017), 223-239.

[2] Drago Roksandić, *Triplex Confinium ili O granicama i regijama hrvatske povijesti 1500. - 1800.* (Zagreb: Barbat, 2003); Alfred J. Rieber, *The Struggle for the Eurasian Borderlands: From the Rise of Early Modern Empires to the End of the First World War* (Cambridge University Press, 2014). Scholarly works of the researchers in the field of Ottoman studies in Croatia (Nenad Moačanin, Kornelija Jurin-Starčević,Vjeran Kursar etc.) are also very significant for the topic.

[3] Hazim Šabanović, „Početak turske vladavine u Bosni", *Glasnik Istorijskog društva BIH* 7 (1955): 37-51; Hazim Šabanović, „Bosansko krajište",*Glasnik Istorijskog društva BIH* 9 (1957): 177-220; Hazim Šabanović, „Vojno uređenje Bosne od 1463. god. do kraja XVI stoljeća", *Glasnik Društva istoričara BiH* 9 (1961): 173-224; *Krajište Isa-bega Ishakovića. Zbirni katastarski popis iz 1455. Godine* (Sarajevo: Orijentalni institut, 1964); Hamdija Kreševljaković, *Kapetanije u Bosni i Hercegovini*, Djela (Sarajevo: Naučno društvo Bosne i Hercegovine,1954); Avdo Sućeska, *Ajani. Prilog izučavanju lokalne vlasti u našim zemljama za vrijeme Turaka* (Sarajevo: Naučno društvo Bosne i Hercegovine, 1965); Avdo Sućeska, „Sličnosti i razlike između odžakluk timara i odžakluka kapetana i ostalih graničara u Bosanskom pašaluku", *Godišnjak Pravnog fakulteta* 20 (1972): 357-364; Adem Handžić, „Prilog istoriji starih gradova u Bosanskoj i Slavonskoj krajini pred kraj XVI vijeka", *Glasnik Društva istoričara BiH* 13 (1963): 321-339; Adem Handžić, „O organizaciji vojne krajine Bosanskog ejaleta u XVII stoljeću: Sjeverna i sjeverozapadna granica", *Prilozi Instituta za istoriju* 23, no. 24 (1988): 45-60; Aladin Husić, „Tvrđave Bosanskog sandžaka i njihove posade 1530. godine", *Prilozi za orijentalnu filologiju* 4 (1999): 189-229.

[4] Fehim Dž. Spaho, „Organizacija vojne krajine u sandžacima Klis i Krka u XVII stoljeću", in *Vojne krajine u jugoslovenskim zemljama u novom veku do Karlovačkog mira 1699.* (Beograd, 1989): 101-103; Seid M. Traljić, „Tursko

in Bosnian-Herzegovinian Ottoman studies, the years when peace agreements were signed—heralding a process of delineating borders—served mostly as temporal markers for the purpose of analysing different time periods in terms of the administrative and military organisation of the Bosnian *eyalet*, as well as many other specificities of the structure of the Bosnian *eyalet*.[5] Due to the time when they were written, most of these scholarly works were objectively precluded from more modern methodological approaches, but they are nonetheless the foundations for any new study of this borderland. Thanks to these works, we are now able to define the territorial extension of the Bosnian *serhat* through time, and then provide a detailed insight into the structure and composition of borderland military forces - frontiersmen of the Bosnian *serhat* – ways of their financing and changes to financing status, changes to the structure of fortress garrisons, differences between *ulufe* (salaried) and *timar* (landed) garrisons in the Bosnian *eyalet* – through the various phases of its emergence and development.

Given that new methodological approaches to the study of borderlands start from the assumption that the borderland was a world in itself, and that the people of the borderland from both sides of the official border had more in common with each other than with the people at the centres of their respective states, the example of Bosnia as a centuries-long Ottoman borderland seems like the ideal subject for the examination of this basic assumption. The most suitable approach to studying borderlands in Bosnia and the region would be to apply the concept of borderland studies with a preference for "connected histories"[6] and "entangled histories"[7] that promote looking for links in the contact zones of the Early Modern Period.

In the past few decades, the trend of applying new technologies in the humanities, along with the application of new methodological concepts, has been on the rise in world historiography. Along with studying new and attractive topics in their papers, studies and thematic collections on

---

mletačke granice u Dalmaciji u XVI i XVII stoljeću", *Radovi Instituta JAZU u Zadru* 20 (1973): 447-458; Snježana Buzov, „Razgraničenje između Bosanskog pašaluka i mletačke Dalmacije nakon kandijskog rata", *Povijesni prilozi* 12, (1993): 1-38; Aladin Husić, "Vojne prilike u splitsko-zadarskom zaleđu u 16. stoljeću (osmanski serhat 1530-1573)", *Prilozi za orijentalnu filologiju* 56 (2006): 125-144. In past several years some of the translations of the *tapu tahrir defters* for Sanjak of Klis to Bosnian language has also been published: *Opširni popis Kliškog sandžaka iz 1550. godine*, obradili: Fehim Dž. Spaho, Ahmed S. Aličić; priredila: Behija Zlatar (Sarajevo: Orijentalni institut, 2007); *Opširni popis timara mustahfiza Kliškog sandžaka iz 1550. godine*, prevela, obradila i pripremila za štampu Fazileta Hafizović, (Sarajevo: Institut Ibn Sina, 2014).
[5] Worth mentioning is Ešref Kovačević, *Granice Bosanskog pašaluka prema Austriji i Mletačkoj Republici po odredbama Karlovačkog mira*, (Sarajevo: Svjetlost, 1973).
[6] Sanjay Subrahmanyam, „Connected Histories: Notes towards a Reconfiguration of Early Modern Eurasia", *Modern Asian Studies* 31, no. 3 (1997): 735-762.
[7] Pascal Firges, Tobias P Graf; Christian Roth and Gulay Tulasoglu, eds., *Well-connected domains: towards an entangled Ottoman history* (Leiden, Boston: Brill, 2014) as well as many others.

borderlands of the Ottoman Empire, in the past decade, Ottoman historians have become aware of or have employed new methodological directions and have ventured into applying new technologies.[8] In Bosnian-Herzegovinian historiography to date, Ottoman studies scholars employed the tools of economics and social science for visualising the historical narrative, meaning that the works of past generations were augmented by charts, graphs and occasionally geographic maps. However, new technologies allow for much greater mobility of various types of information that may serve not just the purposes of visualisation but could also function as databases. In brief, a geographic information system (GIS) is a tool that uses various forms of data as inputs to produce a map as an output. Because these maps are easier to understand than raw data, they can be used as a tool to communicate geographic information to a general audience.[9]

This presentation aims to practically demonstrate the use of new technologies (GIS) to create a visualisation of early modern Bosnia based on sources of Ottoman origin and scholarly works based upon them (*tapu tahrir defterleri, maliyeden müdevver defterleri*). To start with, in order to establish the preconditions for the study of Bosnia in the early modern era as an Ottoman borderland (*serhat*), the borderland belt must be defined. Given that in the early modern era, the concept of linear borders was not yet widely established, the main criteria for proclaiming an area a borderland included the distribution and position of borderland fortresses and their domains. The Ottoman state fostered the Islamic culture of its predecessors in the Near East so it is worth noting that medieval Islamic geography also had the concept of borders and borderlands where border fortresses were situated.[10] Views of cities—characteristic and widespread as distinctive features of illuminated Ottoman manuscripts from the 16th century—were used as documents testifying to the territorial expansion of the Ottoman Empire and as ways to map expanded borders. The idea of presenting the border through images of cities was well-suited to the

---

[8] Caroline Finkel, „Afterword," in *The Frontiers of the Ottoman World*, ed. A.S. Peacock (British Academy, 2009); Amy Singer, „The Ottoman Balkans and the Middle East Compared: How Might This Be Accomplished?" in *Ottoman Legacies in the Contemporary Mediterranean: the Balkans and the Middle East Compared*, eds. Eyal Ginio and Karl Kaser (Jerusalem: The Forum for European Studies, 2013): 23-40; Michael Polczynski and Mark Polczynski, „A Microsoft Excel Application for Automatically Building Historical Geography GIS Maps", *Transactions in GIS* 17, no. 1 (2013): 148–157; Emrah Safa Gürkan, „50 günde devr-i Bahr-ı Sefid: Königsbergli Lubenau'nun kadırgayla imtihanı / Around the Mediterranean in Fifty Days: Reinhold Lubenau's struggle with the galley", *Journal of Ottoman Studies (AHCI)* 43 (2014): 273-300.
[9] Ian N. Gregory, *A place in history: A guide to using GIS in historical research*. 2nd Edition, (Belfast: Centre for Data Digitisation and Analysis, Queens University, 2005); Jack B. Owens, "Toward a Geographically-Integrated, Connected World History: Employing Geographic Information Systems (GIS)," *History Compass* 5, no. 6 (2007): 2014-2040.
[10] The borderland was usually marked by the terms *awasim* (ar.عواصم) or *tuġûr* (ar. ثغور) See: Ralph W. Brauer, „Boundaries and Frontiers in Medieval Muslim Geography", *Transactions of the American Philosophical Society*, New Series, 85, no. 6 (1995): 1-73.

geopolitical reality of the Ottoman borderlands, which were fluid and defined mostly through usurpation of borderland cities. Images of cities offered a vision of the Ottoman Empire as a sum of territories to the members of the ruling elite who collected these images and experienced their Empire as such.[11] In the perception of Ottoman authorities, borderland sanjaks such as the Bosnian sanjak were considered frontiers throughout their existence. For Ottoman travellers, the *serhat* began as soon as they left Rumelia, and in still living folk memory, this included the whole of western Bosnia, and used to include parts of today's Croatia that were within the Ottoman Empire at the time, to the exclusion of eastern Slavonia.[12] The concrete *serhat* as the first line of defence of the Bosnian *eyalet*, and by extension the whole state in the given period, was limited to the belt containing the fortresses where salaried garrisons were stationed. They were financed in a completely different way, that is they received cash payments (tur. *ulufe*), as opposed to the garrisons of fortresses in more peaceful and less exposed interior parts of the *eyalet* whose service was paid for from revenues of the *timar*.[13] On the border with Habsburg military frontiers in Croatia and Slavonia — on what used to be called the bulwark of Christianity or *Antemurale Christianitatis* — in Bosnia, a symbolic bulwark of Islam was established or *Sedd-i Islam*.[14]

What follows is an illustration of the practical application of this technology to visualise the extent of the Ottoman *serhat* in Bosnia in the various phases of its formation and development in the early modern era, based on data from Ottoman sources dated between 1455 and 1587 and academic works based on these sources.[15]

The Ottomans had been present in the territory of the Medieval Bosnian Kingdom for decades before the establishment of Ottoman rule in 1463 with the formation of the Bosnian sanjak. In the Ottoman census of 1455, the area of today's Sarajevo, in the "vilayet of Hodidjed"

---

[11] Kathryn A. Ebel, „Representations of the Frontier in Ottoman Town Views of the Sixteenth Century", *Imago Mundi: The International Journal for the History of Cartography* 60, no. 1 (2008): 1-22.
[12] Nenad Moačanin, „Hrvati pod vlašću Osmanskoga Carstva do razdoblja reformi u Bosni i Hercegovini (1463.-1831.)", in *Hrvatsko-slavonska krajina i Hrvati pod vlašću Osmanskoga carstva u ranome novom vijeku, Hrvatska povijest u ranome novom vijeku 2*, (Zagreb: Leykam International, 2007), 150.
[13] Handžić, "O organizaciji vojne krajine", 45-60.
[14] A number of border towns in the Bosnian *eyalet* were named Sedd-i Islam, in the Klis sanjak, for instance, this was the fortress of Vespoljevac (today Islam Grčki and Islam Latinski), while in the Herzegovina sanjak, the title was given to today's Gabela.
[15] There were also other significant border fortresses in the sanjak of Zvornik and sanjak of Hercegovinia, but this paper will focus only on fortresses stationed in north-western Ottoman borderlands in Bosnia, towards the Habsburg Monarchy, and south-western towards the Venetian Republic.

or "vilayet of Sarayovası", an active garrison of 23 members receiving *timar* from the Sarajevo Valley area were noted in just one fortress, that of Hodidide/Hodidjed.[16]

The first Ottoman census of the Bosnian sanjak dates from 1468-69.[17] Included in it are 300 *sipahi* and 300 soldiers, as well as 17 fortresses with *timar* garrisons: Kličevac, Borovac, Kreševo, Trešnjevo, Prozor, Susid, Vranduk, Bobovac, Hodidjed, Zvečan, Jeleč, Dobrun, Borač, Višegrad, Mileševo, Samobor, Tođevac[18] (map 1). Near the end of the 15th century, the number of *timar* garrisons was reduced, and the censuses note 14 fortresses: Hodidjed, Dubrovnik, Prozor, Akhisar, Susid, Travnik, Vrh Bilica, Vranduk, Bobovac, Kličevac, Višegrad, Dobrun, Jeleč and Zvečan.[19]

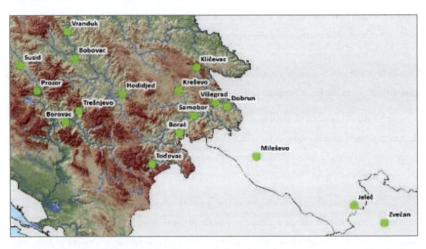

Map 1: Fortresses Bosnian sanjak 1468-69, authors: Elma Korić and Azer Kurtović, 2015. (GIS database: GDi GISDATA d.o.o. Sarajevo; GIS software: ESRI ArcGIS for Desktop)

In the Ottoman-Hungarian Treaty of 1503, apart from the cities in the interior of Bosnia, 19 fortified cities in the "Bosnian *vilayet* borderland" were also recorded: Kamengrad, Ključ, Hlivno, Belgrad/Dlamoč, Vinčac, Komotin, Travnik, Vrhbilica, Vranduk, Doboj, Maglaj,

---

[16] İstanbul, Başbakanlık Osmanlı Arşivi (BOA), *Maliyeden Müdevver Defterleri (MAD)* 544; translation to Bosnian: Šabanović, *Krajište Isa-bega Ishakovića*.
[17] İstanbul, Belediye Kütüphanesi, *Müallim Cevdet Yazmaları*, 0097 (original 0/76); translation to Bosnian: *Sumarni popis sandžaka Bosna iz 1468/69. godine*, Ahmed S. Aličić, (Mostar: Islamski kulturni centar Mostar, 2008).
[18] Cf. Šabanović, "Bosansko krajište"; Handžić, "O organizaciji vojne krajine".
[19] İstanbul, BOA, *Tapu Tahrir Defterleri (TD)* 18 and 24; Husić, "Tvrđave Bosanskog sandžaka".

Belgrad/Akhisar, Susid, Toričan, Fenarlik, Prozor, Bobovac and Dubrovnik, as well as the city of Zvornik and its surrounding area.[20]

Records of an Ottoman census of the Bosnian sanjak from 1516 show that *timar* garrisons were stationed in 14 fortresses: Hodidjed, Dubrovnik, Prozor, Akhisar, Susid, Travnik, Vrh Bilica, Vranduk, Bobovac, Kličevac, Višegrad, Dobrun, Jeleč and Zvečan.[21]

A specific and unique *defter* from 1530 includes, contrary to custom, joint records for garrison members granted an estate for their service (*timar*) and garrison members receiving a salary for their service (*ulufe*). According to A. Husić, the *defter* contains records for 28 cities with a *timar* garrison (Zvečan, Jeleč, Dobrun, Višegrad, Kličevac, Hodidjed, Dubrovnik, Bobovac, Vrh Bilica, Fenarlik, Travnik, Prozor, Akhisar, Susid, Vranduk, Toričan, Sokol, Komotin, Vinčac, Golhisar, Maglaj, Hlivno, Belgrad, Nečven, Sinj, Vrh Rika, Drniš, Jajce) and 18 cities (Doboj, Ključ, Kamengrad, Udbina, Karin, Obrovac, Ostrovica, Skradin, Knin, Bočac, Zvečaj, Banja Luka, Kotor, Tešanj, Kličevac, Bilaj, Novi Grad, Kobaš) with an *ulufe* garrison.[22]

Following the formation of the Klis sanjak in 1537, some of these fortresses came under the administration of the newly founded sanjak, while others remained part of the Bosnian *sanjak*. Given that the status of frontier borderland or *intihâ-i serhad* was temporarily accorded to the Klis *sanjak*, the fortresses belonging to it were in the subsequent period predominantly manned by *ulufe* garrisons. Between 1540 and 1550, 17 garrisons remained stationed in the Bosnian sanjak in the following fortresses: Zvečan, Dobrun, Višegrad, Hodidjed, Dubrovnik, Jajce, Banja Luka, Gradiška, Vinčac, Dobor, Doboj, Bočac, Kotor, Maglaj, Tešanj, Travnik and Vranduk, with a total of 465 *timar* garrison members.[23]

According to a census of frontiersmen of the periphery of the Bosnian *eyalet* from 1586-87, 14 cities are mentioned in the Bosnian Sanjak, of which ten on the River Una and the Prekunje area, two in the area of the Sana River and one on the Sava River. (Kamengrad, Banja Luka, Novi Majdan, Gradiška, Dubica, Jasenovac, Kostajnica, Novi, Krupa, Cazin, Bužim, Ostrožac, Gvozdansko, Zrin). In the Pakrac sanjak, 11 cities are mentioned (Cernik, Dobri Grad, Sirač,

---

[20] Tayyib Gökbilgin, „Korvin Mathias (Mátyás)ın Bayezid II.e mektupları tercümeleri ve 1503 (909) Osmanlı-Macar muahedesinin Türkçe metni", *Belleten*, C. XXII, no. 87 (1958): 369-390; Hazim Šabanović, B*osanski pašaluk*, (Sarajevo: Naučno društvo SR BiH, 1959), 55.
[21] İstanbul, BOA, *TD* 56; Husić, "Tvrđave Bosanskog sandžaka", 196.
[22] İstanbul, BOA, *MAD* 540; Osmanlı Arşivi Daire Başkanlığı, Yayın Nu: 81, Defter-i Hâkânî Dizisi: X, (Ankara: T.C. Başbakanlik Devlet Arşivleri Genel Müdürlüğü, 2006); Husić, "Tvrđave Bosanskog sandžaka", 189-229.
[23] İstanbul, BOA, *TD* 411; Husić, "Tvrđave Bosanskog sandžaka", 202.

Pakrac, Podborje, Velika, Međurić, Kreštelovac, Zdenci, Moslavina), while in the Požega *sanjak*, frontiersmen guarded 7 cities (Požega, Kamengrad, Sv. Mikloš, Voćin, Slatnik, Brezovica and Virovitica). The garrisons were mostly made up of *ulufe* (salaried) garrisons, while some cities also had *timar* (landed) garrisons[24] (map 2).

Map 2: Fortresses of the northern border of the Bosnian *eyalet* in 1586-87, authors: Elma Korić and Azer Kurtović, 2015. (GIS database: GDi GISDATA d.o.o. Sarajevo; GIS software: ESRI ArcGIS for Desktop)

As noted above, on the south-western border in the newly formed Klis *sanjak*, certain administrative transformations took place between the census of 1530 and that of 1540. Some of the fortresses that in 1530 had belonged to the Bosnian sanjak later came under the authority of the Klis sanjak. This is illustrated by Ottoman censuses of the Klis sanjak from 1550.[25] *Timar* garrisons were recorded in 14 fortresses: Livno, Prozor, Susid, Akhisar/Prusac, Fenarlik, Golhisar/Jezero, Sokol, Belgrad/Dlamoč, Sinj, Vrhrika/Vrlika, Knin, Drniš and Nečven.[26] According to F. Hafizović, the fortress of Zvonigrad was later recorded in the same *defter*.[27]

---

[24] İstanbul, BOA, *MAD* 826; Spaho, "Organizacija vojne krajine", 45-60.
[25] İstanbul, BOA, *TD* 440; translation to Bosnian: Hafizović, *Opširni popis*; İstanbul, BOA, *TD* 284; translated to Bosnian: Spaho and Aličić, *Opširni popis Kliškog sandžaka iz 1550*.
[26] Spaho, „Organizacija vojne krajine", 45-60.
[27] Hafizović, *Opširni popis*, 16.

The Ottoman censuses of the 1570s document the existence of a stable fortification belt along this part of the border. According to a 1574 census, F. Spaho notes the following fortresses: Knin, Udbina, Velin, Vrana, Bilaj Barlet, Bilaj Bunić, Boričevac, Ostrovica, Zvonigrad, Obrovac.[28] *Ulufe* garrisons are mentioned in another *defter* from the same period as being stationed in 13 fortresses: Klis, Skradin, Ostrovica, Nadin, Knin, Udbina, Novi, Vrana, Bilaj Barlet, Bilaj Bunić, Bilaj Blagaj, Obrovac and Boričevac.[29]

According to the research of A. Husić, the outermost Ottoman military belt in 1573-74 was made up of 7 fortresses with *timar* garrisons (Nečven, Sinj, Vrhrika, Drniš, Knin, Zvonigrad and Boričevac) and 19 fortresses with *ulufe* garrisons (Udbina, Velin, Bilaj Bunić, Ostrovica, Bilaj Barlet, Vrčevo, Zemunik, Polešnik, Obrovac, Nadin, Karin, Vrana, Rakitnica, Kašić, Dazlina, Drniš, Klis, Lončarić and Kamengrad).[30]

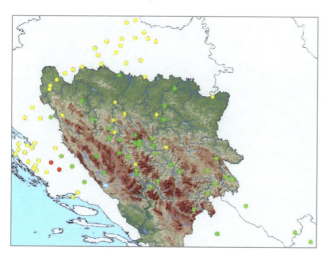

Map. 3: Fortresses of the south-western Ottoman borderland (Bosnian *vilayet/sancak/eyalet* 1468-1587), authors: Elma Korić and Azer Kurtović, 2015. (GIS database: GDi GISDATA d.o.o. Sarajevo; GIS software: ESRI ArcGIS for Desktop)

Legend:

Timar
Ulufe
Ulufe/Timar

---

[28] İstanbul, BOA, *TD* 533; Spaho, „Organizacija vojne krajine", 45-60.
[29] İstanbul, BOA, *TD* 532; Spaho, „Organizacija vojne krajine", 45-60.
[30] İstanbul, BOA, *TD* 526; Husić, „Vojne prilike u splitsko-zadarskom zaleđu", 143.

Conclusion

The territory of the Bosnian *eyalet* in the Early Modern Period represented one of the most turbulent Ottoman borders to the lands of Early Modern Christian Europe. The territory of that border was marked by the fortresses. Based on Ottoman sources, it can be concluded that the garrisons of the fortresses located in the interior of the Bosnian *Eyalet* mostly had *timar* revenues, while the garrisons in the fortress at the outlying end received their salaries in cash. Using the new information technologies, this information can also be visually presented on maps.

Sovereignty and Space through GIS in the Early Modern Polish-Lithuanian/Ottoman Frontier

Michael Połczyński

Abstract

 At its height during the 16th and 17th centuries, the mutual frontier of the Polish-Lithuanian Commonwealth and the Ottoman Empire stretched 1,200 km over the Pontic Steppe region of eastern Ukraine to the heart of Central Europe. Encompassing territories connected to Crimea, the Pontic Steppe, and the Carpathian Mountains within the modern nations of Ukraine, Poland, Slovakia, Romania, Moldova, and Russia, it was the most extensive contiguous land-based frontier shared by a European and an Islamic power during the early modern period. In light of sustained interest throughout the humanities in current and historical relations between Europe and the Islamic world, and in particular the areas of Crimea and Ukraine, this zone of prolonged and intense cultural, economic, and socio-political contact has received little attention as a locus of contact. My research explores processes of conflict, mediation, reconciliation, and disparate notions of sovereignty and legitimacy of rule in the republican/dynastic imperial milieu of Europe's longest early modern frontier with the Islamic world during the 16th century. Apropos of data-driven historical studies on Southeastern Europe and the Ottoman Empire, I am creating a gazetteer for the region using Ottoman, Polish, and other local sources and am employing GIS and related technologies in order to better envision and study these concepts in situ.

 Called the *dzikie pola* ("wild field") by Poles, Ukrainians and Russians and the *deşt-i kipçak* ("Kipchak wasteland") in Ottoman and Crimean sources, this geographic zone hosted multiple coinciding and overlapping frontiers, the existence of which had sweeping ramifications for the shared history of Europe and the Islamic world; confessional frontiers of Christendom/the *Dar al-Islam* as well as Latin/Orthodox lands, political-ideological frontiers between republican and dynastic imperial governments, frontiers between settled agriculturalists and pastoralists, and environmental frontiers between deciduous forests and the steppe. The confluence of these social and natural factors created a liminal zone that was both deep and broad, allowing for the growth of satellite and semi-autonomous frontier societies such as Cossack brotherhoods and the Crimean and Nogai Tatars. The attempts of central powers in Kraków/Vilnius and Istanbul to control their peripheral clients, whose particular usefulness as military auxiliaries was tied to their semi-nomadic, fiercely independent social structures, led to a series of state-building policies in order to maintain control of the Polish-Lithuanian/Ottoman frontier. The results of these policies had wide-ranging implications on political and social climates from Safavid Persia to the kingdom of France, and ultimately helped to shape modern perceptions and identities associated with European and Islamic societies that have since spread to many corners of the globe.

From first diplomatic contact in 1414 to the third and final partition of the Commonwealth in 1795, Polish-Lithuanian/Ottoman relations were driven by two main forces. The first was the larger geopolitical situation in the region, coupled with the grand strategies of both states over the *longue durée*. The second was their shared frontier. The grand strategies of both polities generally aimed to maintain peaceful relations with one another in light of more pressing rivalries with the Habsburgs and Safavids, in the case of the Ottomans, and with Muscovy and the Habsburgs, in the case of Poland-Lithuania.[1] Events on the frontier, however, threatened to upset this balance and consistently proved a serious challenge for power brokers. The constant state of low-level violence that was the order of the day in the Polish-Lithuanian/Ottoman frontier zone was sporadically punctuated by larger incursions and flagrant episodes of unsanctioned inter-regional violence that caused both centers to scramble in order to maintain peace. Disagreements were framed in terms of competing claims to territorial and jurisdictional sovereignty.

Types of Sovereignty

In his book *Boundaries: the Making of France and Spain in the Pyrenees*, Peter Sahlins convincingly argues for three categories of early modern jurisdictional sovereignty:[2]

1.) Jurisdictional sovereignty could be the relationship between subject and ruler. The early modern state inherited the medieval practice of giving precedence to this political bond over the territorial one. Early modern "citizenship", defined in relation to the king, was symbolically affirmed in the oaths of loyalty and allegiance by individuals and corporate groups. Despite there being serious differences in the emerging republican system of Poland-Lithuania and the social order of the Ottoman sultanate, personal allegiance to either monarch by individuals or groups in the frontier created powerful legal bonds that could be leveraged by leaders when making larger claims concerning the legitimacy of their rule.

---

[1] The pragmatism of Ottoman rule that Gábor Ágoston proposes in lieu of a more consistent "grand strategy"[1] usually kept the Ottoman Empire out of conflicts on multiple fronts. Gábor Ágoston, "The Ottomans: From Frontier Principality to Empire," in John Andreas Olsen and Colin S. Gray, eds., *The Practice of Strategy: From Alexander the Great to the Present*, (Oxford, New York: Oxford University Press, 2011), 105-131.

[2] Peter Sahlins, *Boundaries: The Making of France and Spain in the Pyrenees* (Berkeley: University of California Press, 1989), 28-29.

2.) Jurisdictional sovereignty could also emerge from an administration that gave precedence to jurisdiction over territory. Generally conceived, sovereignty consisted of the exercise of authority within a wide range of domains: military affairs, justice, ecclesiastical policies, commercial and economic activities, and taxation. Each of these jurisdictional domains was an administrative circumscription with its own boundaries; these boundaries often failed to coincide, and they remained distinct from the political boundary of the kingdom. In the frontier context this could lead to episodes of condominium or parallel dominium.

3.) Rulers ceded or acquired, in war as in diplomatic settlement, specific political jurisdictions, and rights to domains. These agreements, taking place in the intra-state level, did not always reflect internal narratives of jurisdictional sovereignty. A political jurisdiction or domain may be ceded in a mutually ratified treaty to another state, but this action may be challenged or denied by internal social forces, or publicly repudiated in diplomatic discourse with a third party.

By the turn of the end of the 16th century, the kings of Poland-Lithuania and Ottoman sultans portrayed themselves to their own subjects and to other regional powers as the undisputed masters of their respective sides of a vast shared frontier stretching from the Pontic Steppe to the northern reaches of the Carpathian Mountains. Both monarchs developed narratives affirming their rights to rule based on historical sovereignties of their predecessors and their personal abilities to defend and expand territories of their realms. What was less clear "on the ground" was where, precisely, the power of the Polish King and the Ottoman Sultan began and ended in the vast shared frontier. In the preceding centuries, as the realm of the Ottoman Sultans grew from the Byzantine frontier west and north into the Balkans and east into Anatolia and beyond, Polish and Lithuanian rulers established a loose net of sovereignty over much of the Pontic Steppe, the Principality of Moldavia, parts of the northern Black Sea littoral, and the Danube delta. Meanwhile, Lithuanian involvement in the internal dynamics of the breakdown of the Golden Horde and emergence of the Crimean Khanate continued to serve as the basis for discord and cooperation in the face of Muscovite expansion, continued rivalries within the Horde, and the eventual encroachment of Ottoman power.

The main argument of my thesis is that overlapping relationships forged by Polish, Lithuanian, and Ottoman rulers with the same frontier power brokers in the 14th and 15th centuries resulted in a particularly deep, contested frontier zone, and protracted periods of unresolved condominium in the Polish-Lithuanian/Ottoman frontier into the 17th century. Parallel dominium, for the purposes of this discussion, was extant when frontier clients entered into legally defined or functional relationships of vassalage to more than one sovereign – in this case the Ottoman Sultan, the Kings of Poland, and the Grand Dukes of Lithuanian. Condominium in the region was most often realized through negotiated sovereignty; one major power accepting a client appointed by the other major power as a functional and therefore mutual vassal in the borderlands.

By the 16th century, in addition to unresolved overlapping personal relationships of vassalage or corporate clientage, Polish-Lithuanian and Ottoman rulers had inherited a complex web of claims to territorial sovereignty that dated in some cases to the initial Mongol invasions of Batu Khan in the first half of the 13th century. This resulted in problematic unresolved competing claims to territorial sovereignty by multiple parties.

As a result, king and sultan attempted to wield the changing concepts of sovereignty and legitimization of rule of two antithetical systems of government – a dynastic Sultanate and an emerging *forma-mixta* Republic – in an attempt to firm up their mutual frontiers, eliminate or amalgamate the claims of autochthonous local power brokers, and ultimately disentangle their conjoined sovereignties in a vast and socially diverse borderland. For their part, autochthonous frontier power brokers did what they could to maintain independence, developing their own cultures of local sovereignty that often conflicted with those of their "legal" overlords. In light of the political heterogeneity of the territorial units of this milieu (*forma-mixta* republic, Sunni Hanafi sultanate, Cossack brotherhoods, Chinggisid Khanate, elective voyevodeships, to name a few), episodes of parallel rule and condominium were theoretically anathema to the diverse notions of sovereignty in both the Ottoman Empire and Poland-Lithuania in the 16th century.

Within the distinct national historiographies that deal with Poland-Lithuania and the Ottoman Empire, the intense mediation of conflicting sovereignties often goes unnoticed. When the issue of sovereignty is remarked upon, it is not always understood within the context of the borderlands in which it arose, and usually appears in the form of sudden and ferocious conflict. And yet the Polish-Lithuanian/Ottoman frontier existed for centuries in peaceful states of parallel rule and condominium depending on how king and sultan proved tolerant of one another's cross-border machinations, or the degree to which they could abide the autonomous activities of one another's frontier clients. In many cases, the kings of Poland-Lithuania and Ottoman sultans made use of extralegal crossborder relationships, extending their influence over segments of a neighboring sovereign's frontier territories to push their own internal political agendas. And so the politics of the royal court, *sejm* (parliament), and divan could play out in this distant frontier, at times with immense effect, as was the case with Osman II's failed invasion of Poland in 1620 and his subsequent regicide.[3]

In Ottoman historiography, much has been made of the northern expansion of Ottoman power and the transformation of the Black Sea into an "Ottoman lake" as an essential phase in imperial expansion.[4] A close examination of the region during the 14th and 15th centuries indicates that the establishment of Ottoman rule over the heterogeneous polities of the north Black Sea littorals was immediately and persistently contested by local power brokers as well as by neighboring Poland-Lithuania, which maintained historical claims to sovereignty over borderland territories. The result was that the local reception of Ottoman, Polish, and Lithuanian suzerainties in the region was a multivalent and protracted affair. The entangled relationships of power that existed between the Ottoman Sultan, the King of Poland-Lithuania, and local frontier vassals in the north Black Sea littoral, Moldavia, and the Danube delta persisted into the late16th and 17th centuries, when episodes of intense mediation and conflict were initiated in part to allow the Ottoman Sultanate and the neighboring polity of Poland-Lithuania to hammer and shape their shared frontier into distinct zones of sovereignty more closely resembling the *memâlik-i mahrûse* (well-protected domains) and the *antemurale christianitatis* (Bulwark of Christendom) of the Ottoman imperial and Polish-Lithuanian republican epithets.

---

[3] Baki Tezcan,"Khotin 1621, or how the Poles changed the course of Ottoman history," *Acta Orientalia Academiae Scientiarum Hungaricae* 62, no. 2 (2009): 185-198.
[4] For more see Dariusz Kołodziejczyk, "Inner lake or frontier? The Ottoman Black Sea in the sixteenth and seventeenth centuries", in *Enjeux politiques, économiques et militaires en Mer Noire (XIV-XXI siècles): études à la mémoire de Mihail Guboglu*, eds. Faruk Bilici, Ionel Cândea, Anca Popescu (Brăila: Musée de Brăila - Éditions Istros 2007), 125-139.

Historical GIS

I have been working for some time with GIS and related technologies in order to help me understand the geographical space of the frontier. *GIS* As this region has rarely been studied through Polish-Lithuanian and Ottoman sources, it is very often difficult to figure out how source material is connected and where events occurred. I have found that building a cohesive narrative is impossible without first finding a way to recreate, at least for myself, the spaces in question.

Creating a Gazetteer

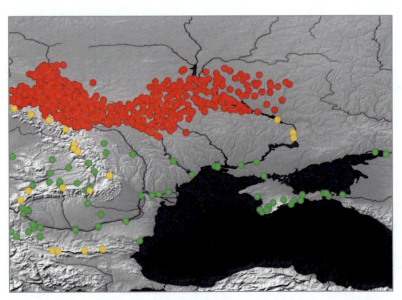

The 16th/17th century Polish-Lithuanian frontier gazetteer as it currently appears. Red icons are Polish-Lithuanian fortifications, green icons are Ottoman fortifications, yellow icons are mountain passes and significant river fords.

One of the most difficult aspects of my research is that there is no useful gazetteer for the places that I study connected to the periods that I focus on. After floundering around for several years, I have recently begun to work on a gazetteer for my dissertation, which I hope will one day serve as the seed for a more complete study of the region in the early modern context.

This is an exciting prospect as some of the earliest accurate maps of the region come from this period; Bernard Wapowski's 1507 maps of the Pontic Steppe, northern Balkans, Crimean and Black Sea littorals; Marcin Broniewski's 1579 *Tartariae Descriptio*; and Guillaume Le Vasseur de Beauplan's suite of maps of Ukraine, Crimea, and Moldavia from the 1640s provide a rich source for locating settlements, fortresses, trade routes, and even the location of forests and other natural features such as the Dnieper river.

Marcin Broniewski's 1507 map of Moldavia, from his *Tartariae Descriptio*.

Georeferencing these maps is helping me to determine the locations of major travel routes. This is particularly useful when trying to understand the movement of goods and peoples. Often enough, those goods were people. Glimpses of the economic importance of the Black Sea slave trade in the Khanate have been offered by studies like Halil Inalcik's publication of the customs register of Caffa from 1487-1490[5]. In his work on slave-hunting and redemption Dariusz

---

[5] Halil Inalcık, *The customs register of Caffa, 1487 - 1490*. (Cambridge, Mass: Harvard Univ., 1995).

Kolodziejczyk offers an estimate of 2,000,000 individuals taken into slavery in the Black Sea region between 1500-1700.[6] Alan Fisher's work on this subject deals mainly with Muscovy's reaction to Tatar raids through reform, expansion, and colonization.[7] Similar to Fisher, Maria Ivanics looks at the practice of slave taking as an integral part of the Crimean Tatar economy.[8] Her thesis states that slave taking was legitimized by Tatar society through the frequent droughts and epidemics that necessitated a constant renewal of agricultural labor on Crimean farms as well as the high profits of the Black Sea slave trade

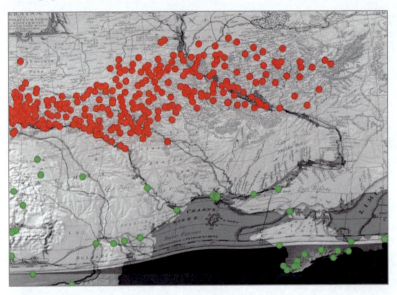

Guillaume Le Vasseur de Beauplan's map of Ukraine, 1648

By georeferencing Beauplan's 1648 map of Ukraine to the gazetteer that I am creating, it is possible to begin to reconstruct historical routes of trading, raiding, and travel, as well as the location of forests, fords, and passes.

---

[6] Dariusz Kolodziejczyk, "Slave hunting and slave redemption as a business enterprise: The northern Black Sea region in the sixteenth to seventeenth centuries," *Oriente Moderno* 86, no. 1(2006): 149.
[7] Alan W. Fisher, *A Precarious Balance: Conflict, Trade, and Diplomacy on the Russian-Ottoman Frontier* (İstanbul: Isis Press, 1999).
[8] Maria Ivanics, "Enslavement, Slave Labour, and the Treatment of Captives in the Crimean Khanate," in *Ransom Slavery along the Ottoman Borders: Early Fifteenth-Early Eighteenth Centuries*, eds. Geza David and Pál Fodor, (Leiden, Boston: Brill, 2007).

Preliminary work on the Polish-Lithuanian side of the frontier, which has much more readily available secondary source material, has resulted in a closer look at the defensive networks established to protect from mainly Crimean Tatar and Moldavian raids and large-scale invasions. Tools such as heat maps give a sense of the intense structuring of the defensive network on the edge of the frontier.

Towards a Linear Boundary/Zonal Frontier Model

I have been trying to develop ways of visualizing the overlapping claims to jurisdictional and territorial sovereignty in the Polish-Lithuanian/Ottoman frontier. In service to this goal I have elected to adopt and modify Peter Sahlins' model of early modern zonal vs. linear boundaries, accepting their co-existence.

In the Polish-Lithuanian/Ottoman frontier context, I have identified two main zones in the 16th century that can be differentiated in terms of their administration, and also in the way that they are imagined by the central powers of both polities. To the west, the frontier was relatively stable, with a mutually recognized linear boundary. The border followed the course of the Dniester River roughly from its source to the Black Sea. It was a relatively straightforward boundary that was rarely challenged: the left bank belonged to Poland-Lithuania, and the right bank belonged to the Ottoman vassal state of Moldavia, and the natural, historically recognized border followed the course of the large Dniester River.

The eastern frontier zone, however, had an entirely different character. Stretching from the Dniester along the northern Black Sea littoral and into the Pontic Steppe as far, perhaps, as the sea of Azov and deep into what is now eastern Ukraine, there were multiple overlapping historical claims to sovereignty that were inherited by the Polish-Lithuanian monarchs and Ottoman sultans through local vassals and power brokers. Disentangling these claims took centuries. By the sixteenth century, conflicting Polish-Lithuanian and Ottoman claims to dominion over the Pontic Steppe Zone were legitimized partly through the historical claims of the Grand Dukes of Lithuania (who were also the kings of Poland by this time) and the Crimean khans.

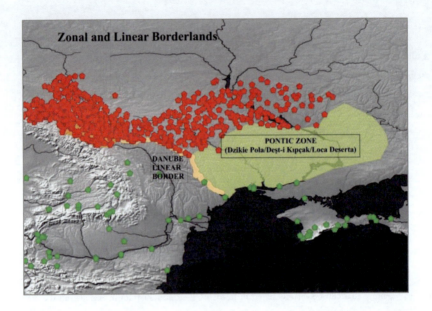

Figurative Littorals

Scholars have begun to challenge the concept of the Black Sea as an "Ottoman Lake". The establishment of Ottoman dominion over key coastal fortresses in Caffa, Cankerman/Özü, Akkerman, and Kilia helped the Ottoman sultans maintain loose control over the coasts, and limit direct access from the Dnieper, Dniester, and Danube Rivers to the Black Sea. To the north of these distinct points of Ottoman direct rule lay the Pontic Steppe Zonal frontier with Poland-Lithuania. This vast space, which proved to be virtually ungovernable by both king and sultan, began just beyond the line of site of the Ottoman fortresses on the Black Sea coast and ended far to the north where Polish-Lithuanian fortified settlements began. What lay in between was a swath of ungovernable territory with few defining features, much like a sea. The Ottoman fortresses of Cankerman, Hacibey, and Akkerman in particular looked out one direction into the (mostly) empty sea, and faced the (far from) empty Pontic Steppe on the other. In a way the Black Sea with its littoral fortresses were mirrored to the north by the fortresses that lined the littorals of the Pontic Steppe, creating an expansive sea of grass next to a vast body of water.

The Pontic Steppe Zone hosted frontiers between settled agriculturalists and pastoralists, and environmental frontiers between deciduous forests and the steppe. In much the same way that the Ottoman sultans attempted to establish control over the littorals of the Black Sea, it became the goal of Polish-Lithuanian and Ottoman rulers to establish control over the figurative, land-locked littorals of the Steppe.

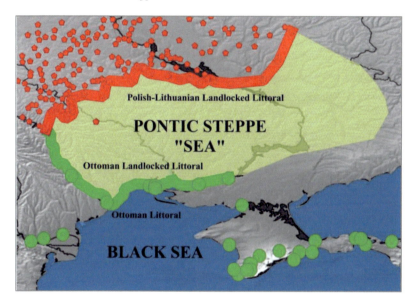

Figurative Littorals

Crimean *Yarliqs* and Conflicting Sovereignties

One challenge offered by this study is to disentangle the multiple overlapping claims to territorial sovereignty in the region. Over time a significant relationship developed between the Giray khans and the Grand Dukes of Lithuania during the early formation of the Crimean Khanate, the successor state of the Golden Horde. The Giray khans acknowledged their early connections to Lithuania, particularly in the *yarliqs* (land grants) they issued to Polish-Lithuanian rulers long after their submission to Ottoman rule. They continued to issue these *yarliqs*, essentially as extortion granting "rights" to the incomes from vast territories stretching from

Smolensk to the Black Sea to the Lithuanian Grand Dukes for nearly two hundred years after the Hordes had exercised any form sovereignty over those territories. In some cases they had never actually controlled them to begin with. In return for recognizing that these lands "belonged" to the Giray khans, who had inherited them from the Golden Horde, and for paying yearly tribute to the khan, Lithuanian rights to sovereignty over those territories would be respected. If not, the Giray khans reserved the right to stage large-scale punitive campaigns. In reality, low-level raiding and slave taking along the frontier was nearly constant, and during times of peace the khans or their relatives could stage large-scale invasions at will even if tribute was paid.

The land grants of the *yarliqs* have been studied as a formulaic bargaining chip, mainly played during periods where Crimean khans were allied with Lithuanian Grand Dukes against Muscovy. In these instances, the khans promised to help return the lands that had been "ceded" to Lithuania in earlier grants but which had taken by Muscovy in recent conflicts. These studies have been productive in helping to understand the role of the Crimean khans in conflicts on the fluctuating Lithuanian/Muscovite frontier. What is perhaps less well-known is how these land grants played out in the Pontic Steppe, where the rulers of Poland-Lithuania, Crimean khans, and increasingly over time, Ottoman sultans vied for territorial control.

By the early 16th century, as Ottoman sultans established direct control over fortresses and territories along the Black Sea littoral, their vassals, the Crimean khans, continued to cede some of these very same territories to the Grand Duke of Lithuania. An unresolved issue that I am still trying to make sense of is that some of these territories had in fact been in possession of the Crimean khans themselves for some time prior to the appearance of Ottoman garrisons. For instance, the region between the Dniester and Dnieper rivers was controlled by the grand dukes of Lithuania already in the 14th century, when Grand Duke Vitold built the Black Sea coastal fortress of Dašov. The fortress appears to have been subsequently abandoned. In 1475 the Giray khans became vassals of the Ottoman sultans. In the late 15th century Mengli Giray Khan occupied the Black Sea littoral and rebuilt the ruins of Dašov as the fortress of Cankerman. In 1538 Süleyman I assumed direct control of the fortress, known in Ottoman sources both as Cankerman and as Özü Kale (Dnieper Fortress). However, Dašov is repeatedly ceded, along with all attending incomes, to the Lithuanian Grand Dukes in the *yarliqs* of 1461-1463, 1472-1474,

1502, 1513, 1514, 1517, 1520, 1532, and 1541.[9] Similarly vague grants are made of the lands connected to the length of the Dnieper River from Kiev to the Black Sea, effectively cutting the Crimean khans' Pontic Steppe territories in half in the same *yarliqs*.

By mapping these instances and overlaying them with other concomitant visualizations of territorial and jurisdictional sovereignty, we begin to see what the kings of Poland-Lithuania and Ottoman sultans were working with when attempting to disentangle legal states of parallel rule and condominium in their shared frontier zone.

A Concise Case Study: the Border Demarcation of 1542

Despite having a shared border since the 15th century, when Ottoman control began to extend into Moldavia and the Crimean Khanate, it wasn't until 1542 that Zygmunt I and Süleyman I attempted to delineate their shared border. In 1530, Ottoman vassal and Moldavian Hospodar Peter Rareș attacked Poland-Lithuania, taking the region of Pokutia and claiming Ottoman acquiescence. The Sultan denied this and allowed a Polish punitive expedition in 1531. Rareș's dethronement in 1538 was finally accomplished when both Polish and Ottoman troops entered Moldavia. The Polish-Moldavian border dispute was ruled by Süleyman I in favor of Poland. Poland re-took Pocutia from Moldavia. Süleyman I took the opportunity to strengthen Ottoman presence in Moldavia, taking the Budjak and the Black Sea fortresses between the Boh and the Dniester rivers, including Cankerman/Özü. In the same action in 1538, Süleyman I also took the castle Tighina on the Dniester River and turned it into an Ottoman fortress, thenceforth called Bender. This transfer of authority is reflected in future *yarliqs* granted by the Crimean khans to Lithuania, which did not include the Black Sea territories that had been in the possession of the khans for some time anyway. Süleyman effectively claimed the lands between the Dniester and the Boh.

Following the Ottoman seizure of the Budjak and the establishment of direct Ottoman control over the Tatar khan's fortress of *Cankerman/Özü* in 1538, and in light of the constant, low-level frontier violence that accompanied frequent raids, kidnapping, theft, and the illegal

---

[9] Dariusz Kołodziejczyk, *The Crimean Khanate and Poland-Lithuania international diplomacy on the European periphery (15th-18th century): a study of peace treaties followed by annotated documents* (Leiden: Brill, 2011). See documents # 1, 4, 8, 12, 14, 18, 24, 29, p. 529-728.

pasturing of animals, Süleyman I and Zygmunt I agreed to undertake a mutual demarcation of their shared frontier. In the Ottoman context, *hududnameler* and *sınurnameler* were issued internally to define boundaries of *vakıfs* and state land (*miri*), and to foreign powers to establish international borders.[10] In the context of international treaties, the Ottomans called them *temessüks*, similar to peace protocols written in two languages (Ottoman and European) and exchanged and attested by both sets of commissioners. They were typically created around the time an '*ahdname* was granted. There is some significance to the fact that *temessük* could mean peace protocol and an agreement acknowledging the location of a given border.[11] In these cases, the acknowledgement of a given border was concomitant with or tantamount to a declaration of peace.

In the same letter of October 1540 regarding the Tatar attacks of the same year, Süleyman I responded to the king's complaints of the illegal pasturing on royal lands of animals owned by the inhabitants of Akkerman, Cankerman, and Kilia.[12] The sultan asserted that the land in question, assumedly somewhere east of the Dniester River, belonged to his vassals, the Tatar khans,[13] and that the land adjoining the Dniester River (*Turla Suyu'nun aşırısında*) belonged of old to his other vassals, the *voyevodas* of Moldavia. Süleyman I informed Zygmunt I that he had attempted to delegate the matter to Lutfi, the *sancakbeyi* of Silistra, and the *kadıs* of Akkerman, but the royal envoy Jakub Wilamowski had refused to meet with the Ottoman provincial officials without first communicating with his sovereign. Süleyman, therefore, set aside the issue of where the border was until the king appointed a royal commissioner who would meet with his own officials. Together they would determine where the historical boundaries of the khans' and the *voyevodas'* (and therefore the sultan's) territories lay. Once the border was set, the sultan promised, he would order his subjects not to cross it, and left it to the king to decide if he would allow herdsmen from the Ottoman side of the border to graze their animals on the Polish-Lithuanian side for a fixed fee.

---

[10] Klaus Kreiser, "Osmanische Grenzbeschreibungen," in *Studi preottomani e ottomani. Atti del Convegno di Napoli (24-26 settembre 1974)* (Napoli: Instituto Universitario Orientale, 1976), 165-72.
[11] For an overview of Ottoman protocols of demarcation see Dariusz Kołodziejczyk, *Ottoman-Polish diplomatic relations (15th-18th century): an annotated edition of 'ahdnames and other documents*. (Leiden: Brill, 2000), 57-67.
[12] Archiwum Głowne Akt Dawnych (hereafter: AGAD). AKW.Dz.Turecki.68.68.148.
[13] "*sâbıkā Tatar hanları tasarruf edegeldikleri Özü Kal'ası'nın sınırıdır,*" AGAD.AKW.Dz.Turecki.68.68.148.

Süleyman Calls for a Border Demarcation, 1542

In April 1542 the issue of pasturage, plundering, and the historical location of the border once again appeared in the communications between Zygmunt I and Süleyman I. The king sent another letter of complaint through his translator, Mikołaj, stating that the sultan's subjects continued to enter his territories to graze their herds, and that they were accompanied by miscreants who plundered his lands.[14] Here we see the confluence of two of the main issues that plagued the frontier: illegal pasturing could evidently provide a cover for raiding. Perhaps raiders accompanied the herdsmen, or perhaps these pastoralists were doing a bit of plundering on the side. Süleyman informed the king that he had told his *sancakbeyi* and *kadi* in Akkerman, and his *kadi* in Bender that the land in question did not belong to the king of Poland. The sultan echoed his ruling from October 1540, claiming that the territory between the Dnieper and Dniester rivers had belonged to the Tatar khans for some time, and was therefore his.[15] The Sultan further explained that the area in question was under the jurisdiction of the directly administered Ottoman fortress of Özü, while the region beyond (i.e. to the west of) the Dniester belonged to the *voyevodas* of Moldavia. Süleyman inferred that the northern border of this territory, which extended east to west through the *deşt-i kipçak* (roughly correlating to the Pontic Steppe), was in dispute. The sultan agreed to a mutual demarcation of this border. In service to this he ordered the *sancakbeyi* of Silistra and the *kadis* of Akkerman and Bender to meet with the king's commissioner on site to undertake the process. They were to rely on the testimony of locals and "reliable" people to determine where the historical borders lay. Once having set the border, the sultan promised to control his subjects.

In May 1542 Süleyman informed Zygmunt I that in October-November 1541 "one hundred infidels from the Polish side [of the frontier] came bringing war to the region of Cankerman,"[16] where they stole 250 sheep and killed two soldiers from the fortress, two Tatars,

---

[14] AGAD.AKW.Dz.Turecki.68.72a. The original document is missing. A copy, prepared by an unknown dragoman of the Porte in Italian resides in AGAD.
[15] AGAD.AKW.Dz.Turecki.68.68.148. This issue, the basis for the proposed border demarcation, was revisited most directly in subsequent communications between king and sultan:
AGAD.AKW.Dz.Turecki.68.78 and AGAD.AKW.Dz.Turecki.68.77. See also Kołodziejczyk, "Inner lake or frontier?," 127.
[16] *"Leh cânibden yüz mikdâr kâfir âlet-i harble Cankerman Kal'ası'na yakın gelip."* AGAD.AKW.Dz.Turecki.68.75.161. Original document, divani script. See also Zygmunt Abrahamowicz, and Zajączkowski Ananiasz, *Katalog dokumentów tureckich: dokumenty do dziejów Polski i krajów ościennych w latach 1455-1672*. (Warszawa: Państwowe Wydaw. Naukowe, 1959.), 72-73, doc. num. 61; Hacer Topaktaş and H. Ahmet Arslantürk, *Kanuni Sultan Süleyman dönemi Osmanlı-Leh ilişkilerine dair belgeler* (1520-1566) (Istanbul: Okur Kitaplığı, 2014), 99-100.

71

and one of the *re'aya*. He was further informed by his border-setting commissioner Osman Paşa, the *sancakbeyi* of Silistra, of another attack in January-February 1542, which resulted in the theft of 150 heads of livestock. Furthermore, a third attack had purportedly occurred in the region of Kilia in April of 1542, where fishermen were molested, Tatar homes were looted, some residents of the suburbs were murdered, one hundred and fifty women and children were enslaved (*nefer avret ve oğlan esir edip*), and 2,000 heads of livestock belonging to the castle's people and local Tatars were stolen.

Around that time, presumably after Süleyman proposed the border-setting joint commission to Zygmunt I, a royal messenger named Şirmed[17] arrived before the *sancakbeyi* of Silistra to discuss the border demarcation process. When asked about the attacks on these Ottoman territories, the messenger replied that, in light of continuous Tatar raids into Poland-Lithuania, there was no lack of conflict and war on both sides (*iki tarafda ber-asl ceng ü cidâl eksik değildir*). The sultan's envoy, Yusuf, was tasked with traveling to Zygmunt I's court and recuperating what was stolen and seeing to it that the perpetrators had been punished.

The seeds of the dispute that ultimately spelled the end for the border demarcation of 1542 were evidently sewn early. The northern border would mainly follow one of two rivers; the Poles preferred the more southerly Kodyma River, while the sultan insisted that the more northerly Sawrań was the historical boundary of his vassals' territory. By late summer of 1542, the commissioners that were given the duty of meeting to set the border were once again engaged in communicating with one another. On September 3rd Osman Şah, *sancakbeyi* of Silistra, wrote to Adam Sieniawski (called here *chorąży*).[18] Evidently Sieniawski had written to his counterpart the *sancakbeyi* asking where, when, and with how many people they would meet to demarcate the border. Osman Şah sent his *subaşa*, Mesih[19], to Sieniawski. He stated that he had already received a letter from the king indicating that they should meet on the 26th of September, and that he would await Sieniawski at that time at the place(s) called Sawrań (ضرص‌اوورراڵن) and Kodyma (قلكددمڤن), and asked that he send his Saxons (كلك‌صرصللرڤق‌سى), as promised.[20] Osman Şah's

---

[17] Zygmunt Abrahamowicz proposed that Şirmed was a Persian name, and that the messenger was likely a Lipka Tatar or an Armenian of Persian extraction in the king's service. Abrahamowicz, and Zajączkowski, *Katalog dokumentów tureckich*, 72, doc. num. 61.

[18] AGAD.MK.Dz.Tatarski.65.5.581. Original document, rik'a/divani script. See also Abrahamowicz, and Zajączkowski, *Katalog dokumentów tureckich*, 73, doc. num. 62. Topaktaş and Arslantürk, *Kanuni Sultan Süleyman dönemi Osmanlı-Leh ilişkilerine dair belgeler*, 101.

[19] This is probably the same Mesih that delivered a letter from Osman Şah to Zygmunt I, in which he was referred to as *voyevoda*, rather than *subaşa*. See: AGAD.AKW.Dz.Turecki.68.85.176. The *saksonlar* may be the Polish commission in this context.

vague reference to the disputed territory (*biz dahi târîh-i mezkûrda Savran ve Koduma nâm mevzi'a varmak kasd olunmuşdur*) bespoke the trouble that was to come. It appears that while Zygmunt I set the time and number of officials that would meet, he did not specify exactly where the meeting should take place. The *sancakbeyi*'s inexact instructions to the Polish commissioners may have been an attempt to avoid conflict over the matter.

Early during the border demarcation process, we see that the tone of Osman Şah's communications with the Polish-Lithuanian side was rather conciliatory. In October 1542, he sent a letter to Zygmunt I through one Süleyman, *çavuş* of the Porte in which the *sancakbeyi* admitted that "in the auspicious and prosperous empire, in the fortresses of Akkerman and Özü, there [were] some people of those fortresses that [drove] their livestock into [the king's] faithless (*ma'rifetinizsiz*) country [in search of pasturage], and to this end some mischief makers [were] crossing [as well]."[20] This seems to be a confirmation of Zygmunt I's accusations of illegal pasturage coinciding with cross-border raiding, which the king voiced in April of that year.[21] Precisely what the *sancakbeyi* meant by "people of Akkerman and Cankerman" is unclear. In the milieu of the frontier, both the Ottoman and the Polish-Lithuanian sides typically referred the inhabitants of directly administered fortresses like Özü or Akkerman collectively as "Turks". This meant that they were more likely to be treated as direct subjects of the sultan without any entangled or intermediate loyalties to the Tatar khan or *voyevoda* of Moldavia. Other local Muslims were referred to as "Tatars," and were further removed in terms of their clientage to the more proximate Tatar khans. In the case of the *sancakbeyi* of Silistra's 1542 letter to the king, the owners of the livestock appear to be residents of Ottoman frontier fortresses, which placed them closer to the authority of the *pâdişâh-ı âlem-penâh*.

Osman Şah also informed the king that the Süleyman had ordered him, as well as the *kadis* of Bender and Akkerman, to act as the sultan's commissioners in demarcating the border with Poland-Lithuania.[22] The *sancakbeyi* continued to state that he would engage commissioners (*ehl-i vukūf*) for the border demarcation. These may have been the Ottoman counterparts to the

---

[20] "…*meşhûm-ı meymûn-ı hümâyununda Akkerman ve Cankerman tabyasında ba'zı kimesneler sizin ma'rifetinizsiz vilâyetiniz sınırına koyunların iledip ol sebeble ba'zı ehl-i fesâd bile geçip…*". AGAD.AKW.Dz.Turecki.68.85.176.
[21] AGAD.AKW.Dz.Turecki.68.72a.
[22] AGAD.AKW.Dz.Turecki.68.85.176. Original document, divani script. See also Abrahamowicz, and Zajączkowski, *Katalog dokumentów tureckich*, 74-75, doc. num. 64. Topaktaş and Arslantürk, *Kanuni Sultan Süleyman dönemi Osmanlı-Leh ilişkilerine dair belgeler*, 105.

"Saxons" that Osman Şah asked Sieniawski to bring. The envoy that delivered the message, the *voyevoda* Mesih,[23] also brought a copy of the sultan's directive to the Ottoman commission, and asked that the king dispatch his own representatives to help set the border. Osman Şah was already in contact with the Polish commissioner Adam Sieniawski, so this seems to have been a plea directly to the king to order his commissioners to conclude the border demarcation process in a timely manner.

In mid-October 1542, the border commissioners failed to meet. The main issue that forestalled a productive outcome was that the two sides could not agree upon which river would serve as the border stretching from west to east- the northerly Sawrań (claimed by the Ottomans) or the southerly Kodyma (claimed by the Poles) both of which are tributaries of the Boh River. Several documents are preserved that detail the Ottoman perspective of why negotiations broke down sometime after October 15th. These are based on a missing document written by the head Ottoman commissioner, Osman Şah, the *sancakbeyi* of Silistra, to the Süleyman I. The missing document contained an account of why the border demarcation failed. Though the original missive has not been located, three other Ottoman documents pose as copies or else paraphrase the lost original.

The first document, undated, was composed in the Polish idiom at Bender, the Ottoman fortress where Osman Şah based his operations during the failed commission.[24] The letter was sent by the *sancakbeyi* to Zygmunt I through a royal envoy sometime after Osman Şah forwarded his original report to the Porte, and consists mainly of a flawed translation of the Osman Şah's account. The document boasts an Ottoman official's seal, but not that of Osman Şah.[25] The second document was prepared at the Porte, and claimed to be a copy of Osman Şah's original letter to the Sultan. Süleyman sent this document to Zygmunt I along with his own letter concerning the events in question.[26] This appears to be the most faithful copy of the lost original. The third document is Süleyman's letter to Zygmunt I, which paraphrases the *sancakbeyi's* narrative

---

[23] This is likely the same individual that delivered a letter form Osman Şah to Sieniawski on September 3rd, in which Mesih is referred to as *subaşa* rather than *voyevoda*. See: AGAD.MK.Dz.Tatarski.65.5.581.
[24] AGAD.AKW.Dz.Turecki.68.84.174.
[25] Osman Şah's seal is clearly visible on AGAD.AKW.Dz.Turecki.68.83a.173a, and AGAD.AKW.Dz.Turecki.68.85.176., respectively.
[26] AGAD.AKW.Dz.Turecki.68.77.164.

of the failed commission.[27] By comparing the three versions of Osman Şah's account it is possible to reconstruct his narrative, and determine Süleyman's response.

First, however, there is an unresolved issue regarding the dating of these documents. In an undated letter from the *sancakbeyi* of Silistra to Mikołaj Sieniawski, Bernard Pretwicz, and the other border-setting commissioners, Osman Şah informed his Polish counterparts through his messenger Ferhad, "*voyevoda* of Akkerman, Silistra, and Bender", that on the 15th of that month he had arrived at the Ottoman fortress of Bender.[28] He went on to state that after two days he would arrive at the Sawrań river, as agreed, and asked that the Polish commissioners meet him there. It is unclear at what point this agreement was made. Following this, Osman Şah claimed to have stayed in the steppe for a period of four days, awaiting his Polish counterparts, who never arrived. This means that the Ottoman commission was in the field until around the 21st of October. Problematically, the two documents prepared at the Porte (i.e. Süleyman's letter and the copy of the *sancakbeyi's* report) on 1-10 Şaban 949 h. (10-19 October, 1542) antedate the events they claim to talk about. They certainly do not allow for the time required for the news to travel from Bender to the Porte.

The three versions of Osman Şah's narrative of the failed demarcation offer clues as to why the border demarcation of 1542 was a failure. In them, we learn that before setting out for the arranged meeting in the *deşt-i kıpçak*, and likely before relocating his team of commissioners along with the *kadis* of Akkerman and Bender to the Ottoman frontier fortress at Bender, the *sancakbeyi* of Silistra gathered the affidavits of trusted witnesses (*mu'temedün-aleyh kimesneler şehâdet edip*) in the Ottoman fortress of Akkerman attesting to the historical borders of the Tatar khans' domain.[29] We learn from his letter to the Padishah that these witnesses included the fortress of Akkerman's *azebler ağası* Haydar, and the *kethudâs* Habib, Hacı İbrahim, Hacı Mehmed, the Tatar Ali, Mehmed Ağa from the fortress of Özü, the *mü'ezzin* Hoca and trustworthy inhabitants of Kilia.[30] These witnesses, who were evidently thought to be of an age that they could reliably recall the position of the borders before Süleyman assumed control of the fortress at Özü in 1438,

---

[27] AGAD.AKW.Dz.Turecki.68.88.165.
[28] AGAD.AKW.Dz.Turecki.68.83a.173a. Original document, Ruthenian language. See also: Abrahamowicz, and Zajączkowski, *Katalog dokumentów tureckich*, 75, doc. num. 65.
[29] AGAD.AKW.Dz.Turecki.68.77.164.
[30] In the Polish language document sent from Osman Şah to Zygmunt I, the names are rather garbled: "*Hadzi Breim, Habib Kihay, Tataralia, Loczakow Machmet Aga, Misz Godz y wszystkich inszych ludzi dobrych*", AGAD.AKW.Dz.Turecki.68.84.174.

contested that the border of the Tatar khan's domain in the north was the northerly Sawrań River. It then ran to the east down the Boh River (*Ak Suyu*) to its confluence with the mouth of the Dnieper River (*Özü Suyu*), and then on to the Black Sea. West of the headwaters of the Sawrań, they swore, it followed the "well-known" valley called *Değirmenderes* to the village of *Davudova* (ددااوودد اووء) in the lands of the *voyevoda* of Moldavia on the banks of the Dniester.[31] The result, according to the *sancakbeyi*, was that neither the king of Poland-Lithuania, nor the *voyevoda* of Moldavia had any claim to that space, which belonged to the sultan. Furthermore, the Tatar khan had been collecting taxes from the region for thirty or forty years.[32] Given that the sultan had only enforced his direct authority over the Black Sea fortress of Özü four years prior to the border demarcation attempt of 1542, it is interesting that the age of the witnesses should be emphasized in Ottoman documents. Perhaps the sultan's authority in the area predated 1538?

Significantly, the Polish language letter sent by the Ottoman commissioner, the *sancakbeyi* of Silistra Osman Şah, to Zygmunt I detailing the events in question makes no mention of the local Muslim witnesses' claim regarding the placement of the northern border. This version states that the eastern border followed the Dnieper River to the Black Sea, and the western border ran from Jahorlik down the Dniester to the Black Sea. It also mentions that the area around Özü (perhaps referring to the entirety of the disputed territory) stretched from the "*Rarsulay*" to the "*Ozunyazin*", and terminated at the sea.[33] In this document, the settlement of Jahorlik appears to take the place of *Davudova* on the Dniester River as the northernmost point of the western border, and the "*Değirmenderes*", or perhaps the entirety of the northern border, seems to have been replaced by the area between "Rarsulay" and "Ozunyazin".

Another event in the Ottoman commissioner's account points to a possible cause for the breakdown of the border demarcation of 1542. The Ottoman commission was given cause to

---

[31] *"sınır Savran nâm mahalle müntehîdir ondan sağ cânibi Aksu'ya ondan Özü Suyu'na ondan Karadeniz'e varınca değin ve sol cânibi Değirmenderesi demekle ma'rûf vâdi ve Boğdan Vilâyeti'nden Davudova nâm karyenin yukarı yanında Turla Suyu'na gelince mahdûddur mezkûr mahdûd olan sınırı"*, AGAD.AKW.Dz.Turecki.68.77.164. The Sultan's letter contains a nearly identical passage: *"sınır Savran nâm yere yarır ondan sağ tarafı Aksu'ya ondan Özü Suya'na ondan Karadeniz'e varır ve sol tarafı Değirmenderesi demekle ma'rûf dere Boğdan Vilâyeti'nden Davudova nâm karyenin yukarı yanından Turla Suyu'na gelince sınırdır"*, AGAD.AKW.Dz.Turecki.68.78.165. Osman Şah's Polish language letter to the king contains the following version: "Granica Oczakowska postawiona poprawey do Dniepru, od Dniepru do Czarnego Morza, a po lewey stronie od Miasta Jahorlik, y kiedy Han Tatarski Oczakow tryzmał, tedy pole miejsca Oczakowski brał oddzięciną zowią Rarsulay Ozunyazina Zawarł, A tam brał za Morskich".

[32] *"otuz kırk yıldan ziyâde Tatar hanları zabt edip zikr olan mahallerde koyunları olan kimesnelerin resm-I oltağın ve beytül-mâl ve sâir bâd-ı hevâsın hân alıp âdet-i ağnamı mîrî için zabt olunu gelmişdir"* AGAD.AKW.Dz.Turecki.68.77.164.

[33] *"Granica Oczakowska postawiona poprawey do Dniepru, od Dniepru do Czarnego Morza, a po lewey stronie od Miasta Jahorlik, y kiedy Han Tatarski Oczakow tryzmał, tedy pole miejsca Oczakowski brał oddzięciną zowią Rarsulay Ozunyazina Zawarł, A tam brał za Morskich"*, AGAD.AKW.Dz.Turecki.68.84.174.

believe that the Poles were amassing a large army on the frontier, in the very area of the proposed demarcation. While the *sancakbeyi* was at his forward base of operations in Bender, a letter arrived from Peter, *voyevoda* of Moldavia, claiming Polish commanders were at the border with 12,000 troops and that they had no intention of carrying out the demarcation of the border.[34] Osman Şah's conciliatory Polish language letter to Zygmunt I indicated that Peter was concerned that the Polish force was gathering to invade his lands (i.e. Moldavia). This too seems to have been taken with a grain of salt by the *sancakbeyi*, who claimed to have laughed at Peter's report, before looking to his military commanders and kadis (*"idzie Dwanascie Tysięcy nad swoią głową, a nie nad granicą, wtedym się smiał, y patrzyałem Rotmistrzow w Kahajow"*).[35]

Having consulted the trusted witnesses from Akkerman, Silistra and Özü, and evidently unconcerned by Peter's report, Osman Şah traveled for four days until he reached the grave of a well-known local saint (*ma'rûf azîz*), "Danyal-Ata", in the area of Deligöl (*Deligöl nâm mevzi'de*).[36] Once there, a messenger, identified as Przewalski (پرزوورروالجچككى in the sultan's letter to the king, arrived from Sieniawski asking where the commissions should meet and how many men they should bring.[38] Osman Şah instructed them to meet at the Sawrań River and to bring three hundred men and that he would do the same. The *sancakbeyi* dispatched the *voyevoda* Ferhad along with ten men from Kilia, who probably travelled back with Przewalski to deliver Osman Şah's response to the Polish commissioners.

On the fifth day of travelling north through the *deşt-i kıpçak*, Ferhad encountered delegates from the Polish commissioners. The Ruthenian language letter that he carried from Osman Şah recognized that the Poles claimed the northern border to be the Kodyma river.[37] The Ottoman commissioners, however, insisted that their witnesses from Akkerman and Kilia had sworn that the border, for the last sixty years, had been the Sawrań river.[38] As evidence, they further claimed

---

[34] "*Boğdan voyvodası olan Petri Voyvoda'nın âdemi ve mektûbu gelip zinhâr öte yakaya geçmeyesin zirâ Lih beyleri on iki bin âdemle hıyânet kasdına gelmişlerdir sınır kestirmek ihtimâli yokdur deyü*", AGAD.AKW.Dz.Turecki.68.77.164.
[35] AGAD.AKW.Dz.Turecki.68.84.174.
[36] In Osman Şah's letter to the king, Deligöl is called "Szalianie". AGAD.AKW.Dz.Turecki.68.84.174. AGAD.AKW.Dz.Turecki.68.78.165.
[37] AGAD.AKW.Dz.Turecki.68.81.169. Original document, Ruthenian language. See also Abrahamowicz, and Zajączkowski, *Katalog dokumentów tureckich*, doc. num. 66.
[38] This timeline conflicts with another that was presented in several other Ottoman documents, acknowledging that the Khan had control of the region for thirty to forty years. See: AGAD.AKW.Dz.Turecki.68.77.164, and, AGAD.AKW.Dz.Turecki.68.78.165. Osman Şah states "*…wte czasy woyska swoie ruszały ku mnie do Kodyzni…*," AGAD.AKW.Dz.Turecki.68.84.174.

that grazing fees had been collected by the Tatar khan and that the Ottoman sultan had received *"horszczyna"* from the same territories. The *sancakbey* of Silistra informed them, therefore, that the border would be at the Sawrań River. In response, the Polish delegates stated that, even if they should loose their heads, the border would be the Kodyma and not the Sawrań River.

Ferhad and his companions from the fortress returned and relayed the news, adding that the Poles had come with over twenty thousand armoured troops, over two thousand harquebusiers (*tüfengci*), and one hundred cannons. By the time this news was received, the *sancakbeyi* may have already arrived at the Kodyma River.[41] It seemed to the Ottoman commissioner that the Poles had come for war, and not for a peaceful border demarcation. Taking the reported buildup of Polish troops as a sign, Osman Şah decided that the matter was closed, returned to his *sancak* and contacted the sultan for further instructions. The veracity of these claims, as well as the earlier letter form the Moldavain voyevoda, remains untested. If there was a build-up of Polish-Lithuanian forces in the southern frontier at this time, the numbers found in Ottoman documents seem greatly inflated.

After receiving word from Osman Şah that the demarcation was a failure, Süleyman I made a copy of the *sancakbeyi*'s account and sent it to Zygmunt I, along with his own letter.[39] The sultan agreed that Osman Şah should oversee the demarcation of the northern border along the Sawrań River, according to the memory of the sworn witnesses from Akkerman and Kilia. The sultan's letter paraphrased his commissioner's narrative with a few more details. Süleyman agreed that the Tatar khans had occupied this territory for thirty or forty years[40] and stated that they received grazing fees and taxes from those lands. The sultan also clarified that the sheep taken from the region were a payment of *hass* to the sultan (*âdet-i ağnâmları hâssa-i hümâyûnum cânibinden zabt olunur*).[41] Süleyman asked Zygmunt I why the Polish commissioners had come with such a force, and why they did not agree to the terms proposed by the Osman Şah (i.e. that the border was at the Sawrań). Süleyman presented as further evidence of his dominion over these lands that

---

[39] AGAD.AKW.Dz.Turecki.68.78.165. Original document, divani script. See also Abrahamowicz, and Zajączkowski, *Katalog dokumentów tureckich*, 77-79, doc. num. 68; Topaktaş and Arslantürk, *Kanuni Sultan Süleyman dönemi Osmanlı-Leh ilişkilerine dair belgeler*, 106-108.

[40] This contradicts Osman Şah's Ruthenian language letter to the Polish commission that the territory had belonged to the Tatar Khans for sixty years. AGAD.AKW.Dz.Turecki.68.81.169.

[41] *"otuz kırk yıldan ziyâde Tatar hanları zabt edip onda koyunları yürüyenlerin resm-i otlağını ve beytü'lmâlini ve sâir bâd-ı hevâsını hanlar alıp âdet-i ağnâmları hâssa-i hümâyûnum cânibinden zabt olunur"*, AGAD.AKW.Dz.Turecki.68.78.165. This payment corresponds to the *horszczyna* mentioned in: AGAD.AKW.Dz.Turecki68.81.169.

there were ruins of Muslim graves, mosques, and schools in this place. These monuments, and remnants of Muslim life, put the land that they occupied lawfully within the *ehl-i İslâm*.[42]

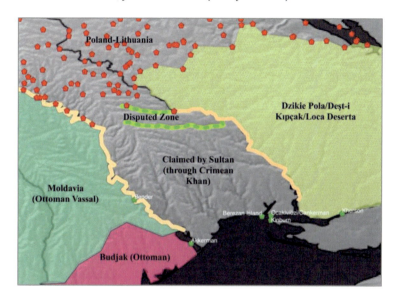

On the 28 of October, after the Polish-Lithuanian and Ottoman commissions failed to meet, Osman Şah wrote once again in a conciliatory manner to the Polish border commissioners. He claimed that the entire affair was a failure because the Poles had not been able to tell him where the border was meant to be.[43] The *sancakbeyi* reiterated that his witnesses had stated that the historical border was the Sawrań River, but that for the sake of friendship between the sultan and the king, Osman Şah agreed that the border should be the Kodyma River. Of course, he stated, he needed to write to the sultan regarding this matter. First, however, he needed to hear definitively from the Polish commissioners regarding how they wanted to demarcate the border, dispairing the idea of waiting around in the *dzikie pole* for the arrival of commissioners. In the end, it would be nearly one hundred years before the first successful mutual border demarcation was completed between Poland-Lithuania and the Ottoman Empire in 1633.

---

[42] "*zikr olunan sınır içinde ehl-i İslâmdan nice kimesnelerin makbereleri ve nice mescidler ve medreseler alâmetleri dahi bulunmuş bu hususlar dahi sahîh sınır idüğüne delâtet eder hakk üzere sınır kesilmeğe*", AGAD.AKW.Dz.Tureckі.68.78.165

[43] AGAD.AKW.Dz.Tureckі.68.82.171. Original document, Ruthenian language. See also Abrahamowicz, and Zajączkowski, *Katalog dokumentów tureckich*, 76-77, doc. num. 67.

Representations of Turkey in Bosnian Mainstream Printed Media (2003-2014): A Corpus-Assisted Critical Discourse Analysis

Dino Mujadžević

Abstract

The issue of the contemporary rise of Turkish influence in Bosnia and other Balkan countries has been a controversial topic among scholars. The 2000s and 2010s have witnessed a notable rise of Turkish official foreign policy, economic, cultural, and religious activity in the region under the Islamist AKP Party. Perceptions of this development have been mainly limited to two polarized views: a positive view that stresses cultural links and possible economic benefits, and a negative view that focuses on the perceived danger of the neo-Ottoman imperialism. Bosnia and Herzegovina, with its large Muslim population (ca. 50%), large Ottoman cultural heritage, and recent history of inter-communal war and ethnic cleansing of the Muslim (Bosniak) population is the focal point of Turkey's foreign policy in the Balkans. As Turkey's elite sees the establishment of its presence in Bosnia as highly symbolically important, the Turkish official and non-official actors have in recent years launched a series of cultural, media-related, educational, religious and, to a lesser degree, economic projects, mainly in predominantly Bosniak areas of Bosnia and Herzegovina. Whereas the level of Turkish humanitarian and other help, as well as economic investments, lag behind those of Germany, Austria, Slovenia, and Croatia, it seems that Turkish actors in Bosnia and their local allies mainly focus on activities aimed to influence public discourses for the benefit of Turkey. This paper uses the theoretical framework of Critical Discourse Analysis and the corpus-linguistic methodology to analyze how the representation of Turkey in Bosnian printed media was used to shape public opinion on Turkish foreign policy towards Bosnia and Herzegovina between 2003 and 2014. The paper focuses on the big picture of media representations of Turkey in the given period. For this purpose, a corpus of roughly 20 000 articles dealing with Turkey from major Bosnian media was created from a privately owned media collection. Thereafter, a collocation analysis of the search words with the meaning of Turkey and Turkish, and a concordance analysis of the extracted collocates was conducted. The results were qualitatively interpreted to establish which words were used as parts of discourses supporting or obstructing Turkish foreign policy in Bosnia and Herzegovina. The paper concludes that the representation of Turkey in the context of reporting on Turco-Bosnian diplomatic and economic relations was heavily influenced by the pro-Turkish discourse.

Introduction

Turkey under the rule of conservative AKP (*Adalet ve Kalkınma Partisi*) has shown a great deal of interest in Bosnia and Herzegovina and has managed to establish its influence in this Balkan country. This influence is especially strong with Bosniak conservative political and mainstream Islamic religious actors.[1] Additionally, Turkish state actors have become increasingly visible

---

[1] For Turkish official and unofficial foreign policy, including religious actors, in the Balkans since 1990s see: Kerem Öktem, *New Islamic actors after the Wahhabi intermezzo: Turkey's return to the Muslim Balkans,* Paper presented at the conference "After the Wahhabi Mirage: Islam, politics, and international networks in the Balkans" (Oxford: European Studies Centre, University of Oxford, 2010), 21-25; Birgül Demirtaş, "Turkey and the Balkans: Overcoming

through their programs of financing the renovation of Ottoman historical heritage, mosque building, and developmental aid. Nevertheless, the Turkish foreign policy towards Bosnia and Herzegovina under the AKP has not merely been a matter of foreign policy, but also an integral part of Turkey's internal political dynamics.

Contemporary Turkey's attitude toward Bosnia has been heavily influenced by the presence of a large Muslim population and by the Ottoman cultural heritage in the country as well as by perceptions of the 1992-1995 Bosnian war. During the 1992-1995 war and its aftermath, the Turkish conservative scene profited from the situation by using the narrative of an endangered ex-Ottoman Muslim population in Bosnia, threatened with extinction, for the plight of which Kemalist Turkey had no concern, the only true supporters of which were, supposedly, the conservative Turks, who insisted on providing assistance to the endangered Muslim communities related to Turkey on the basis of Islamic and Ottoman cultural solidarity. The AKP government has, ever since it came to power in 2002, been striving to acquire the role of Bosnia's protector and to forge special relations with Bosnia.[2] The topic of Bosnia – as well as of the Balkans in general – emerged as an important topic as part of a foreign policy that increasingly championed the use of the Ottoman heritage as a foreign policy tool. In the post-2007-08 period in particular, when Turkish foreign policy took a more conservative turn, its discourse on Bosnia produced by the representatives of the Turkish state and public institutions as well as of non-official activists relied on an exclusively positive view of the Ottoman historical heritage asserting simultaneously Turkey's role as the region's leader and the protector of regional stability and the Bosnian statehood as well as of the very existence of Bosnian Muslims (Bosniaks).

On the other hand, a significant part of the Bosniak population and elite – primarily the leadership of conservative party SDA (*Stranka demokratske akcije*) and by far the largest Muslim organization, Islamic Community in Bosnia and Herzegovina (ICBH) – have eagerly accepted and supported the notion of special relations with Turkey, in which they saw a possibility for the affirmation of the Bosnian Muslim identity, as well as for political security and economic

---

Prejudices, Building Bridges and Constructing a Common Future", *Perceptions. Journal of International Affairs*, Summer 2013, 163-183.

[2] For the Turkish role in Bosnia under AKP see also Alida Vračić. & Kerem Öktem. "Two views on… The Balkans: Alida Vracic and Kerem Öktem," *Turkish Review*, 1 September, 2013, http://www.turkishreview.org/interviews/two-viewson-the-balkans-alida-vracic-and-kerem-Öktem_540292 (accessed March 10, 2016); Dino Mujadžević, *Asserting Turkey in Bosnia* (Wiesbaden: Harrassowitz, 2017).

prosperity.[3] In addition to purely political and economic influence (deemed by many as rather minor), the Turkish presence among Bosniaks and other Balkan Muslim groups displays strong cultural, educational, and religious features. The discourses of both the Bosniak and the Turkish conservative scenes, the main actors in this development, have heavily relied on the Ottoman legacy, which provided the general framework of communication. While completely dominant within the conservative Muslim media in Bosnia, Turkish influence and pro-Turkish activism, albeit in a less direct form, has also had some impact on the mainstream Bosnian media, especially in those parts of the country with a Bosniak majority.

This paper investigates the representations of Turkey in the mainstream Bosnian printed media that were used to support or criticize Turkish foreign policy towards Bosnia and Herzegovina between 2003 and 2014. For that purpose, the corpus of all available electronically encoded mainstream Bosnian newspaper and magazine articles was collected and investigated with the assistance of corpus research methods. While support for Turkish foreign policy – referred here as pro-Turkish discourses – encompasses many different references and images, due to the limitations of this method which demands a focus on a limited number of research words, I will analyze only the discursive use of the concepts of "Turkish" and "Turkey". That means that the analysis will deal only with texts that are explicitly associated with the representation of Turkey and not with those that, for example, deal with the Ottoman Empire without mentioning the word "Turkey" or "Turkish".

In other words, the price to be paid for conducting a computer-assisted analysis of this large body of material will be a narrowing of the focus of the research which may result in over-representation of articles that deal with issues linked with contemporary Turkey although in Bosnian "Turkey" and "Turkish" are also often used to denote the Ottoman state and Ottomans respectively. The qualitative analysis will be applied to the results of the corpus analysis to investigate the language patterns in the results of corpus analysis and detect possible evidence of the discourses related to the Turkish foreign policy toward Bosnia. The analysis will go into the big picture, the overall tendencies of such a discursive media construction of Turkey in the mainstream Bosnian printed media.

---

[3] For the general currents among contemporary Bosnian Muslims including the convergence between conservatism and ethnic nationalism see Dino Abazović, *Bosanskohercegovački muslimani između sekularizacije i desekularizacije* (Zagreb – Sarajevo: Synopsis, 2012); Mujadžević, *Asserting Turkey in Bosnia*.

Research Procedure

In this paper, I will focus on the particular version of the discourse analysis theoretical framework known as Critical Discourse Analysis (CDA), described by major authors as being both a theoretical perspective and research method. It uses the conceptualization of language as a form of social praxis and attempts to make people conscious of the mutual influence of language and social structures. It provides insight into the content of the textual material as the outside representative of discourse and connects it to its producers and their motives.[4] Generally speaking, CDA practitioners focus on research into the opaque and the transparent manifestations of power, ideology, control, dominance and discrimination in language. For CDA, language is not powerful on its own – it gains power by the use people make of it. CDA also shows that texts are not isolated occurrences and are produced by particular reasons, the key questions being "How do (the more) powerful groups control public discourses?"[5] According to Jäger, the purpose of CDA is to extract the discourse information (structures, practices) that is inscribed in various texts. The term text includes both written texts and transcripts of spoken interaction and it is considered narrower than discourse. Jäger stresses the role of discourse as being the effective expression of power, but also maintains that the discourse is reinforced and protected by power. According to Jäger, discourse(s) can be criticized from several viewpoints, especially for their inner contradictions, but he accepts that even the critics of a discourse cannot function outside discourse(s) and that the discourses cannot be reduced to notions such as "false ideology". This is equally valid for all types of discourses: everyday life, political, media, educational, etc. The Jäger version of CDA is particularly useful for an interpretative analysis based on textual material since it enables the researcher to establish theoretically firm relationships between the texts, their authors as (co)producers and their specific positions, between general concepts and the societal context, i.e. political power-relations.[6]

Jäger accepts the proposition that CDA can make use of quantitative methods, e.g. to determine the appearance frequency and centrality of a specific term/phrase in a discourse. To facilitate historical comparison, he suggests that several successive quantitative synchronic analyses

---

[4] On CDA see, Norman Fairclough, *Language and Power* (London: Longman, 1989); Theun van Dijk, "Critical Discourse Analysis," in D. Schiffrin, D. Tannen and H. E. Hamilton, eds., *The Handbook of Discourse Analysis* (London: Blackwell, 2001), 352-71; Siegfried Jäger, *Kritische Diskursanalyse*. 4. erw. Aufl. (Duisburg/Münster: DISS – Unrast Verlag, 2004); Theun van Dijk, "Ideology and discourse analysis", *Journal of Political Ideologies*, 11, no. 2 (2006): 115-140; R. Wodak, R. and M. Meyer (eds.), *Methods of Critical Discourse Analysis* (London: Sage, 2006).
[5] van Dijk, "Critical Discourse Analysis," 355.
[6] Jäger, *Kritische Diskursanalyse*, 120-127; Siegfried Jäger, "Theoretische und methodische Aspekte einer Kritischen Diskurs- und Dispositivanalyse," in Reiner Keller, Andreas Hirseland, Werner Schneider, Willy Viehöver, eds., *Handbuch Sozialwissenschaftliche Diskursanalyse* (Opladen: Leske – Budrich 2006), 83-114.

should be performed and then compared in order to show changes and continuities inside the discourse.[7] One of the quantitative methods suitable for CDA is definitely the corpus-assisted approach. Corpus-assisted CDA can be described as the study of digitized textual corpora by the application of both the qualitative CDA and quantitative computer-generated methods of corpus analysis. This produces interdisciplinary synergy between corpus-linguistic methodology with purely qualitative discourse and social studies on the basis of digitized textual corpora.[8] The quantitative part of the research includes corpus analysis techniques with extracted data as a result. Generally speaking, corpus analysis is a computer-assisted investigation of the electronically encoded examples of naturally occurring language. The results of corpus analysis are intended "to be used as a standard reference with which claims about language can be measured". The quantitative corpus-assisted method is here only used to supplement and assist qualitative CDA because a computer-assisted method can only reach a limited number of features of text and only hardly or not at all analyze the text as a whole.[9]

The interpretative part includes theoretical, methodological, and contextual research, as well as data interpretation in accordance with the CDA theoretical framework. The advantage of the corpus-assisted over the qualitative approach in CDA is that a very large amount of textual material can be researched. Although highly detailed and focused, purely qualitative CDA is limited to smaller textual materials. The corpus-assisted approach provides much more extensive, empirically backed information for CDA than more traditional, purely qualitative, methods. An advantage of corpus-assisted CDA is that non-apparent discourse-related data from digital textual sources can be extracted from textual material providing complete data for CDA interpretation. Some of the patterns may have already been recognized by qualitative research, but a corpus-driven approach can help CDA to become aware of discursive phenomena, which were previously not even noted.[10] A frequent criticism of research based on the corpus methodology is that it tends to disregard context.[11] Corpus-assisted CDA has been developed in the Netherlands and the UK

---

[7] Jäger, „Theoretische und methodische Aspekte einer Kritischen Diskurs- und Dispositivanalyse."
[8] For more on this synergy see Paul Baker, Costas Gabrielatos, Majid Khosravinik, Michal Krzyzanowski, Tony McEnery and Ruth Wodak, "A useful methodological synergy? Combining critical discourse analysis and corpus linguistics to examine discourses of refugees and asylum seekers in the UK press," *Discourse and Society* 19, no. 3 (2008), 274-276.
[9] Paul Baker, *Using Corpora in Discourse Analysis* (London - New York: Continuum, 2006), 2.
[10] P. Baker, C. Gabrielatos and T. McEnery, *Discourse Analysis and Media Attitudes* (Cambridge: Cambridge University Press, 2013).
[11] Baker, Gabrielatos, Khosravinik, Krzyzanowski, McEnery and Wodak, "A useful methodological synergy?", 273-274.

since the early 1990s. In the 2010s Lancaster University in the UK, which hosts the CASS (Centre for Corpus Approaches to Social Studies), became a leading center for corpus-assisted CDA.[12]

I will use two corpus analysis techniques: collocation analysis, the chief technique, and concordance analysis, an auxiliary method. The purpose of these two corpus techniques is to extract information on the immediate textual context of chosen search words in the given textual corpora. Textual surroundings can show associations and connotations of the words and the assumptions they embody,[13] which can, in return, point to the semantic structures and the discursive practices related to the search term(s). Collocation analysis is the examination of words that tend to co-occur more frequently with the words that are under analysis, based on calculations by computational tools. This technique is useful to determine the most significant relationships between words based on co-occurrence in a corpus. The procedure to calculate the collocation of search terms will be based on the standard five-word window to the left and to the right of the word under analysis. The calculation is not based on a simple frequency count of co-occurrence but uses the statistical test known as Mutual Information (MI). The MI test tends to take into account the cases when two words occur together as well as apart from each other and assign higher priority to those that are generally found together. It is calculated by an algorithm that computes the expected probability that two words will be collocated, based on their relative frequencies and the overall size of the corpus, and the actual number of co-occurrences. The final value expressed as a number indicates the strength of the collocation of two words. Extracted words that tend to co-occur with the search words (collocates) are especially important for discourse analysis because they point to the language specifically associated with the word under analysis. If a word has a higher statistical chance of co-occurring with another it points to the deliberate choice of words in the discourse involved.

Concordance analysis investigates concordances of words. A concordance is a list of all occurrences of a particular search in a corpus generated by a computational tool, which puts the word in the middle of a line (a concordance line) and shows you what the surrounding text looks like. Each concordance line shows an occurrence of the search term in its full textual surroundings enabling us to look at the words and phrases which occur to the left- and right-hand sides of the

---

[12] For the development of the corpus-driven CDA see Baker, *Using Corpora in Discourse Analysis*, 5; T. McEnery and A. Hardie, *Corpus Linguistics. Method, Theory and Practice* (Cambridge: Cambridge University Press, 2012); Baker, Gabrielatos and McEnery, *Discourse Analysis and Media Attitudes*.
[13] Michael Stubbs, *Text and Corpus Analysis. Computer-Assisted Studies of Language and Culture* (Cambridge, Massachusetts: Blackwell, 1996), 172.

search term(s). For example, if we investigate a particular collocate, our computer tools will provide us with all its occurrences, including sections of the texts preceding or following the particular collocate under analysis. The number of places (i.e. words) to the right and left can vary. In contrast to collocation analysis, concordance analysis doesn't point just to statistically often co-occurring words but allows access into much broader co-text. In the framework of this research concordance analysis will be used to examine the exact context of collocates. This technique is more labor-intensive than collocation analysis, but it will nevertheless give more room for interpretation to the researcher. Concordance analysis, although enabled by a computational tool (a concordancer), actually represents a gradual transition to the qualitative analysis of digitally extracted data.[14] The tool which will be used for collocation and concordance analyses is the AntConc. It is free software, which was developed by the British linguist Lawrence Anthony.[15]

As previously mentioned, quantitative analysis is only a part of the corpus-assisted CDA approach. Computational processing of the corpus alone cannot give us the list of discourses within the textual material, just data that may or may not include discourse-relevant language patterns. Therefore, the next step in the research will be to detect and interpret the language patterns on the basis of the data extracted from the corpus. The interpretation in accordance with the tradition of the qualitative CDA will concentrate on subjective scanning for discourse-related language patterns, based on repetition, as evidence of structures. The research into discourse structures will include the detection of topical structures (macro-topics and discourse strands as their thematically organized parts), as well as their lexical, grammatical, rhetorical, syntactical and stylistic and other properties ("the text surface", "local structures", "discursive devices") including the use of symbolism, metaphors and common schematic structures (argumentation strategies and meaning distribution such as implications and hints).

Semantic preference and discourse prosody are especially important in the framework of corpus-assisted research. An investigation of these language properties aims to explain why particular discourse patterns appear around collocates. Semantic preference is the tendency of a word to co-occur with a set of semantically related words, which can in turn denote topic structure in a discourse. Discourse prosody is an interrelated concept in which there is co-occurrence of a word with a set of related words that suggests a discourse. The former denotes aspects of meaning

---

[14] For more on these techniques see McEnery & Hardie, *Corpus Linguistics. Method, Theory and Practice*.
[15] For more about the AntConc see *Laurence Anthony's Website*, http://www.laurenceanthony.net, (accessed on March 10, 2016).

that are independent of speakers, whereas the latter concentrates on attitudes. Concordance analysis offers a lot of space for qualitative analysis. It assures that the meaning and discursive use of words will be properly understood by taking into account their textual surroundings.

Sources

Printed media have been chosen for this research according to both availability and influence criteria. First and foremost, post-2000 Bosnian printed media data – as it is the case with similar material almost everywhere – are nowadays relatively easy to obtain in electronic form. Despite the fact that electronic media, especially TV, represent the chief source of news for the population and account for the lion's share of the advertising market, Bosnian printed media might still retain a great deal of importance in shaping opinions, as well as in setting agendas regarding certain topics in the society.[16] Research in several Western countries has shown that newspapers do have considerable power to influence public opinion[17] and, with due caution, these results can be applied also to the Bosnian printed media landscape. Additionally, since in the early 2000s online editions for most of the printed media emerged, one can argue that they reach more people than is visible in circulation numbers. Due to its role in constructing ideologically motivated versions of reality, journalism in the UK was famously described as an "argumentative discourse genre."[18] There is no reason not to use this definition for Bosnian media; indeed, it is even more relevant. As in other countries, the Bosnian media attempt to exert social and political influence according to the interests of the owners and authors while balancing this objective with the need to reflect the views of audiences, public interest, and standards of professional reporting. The legacy of the Bosnian war 1992-1995 and ethnic division still looms large over this country adding complexity, even occasional tensions, to the media scene.[19] In 2013, the US-based Freedom House categorized the Bosnian media as "partly free," which indicates the continued presence of highly ideologically charged and often manipulated media reporting.[20]

---

[16] "Bosnia-Herzegovina profile – Media," www.bbc.com, http://www.bbc.com/news/world-europe-17211939, (accessed on March 10, 2016).
[17] Teun A. van Dijk, *Racism and the Press* (London and New York: Routledge, 1991).
[18] Baker, Gabrielatos and McEnery, *Discourse Analysis and Media Attitudes*, 3.
[19] L. Woodward, "A one sided story: Bosnia and Herzegovina's media landscape," available at https://rising.globalvoicesonline.org/blog/2014/07/23/a-one-sided-story-bosnia-and-herzegovinas-media-landscape/, accessed on March 10, 2016.
[20] "Bosnia-Herzegovina profile – Media".

There are no studies that document the prevalence of reporting on Turkey in Bosnian printed media in the period under analysis as compared to similar topics, e.g. reporting on other countries. Nevertheless, as an indication of the "news value" of Turkey in the Bosnian printed media I offer the following data: in the *infobiro.ba* media collection, between 1 January 2003 and December 31 2014, the noun "Turkey" in Bosnian in nominative singular (*Turska,* nota bene the adjective Turkish in the feminine nominative singular, *turska*, has the same form!) appears in 16 223 articles of the collection, whereas the noun "Germany" in the nominative singular (*Njemačka*, also sharing the grammatical form with the adjective "German", *njemačka*, in feminine nominative singular), came up exactly half as much, just 8101 articles. Although not a definitive proof, this can be taken as an indication that Turkey as a news topic in the Bosnian press attracted at least as much attention as reporting on Germany, a country with much more political and economic influence in Bosnia. This, in turn, indicates other factors that influence frequent reporting on Bosnia. As I will demonstrate later in the paper, the creation of such a number of media texts is also linked to two factors: a) Turkish official and non-official foreign policy actors in Bosnia are focused on cultural public diplomacy and *ipso facto* media influence; b) the readiness of Bosnian media to support these efforts or, in less number of cases, to criticize them.

The searchable archive of Bosnian newspaper and magazine articles in digital form *infobiro.ba* was the obvious choice for this type of research due to its online access and the fact that it covered the most influential printed media from major Bosnian centers like Sarajevo, Banja Luka and Mostar including simultaneously media of different ideological and ethnic background. It includes digitized articles from daily newspapers (*Oslobođenje, Dnevni avaz, Nezavisne novine, Dnevni list*), weeklies (*Dani, Slobodna Bosna, Reporter*), agencies (ONASA), etc. This media archive enables thousands of articles to be downloaded onto a PC in a very short time and very specific searches can be carried out. Still, due to the limitations of this collection, my research could not include smaller magazines representing ideologically extreme positions (including various Islamic conservative, leftist, as well as Serb and Croat ethnic nationalist publications). Nevertheless, the media that have been chosen exert by far the biggest impact on the population, due to their cumulative circulations and the discursive place they occupy in various communities across Bosnia.

Quantitative Analysis

The first task was to create the research corpus. For an article from *infobiro.ba* from the period 2003-2014 – the year 2002 was not available – to be included in the corpus, it needed to contain at least one of these words: *Turska, Turske, Turskoj, Tursku, Turskom, turski*. These search words were chosen because they are typically associated with Turkey in Bosnian language media. This search elicited 20 211 articles containing these keywords from Bosnian printed media and those files were downloaded. As I planned to research the big picture of historical discursive praxes between 2003 and 2014, we will tackle our main corpus data as a whole. The second step was the creation of lists of collocates of the search terms that signify the meaning of Turkey (*Turska*) and/or Turkish (*turski, turska, tursko*). In addition to being semantically related, these two words are also grammatically related in Bosnian/Croat/Serb languages: the word "Turkey" is actually substantive of the adjective "Turkish" (nominative singular feminine) and they share all grammatical forms. By examining the textual surroundings of the noun Turkey and the adjective Turkish we tackle the most common patterns of the media construction of Turkey in Bosnian newspapers and magazines. These patterns are the starting point for the investigation of the presence and structure of discourses on Turkish foreign policy towards Bosnia. The regular expression \btursk(a|e|oj|u|o|om|i|og|im|ih)\b will be used for the AntConc collocation analysis procedure in order to cover all declination cases of both the noun "Turkey" and the adjective "Turkish" (in all three genders). This regular expression includes the following search terms: *turska, turske, turskoj, tursku, tursko, turskom, turski, turskog, turskog, turskom, turskim* and *turskih*. Span around the node word was 5, which means that 5 words to the left and 5 words to the right of the search terms underwent collocation analysis. The minimal frequency of a collocate taken into account was 10. Collocates which had lower frequency were mostly personal nouns and words with spelling mistakes, so I decided to omit these. The cut-off point for significance for each of the statistical measures was established at 8. Collocates with lower significance were not taken into consideration. This procedure rendered 1078 collocates – roughly 1/5 of all collocates of the search terms. The top 100 extracted collocates are listed in the table at the end of this paper.

Qualitative Analysis

The extracted collocates constitute vocabulary that has been used for the construction of an image of Turkey in Bosnian newspapers and magazines between 2003 and 2014. The concordances of the collocates also reveal how the reporting on Turkey was discursively used to support or criticize Turkish foreign policy towards Bosnia. They show that these discourses were consistently present in a significant degree only when collocates were used for reporting on two macro-topics in the research corpus of Bosnian printed media: *Turco-Bosnian diplomatic relations* (184 collocates) and *Turco-Bosnian economic relations* (195 collocates). These collocates and their concordances will be presented in the next chapters. A collocate was classified to a macro-topic too if most of its instances belonged to this group. Other collocates that very often dealt with topics like sports, culture, history, or internal or foreign Turkish politics (not related to Bosnia!) only rarely or never contained supporting or critical discourses on Turkish foreign policy.

The pro-Turkish discourse was, in the framework of these two macro-topics, conveyed predominantly in an indirect fashion. The collocates that were used for the construction of the pro-Turkish discourse appeared predominantly in news texts which were commonly paraphrases of official statements by politicians, businessmen, or diplomatic *communiqués*. The authors of such pro-Turkish texts did not express either open support for Turkish foreign policy or open criticism. Nevertheless, their frequency and the tendency to allow Turkish or Bosnian pro-Turkish officials to voice their opinions without scrutiny and to report statements of Turkish officials and Turkish institutions *in extenso* and *verbatim* point to the existence of the subtle, but very widespread, pro-Turkish discourse in these texts. Information about Turkish foreign policy activities tended to be reported in detail and without any critical distance, which suggests pro-Turkish discourse prosody. Thus, I argue that a large number of non-opinionated and descriptive articles is by itself an effective discursive strategy aimed at supporting Turkish foreign policy interests. Moreover, the style of these reports mostly resembles the style of official statements or reporting by the state news agencies. For example, by repeating details without commentary about visits of Turkish delegations and by quoting large parts of official statements during those visits, some media tend to highlight the omnipresence of Turkish official and non-official foreign policy actors and create a supportive atmosphere for their activity, as in this example:

> A delegation of businessmen and mayors of municipalities from the Republic of Turkey yesterday visited the municipality of Vogošća, to get familiar with economic capacities available to Vogošća because they are interested in investing, said Džejna Pinjo from the information service of the municipality yesterday. This is the first time that the Turkish delegation is visiting our community. The delegation consisted of five mayors of municipalities, four businessmen and a journalist, and after being received by the Mayor Asim Sarajlić, and with him his assistants, the Turkish delegation

visited the new and the old industrial zone, and the facilities of "Farmavita" and "Mimsaž", said Pinjo. She added that they also discussed the twinning of the municipalities Bakirpaša and the municipality Vogošća. The Mayor of the Municipality Bakir-pasha Kokut Abdullah, who also headed this delegation, expressed his wish that the municipalities of Vogošća and Bakir-pasha should become twin towns, said Pinjo. (*Nezavisne novine*, 25 March 2006)

On the other hand, discursive criticism of the Turkish foreign policy toward Bosnia was conducted in an open manner as well as indirectly by the pursuit of chosen topics, like economic problems or failures of Turkish investment. The motivation for producing either of these two discourses in the mainstream Bosnian printed media is rather complex and it seems to range from direct economic interests, political agency and/or ethno-nationalist ideology and bias of authors, media owners and power structures like business and political interests that influence a particular media outlet. Although printed media from the parts of Bosnia where Bosniaks demographically dominate have tended to publish more supportive texts related to Turkish foreign policy in Bosnia, printed media in Serb- or Croat-dominated parts of that country published a significant number of articles that can be considered vaguely pro-Turkish. The political orientation of the media seemed to matter a lot, but it also curiously depended on in which part of Bosnia a particular printed media outlet was situated: liberal weekly *Dani* from Sarajevo where Bosniaks constitute a majority published mainly critical articles on Turkish foreign policy toward Bosnia, while a liberal daily from Bosnian Serb dominated Banja Luka, *Nezavisne novine* published a great number of texts that fall into the category of pro-Turkish discourse.

Turco-Bosnian Diplomatic Relations

184 collocates of the search terms that were associated with official activities of Turkish and Bosnian diplomats or high-ranking officials in the framework of bilateral relations between the two countries form a distinctive semantic group (Table 1). Nevertheless, collocates from this group were largely related to the Turkish classical and public diplomatic activity in Bosnia – such as meetings with Bosnian officials or ceremonial openings of the buildings whose reconstruction was financed from Turkey. Furthermore, most of the collocates belonging to this macro-topic were predominantly used in the framework of the pro-Turkish discourse. The presence of this macro-topic in the corpus does not surprise and it corresponds to the contextual information we have. As various sources document, Turkish official foreign policy actors were very active in

Bosnia. Besides the huge number of visits and meetings with Bosnian, and especially Bosnian Muslim officials, the public diplomacy efforts of the Turkish state actors, like humanitarian donations and financing of cultural and media projects, were relatively large. As I will show below, the collocates from this macro-topic indicate that these focused public diplomacy efforts, together with the support of sympathetic media, are succeeding in shaping the dominant perception of Turkish official foreign policy in Bosnia as something positive.

Table 1: collocates used in context of reporting on the Turco-Bosnian relations[21]

Adjectives	**Relations:** **bilateral** [*bilateralni* (50), *bilateralne* (31)], **brotherly** [*bratske* (10)], **friendly** [*prijateljska* (19), *prijateljske* (51), *prijateljskih* (30)], **unbreakable** [*neraskidive* (10)], **trilateral** [*trilateralni* (19), *trilateralnom* (11)] **Diplomacy:** **honorary** [*počasni* (60), *počasnim* (45), *počasnog* (31)], **newly-appointed** [*novoimenovani* (16), *novoimenovanog* (18), **introductory** [*nastupni* (15), **farewell** [*oproštajnu* (12)], **official** [*službenoj* (15)] **Turkey:** **ready** [*spremna* (71)] **Other:** **communicational** [*komunikacione* (11)], **forestry** [*šumarskih* (12)]
Adverbs	**strongly** [*snažno*]
Nouns	**Diplomacy:** **ambassador** [*ambasador* (411), *ambasadora* (166), *ambasadoru* (46), *ambasadorima* (20), *ambasadorica* (66), *ambasadorice* (11), *ambasadoricom* (16), *ambasadoricu* (12) *veleposlanik* (26), *veleposlanika* (10)], **attache** [*ataše* (26)], **consulate** [*konzulat* (29), *konzulata* (38)], **chairman** [*predsjedavajucim* (11)], **deputy** [*zamjenikom* (11)], **embassy** [*ambasada* (145), *ambasade* (510), *ambasadu* (56), *ambasadi* (61), *ambasadom* (28)], **entrusted** [*povjerena* (10)], **credentials** [*akreditive* (10)] **delegation** [*delegacija* (310), *delegacije* (182) *delegaciju* (109), *delegacijom* (53), *delegaciji* (39). *izaslanstvo* (17)], **diplomacy** [*diplomatija* (38), *diplomatije* (168), *diplomacije* (21)], **guest** [*gosta* (27), gosti (119), *zvanica* (11)], **consul** [*konzul* (148), *konzula* (62)], **mayor** [*nacelnikom* (10)], **minister** [*ministar* (528), *ministru* (32), *ministrom* (97), *ministrima* (15)], **official** [*zvaničnik* (11), *zvaničnika* (43), *zvaničnici* (55), *zvaničnicima* (24)], **parliamentarian** [*parlamentarac* (11), *parlamentarci* (13)], **representative** [*predstavnici* (316)], **visit** [*posjeta* (154), *posjeti* (192), *posjete* (225), *posjetu* (156), *posjetom* (15)] **Assistance:** **donor** [*donator* (13)], **donation** [*donacija* (16), *donaciju* (16)], **grant** [*grant* (17)], **gratitude** [*zahvalnost* (27), *zahvalnosti* (18)], **humanitarian** [*humanirarna* (18)], **support** [*podršci* (27)] **Military:** **contingent** [*kontingent* (33)], **brigadier** [*brigadir* (17)], **EUFOR** [*eufor* (89), *eufora* (10)], **battalion** [*bataljon* (32), *bataljona* (44)], **command** [*komandu* (10)], **helicopter** [*helikopteri* (10)], **officers** [*oficiri* (13)], **ship** [*brod* (70), *broda* (38), *brodovi* (21), *brodovima* (14), *brodom* (13)], **soldier** [*vojnici* (78), *vojnike* (21)] **Actors:** **Vefahan Ocak** [*vefahan* (91), *vefahana* (20), *vefahanom* (14), *odžak* (50), *ocak* (18), *ocaka* (12), *ocakom* (10)], **Bülent Tulun** [*bulentom* (31), *tuluna* (27), *tulun* (86), *tulunom* (24)], **Melek Sina Baydur** [*melek* (10), *bajdur* (67), *baydur* (41)], **Osman Aksakal** [*aksakal* (15)],

---

[21] Collocates in Bosnian, Croat and Serb languages are listed in italics next to the number of occurrences of a collocate in the corpus. English lemma version is given in bold letters. Collocates are grouped according to grammatical categories and semantic groups.

	Metin Ergin [*metin* (28), *ergin* (23)], Ali Babacan [*babadžan* (29), *babacan* (34)], Bešir Atalay [*atalaj* (13)], Ahmet Kemal Baysak [*kemalom* (28), *bajsak* (54), *bajsaka* (10), *bajsakom* (14), *baysak* (28), *baysakom* (12)], Tolga Bermek [*bermek* (10)], Haris Silajdžić [*silajdžića* (16)], Osman Kahveci [Kahveci (11)], Nada Janković [*jankovic* (13)], TİKA [*TİKA* (108), *razvojna* (20), *razvojne* (38)]
	Criticism: Darko Tanasković [tanaskovic (15)], influence [*uticaju* (11)], mother [*mati* (27), *majku* (36)], neo-Ottomanism [*neoosmanizam* (13)]
	Location: Vilsonovo šetalište [Vilsonovom (43), šetalištu (41)]
Verbs	Relations: advance [*unaprijediti* (29)], assign [*pridaje* (27)], improve [*unaprijediti* (29)]
	Diplomacy: arrive [*doputovala* (10)], depart [*otputovati* (29), *otputovao* (26), *otputovali* (11)], discuss [*razgovarao* (130)], meet [*sastao* (34), *susreli* (12)], receive [*primio* (109)], stay [*boravi* (42), *boravila* (35)], visit [*posjetio* (67), *posjetiće* (13) *posjetila* (66), *posjetili* (69), *obišla* (11)]
	Turkey: call for [*priziva* (13)], count on [*računati* (12)], interfere into, [*miješati se* (27)]
	Assistance: donate [*donirao* (13), *donirala* (34)], finance [*finasirati* (35), *finansira* (45)], help [*pomagati* (14), *pomogla* (23)], support [*podržavati* (16), *podržava* (96)], promise [*obecala* (12)], primiti (to accept, to receive), renovate [*obnavlja* (18)], thank [*zahvalio* (64)]

Special relations. This pro-Turkish discourse strand in the Bosnian mainstream printed media aims to affirm the putative importance of Bosnia for official Ankara – but also *vice versa* – by framing the relations between the two countries as something special. The language used in the framework of the discourse strand of special relations points to the fact that its origin lies in official Turkey's objective to pose as the protector of Bosnia and Bosnian Muslims, and the wish of the Bosnian Muslim political elite to seek patronage with official Ankara. Very revelatory of this type of approach is a statement of Turkish minister Faruk Şahin, who during his visit to Sarajevo in September 2013 stated that Bosnia has "a special place in Turkey and in the hearts of the Turkic peoples."[22] Bosnian printed media usually constructed this discourse strand by combining elements from the Bosnian and Turkish official foreign policy discourses, but Turkish foreign policy is almost always constructed as having the initiative in this relationship.

The frequent, uncritical, detailed, descriptive and supposedly neutral reporting on official and ceremonial features of the diplomatic activities between Bosnia and Herzegovina and Turkey – especially visits by Turkish officials to Bosnia and activities of Turkish diplomats in this country – constituted by far the largest part of the discourse strand of special relations. While saturating the media space with constant references to Turkish diplomacy, this type of reporting constructed it also as very active and omnipresent in Bosnia, which implied the conclusion that Turkey assigns special importance to this country. The adjective "friendly," usually co-occurring as a qualifier of

---

[22] *Dnevni list*, 9 November 2013, accessed through *infobiro.ba*

the noun Turkey, was often used as part of this discourse strand as part of statements uttered by Bosnian and Turkish foreign policy actors and as quoted in printed media texts by Bosnian journalists. Although concordance analysis of these collocates reveals that some of the occurrences of the adjective "friendly" were used as a part of the stereotypical diplomatic vocabulary, most of the examples document its discursive use with the aim of constructing Turkey as a state that insists on some sort of special feelings towards Bosnia on a level that is more than diplomatic courtesy:

Davutolu je još jednom pokazao da prijateljska Turska ostaje uz BiH i da podržava ...
Davutoğlu has once again shown that Turkey remains friendly with Bosnia and Herzegovina and that he supports ...
(*Dnevni avaz*, 2 November 2011)

Ovo je još jedna potvrda višestoljetnih prijateljskih odnosa između BiH i Turske.
This is further evidence of centuries of friendly relations between BiH and Turkey.
(*Dnevni avaz*, 3 September 2006)

Dvije delegacije konstatuju da između prijateljskih država BiH i Turske ima najviše potpisanih međunarodnih ugovora.
The two delegations recognize that the number of signed international agreements is the greatest between the friendly countries Bosnia and Turkey.
(*Dnevni avaz*, 19 December 2012)

The adjective "unbreakable" was predominantly used in similar contexts in order to stress the high level of friendliness between Bosnia and Turkey, as in these examples:

Turski reis potencirao neraskidive veze između dva naroda i dvije države
The Turkish grand mufti stressed the unbreakable link between the two peoples and two states
(subtitle, *Dnevni avaz*, 15 August 2009)

Neraskidive niti Bošnjaka i Turaka
Unbreakable ties of Bosniaks and Turks
(title, *Oslobođenje* 2010, 11 June 2010)

Muratović: Tursku i BiH spajaju neraskidive veze
Muratović: Turkey and Bosnia and Herzegovina are joined by the unbreakable bond
(title, *Dnevni avaz*, 30 April 2004)

The adjective "brotherly" was also occasionally used to describe Turco-Bosnian relations as special, even very special although this collocate was often used to refer to fraternization of Bosnian and Turkish towns or, rarely, in an ironic meaning:

Pozidju konzula Cilek je već poćeo koristiti kako bi približio dvije *bratske* zemlje, ...
Cilek has already begun using the position of consul to bring the two brotherly countries closer together... (*Dnevni avaz*, 9 August 2010)

Između BiH i Turske postoje duboke i bratske veze, a posjeta ovog broda jedan je vid demonstracije veoma dobrih odnosa.
Between BiH and Turkey there are profound and brotherly ties, and the visit of this ship is just one form of demonstration of the very good relations. (*Dnevni avaz*, 19 May 2009)

The verb "to assign" was arguably the most important verb in the framework of this discourse strand. The verb "to assign" was predominantly used as the part of the phrase "to assign importance" – usually "great importance" – in sentences whose subject was "Turkey". As concordance lines reveal, this phrase was used to describe Turkish foreign policy positions that stress the supposed importance of Bosnia for Turkey. Most of the examples were related to pledges of the preservation of the territorial integrity and/or sovereignty of Bosnia by Turkish actors which were highlighted by sympathetic journalists, as in these examples:

To je razlog što Turska *pridaje* veliki značaj teritorijalnom integritetu BiH, njenom suverenitetu ...
This is the reason why Turkey attaches great importance to the territorial integrity of Bosnia and Herzegovina, to its sovereignty ... (*Oslobođenje* 14 September 2012)

Turska *pridaje* veliku važnost vašoj zemlji istaknuo je Unluer. Prema njegovim riječima, većina ljudi u Turskoj danas, umjesto u druge zemlje regiona, želi doći u BiH, ...
Turkey attaches great importance to your country, said Unluer. According to him, most people in Turkey today, want to come to BiH in preference to other countries in the region. (*Dnevni avaz*, 22 May 2012)
Predsjednik Turske Abdullah Gul ukazao je na važnost koju Turska pridaje odnosima s BiH ...
The President of Turkey Abdullah Gul underlined the importance that Turkey attaches to the relations with Bosnia and Herzegovina. (*Dnevni list*, 16 May 2013)

Collocates that refer to classical and public diplomatic and military activities in Bosnia (e.g. "diplomacy", "delegation", "ambassador", "brigadier", "contingent" etc.; verbs like "to visit", "arrive" etc.; adjectives like "official", "introductory" etc.) or names of politicians and diplomats themselves (Ali Babacan, Vefahan Ocak, Melek Sina Baydur, etc.), the largest part of the vocabulary associated within the macro-topic of Turco-Bosnian diplomatic relations, were mainly used as part of this discourse strand.

Turkey as a help provider. This discourse strand has aimed to construct the Turkish governmental and allied non-governmental actors from the Turkish conservative scene as providers of various kinds of help to Bosnia during the period under analysis. As previously noted, these efforts, which include financial support for various cultural (renovation of the Ottoman architectural heritage etc.) and humanitarian (donations to hospitals etc.) projects, are part of the Turkish public diplomacy campaign, which is in return supported by sympathetic Bosnian newspaper media. The lists of the search term collocates contain slightly fewer collocates exclusively or predominantly related to this discourse strand than to the discourse strand of special relations. The verbs "to support," "to promise," "to count on," the noun "support", the adverb "strongly," and the adjective "ready" were very often used in politicians' statements to express the willingness of official Ankara to support Bosnia in various ways, as in these examples:

Od ratnih dana do danas, Turska se trudila _podržavati_ BiH u svim oblastima, što će i nadalje činiti.
From the days of the war up to this day, Turkey has tried to support Bosnia and Herzegovina in all areas, which it will continue doing.
(*Dnevni list*, 19 November 2013)
"Turska je _spremna_", kazao je Erdoan, "prenijeti BiH svoja iskustva na putu ka Evropi."
"Turkey is ready ", said Erdoğan,"to transfer its experience to Bosnia and Herzegovina on the road to Europe."
(*Oslobođenje*, 17 February 2005)

Turska će intenzivnije _pomagati_ BiH.
Turkey will help Bosnia and Herzegovina more vigorously.
(title, *Dnevni avaz*, 23 September 2010)
BiH može _računati_ na punu _podršku_ Turske"
"Bosnia and Herzegovina can count on the full support of Turkey "
(title, *Oslobođenje*, 11 December 2009)

Erdogan: Bosna uvijek može <u>računati</u> na nas
Erdoğan: Bosnia can always count on us
(title, *Dnevni avaz*, 4 May 2008)

The collocates "to donate", "to finance", "to renovate" and the noun "donation" in most instances appeared in the context of reporting on more concrete ways of helping Bosnia through means of financing projects, usually the restoration of the Ottoman historical heritage sites. The collocate referring to the main actor of the Turkish state in the field of public diplomacy, Turkish developmental agency ("TIKA"), was especially important in this respect. The verb "to help" was also sometimes used as part of this discourse strand:

Turski bataljon donirao sedam kompjutora
The Turkish battalion donated seven computers
(title, *Oslobođenje* 9 January 2006)

Prema nedavnoj odluci vlade Republike Turske, ova će država finansirati kompletnu obnovu, sanaciju i revitalizaciju stanja Višegradske ćuprije …
According to a recent decision of the government of the Republic of Turkey, this state will finance the complete restoration, rehabilitation, and revitalization of the state of the Višegrad bridge …
(*Oslobođenje* 12 May 2007)

Direkcija vakufa Turske obnavlja Isa-begov hamam
Turkey's Directorate of pious foundations renovates Isa-beg's bath
(*Oslobođenje*, 5 February 2008)

Sporazumom se realizira donacija vlade Turske u iznosu od …
The donation of the government of Turkey in the amount of … is being realized according to an agreement.

Davutoglu je jucer u Banjoj Luci obišao gradilište Ferhat-pašine džamije i razgovarao s banjoluckim muftijom Edhemom ef. Camdžicem o izgradnji ovog vjerskog objekta, ciju obnovu je <u>pomogla</u> Turska uprava za međunarodnu suradnju i razvoj (TIKA).
Yesterday in Banja Luka Davutoğlu visited the construction site of the Ferhat Pasha mosque and talked to the Banja Luka mufti Edhem ef. Čamdžić on the construction of a religious building, whose restoration was supported by the Turkish Directorate for International Cooperation and Development (TİKA).

(*Dnevni list*, 21 January 2011)

Nakon zimske pauze, ponovo su poceli radovi, koje finansira turska razvojna agencija „TIKA", a cija je vrijednost veca od pet miliona maraka.
After the winter break, the construction whose value exceeds five million marks has begun again, funded by the Turkish Development Agency or TİKA
(*Dnevni avaz*, 15 May 2007)

    Investigation of concordances suggests that this discourse strand of Turkish assistance is very often interconnected with the discourse strand of special relations. It is often used to assist the argumentation of the promotion of special relations. The architecture renovation projects financed by Turkish authorities and other Turkish actors tended to attract the attention of Bosnian newspapers during the visits of high-ranking Turkish politicians, which were primarily used to promote the concept of special relations between the two countries and help the renovation of the Ottoman architectural heritage, as proof of that. These occasions were then used to open the renovation sites and stress the special place taken by Bosnia in Turkish foreign policy.

    Criticism. The critical discourse towards Turkish foreign policy was less present within the macro-topic of Turko-Bosnian diplomatic relations than the pro-Turkish thread. The number of collocates from this macro-topic that were exclusively or predominantly associated with any kind of criticism of Turkish foreign policy toward Bosnia was very small. References to the "neo-Ottomanism," a putative ideology of Turkish foreign policy as suggested by some critics of Turkey, did not gain ground in Bosnian mainstream newspapers, although subtle insinuations against Turkish foreign policy ambitions in Bosnia did surface from time to time. The collocate "neo-Ottomanism" was above the threshold of significance set for this research, but most of the occurrences of this word were related to the reporting and even criticism of the book by Darko Tanasković, the main proponent of the neo-Ottoman allegations in the Western Balkans. Similarly, two other collocates, the verb "to intervene in" and the noun "influence", were predominantly used by critics of Turkish foreign policy towards Bosnia, for example by Milorad Dodik, the president of the Republika Srpska. Dodik and other Bosnian Serb politicians on several occasions accused Turkey of interfering in the affairs of Bosnia and Herzegovina using the argument of Turkish putative threat against the sovereignty of Bosnia and Herzegovina. Ironically, such statements were almost exclusively reported as part of critical articles on these politicians. Only three collocates from our list, two of them with meaning "mother" can be seen as belonging, at least partially, to the critical discourse *per se*. On several occasions, the former religious leader of Bosnian Muslims, the then influential reis-ul-ulema Mustafa Cerić publicly called Turkey "our mother" (i.e. the Bosnian Muslim mother).[23] This created a wave of criticism and ridicule of Cerić and similar-minded people from the Bosnian Muslim elite for conservatism and sycophancy towards foreign leaders, i.e. Turkish political elite, and for lack of patriotism and sensitivity for the Bosnian multi-ethnic context and modern needs of the country. This wave of criticism also influenced the appearance of these collocates on the list. Here are some examples:

Odatle to ocajnicko okretanje „maticama", identificiranje s njima: „maticna zemlja Hrvatska", „maticna zemlja Srbija", ili za Bošnjake u verziji Mustafe Cerica: „Turska nam je mati, tako je bilo i tako ce ostati!"
This desperate turning to "national homelands" and identifying with them comes from there: "mother country Croatia ", "mother country Serbia," or for Bosniaks in the version Mustafa Cerić: "Turkey is our mother so it was and so it will remain!"
(*Dani*, 20 June 2006)

Often these collocates were to be found in ironic contexts, which were nevertheless meant to be critical of the Turkish role in Bosnia:

Ako je, dakle, Turska (druga) majka Bošnjacima, a Srbija i Turska dvije sestre onda je, koliko se razumijem u rodbinske veze, sada Srbija tetka Bošnjacima …
If, therefore, Turkey is (the second) mother to Bosniaks, and Serbia and Turkey are two sisters, then, as I understand the family ties, now Serbia is the aunt to Bosniaks …
(*Oslobođenje*, 25 July 2009)

The Bosnian verb meaning "to call for"/ "to invoke"/ "to evoke" – usually with "Turkey" as its object - was also often used in the context of the critical discourse of the Turkish foreign policy in Bosnia:

Onaj ko ovde priziva Tursku, on opravdava, pomaže i legitimira „Veliku Srbiju" …
Whoever here invokes Turkey, justifies, legitimizes and helps "Greater Serbia" …
(*Oslobođenje*, 1 July 2010)
… ovih dana priziva Tursku drugu majku u pomoć …
… these days calls upon Turkey, the second mother, for help …
(*Oslobođenje*, 14 October 2010)

---

[23] Mustafa Cerić, "Mustafa Cerić: „Naša Majka je Turska!", youtoube.com, https://www.youtube.com/watch?v=r-gCPvGg3go (accessed January 30, 2020).

Turco-Bosnian Economic Relations

Turco-Bosnian economic relations were the second-largest macro-topic of the corpus according to the number of collocates (195). As was the case with the macro-topic of Turco-Bosnian diplomatic relations, this macro-topic also included media discourses in support and against Turkish foreign policy towards Bosnia. Collocates that are exclusively or mostly used in the framework of the pro-Turkish discourse were more numerous. During the period 2003-2014, the Turkish foreign policy through official and unofficial means coordinated efforts to advance Turkish economic presence in Bosnia and used economic issues, especially the need to advance trade and investment. This was an important part of official statements and public relations efforts. For example, the Turkish Deputy Prime Minister Ali Babacan during his visit to Sarajevo said that "Turkey is ready to invest in infrastructure and energy projects."[24]

Whereas Turkish officials often presented investment in Bosnia as a national or governmental project, in reality the Turkish business actors, despite all the official exhortations and incentives, were resolved to invest primarily on the basis of their own, rather than political, national or religious interests. Nevertheless, the Bosnian media and public tended to see the presence of Turkish investments and trade with Bosnia as a constituent part of official foreign policy, even in cases when they were reporting on private initiatives. This was visible equally in texts that supported and that criticized Turkish foreign policy toward Bosnia. Collocates related to Turkish diplomatic activities often appeared in texts that focused on economic issues and *vice versa*: reporting on official diplomatic activities almost always included some sort of economic issues and texts focusing on Turco-Bosnian economic issues often mentioned Turkish foreign policy. Despite being such an important part of Turkish foreign policy discourse, especially in the light of the claims of special relations, the actual role of trade and investment from Turkey in Bosnia was not that impressive. For example, Turkey was in 2013 only the ninth exporter to Bosnia (218 million $). Bosnia's imports from Turkey were actually three times smaller than those from Germany (735 million $) or Switzerland (685 million $). The discrepancies were even higher when we consider exports from Bosnia: 88 million $ to Turkey, but 685 million $ to Germany.[25]

---

[24] *Infokom*, April 1, 2011 (accessed through *infobiro.ba*).
[25] *Politička romansa: odnosi između Turske i Bosne i Hercegovine*, 33.

Table 2: Collocates used in the context of Turco-Bosnian economic relations

Adjectives	**General**: Bosnian-Herzegovinian [*bosanskohercegovačko* (14)]. **banking** [*bankarsko* (15), *bankarsku* (10)], **central** [*centralni* (19), *centralnog* (16)], **civilian** [*civilna* (20)], **productional** [*proizvodna* (64)], **economic** [*privrednu* (27), *privrednih* (55)], **Investment:** interested in [*zainteresirana/turska* (59), zainteresirani (33), zainteresirane (14), zainteresovani (27), *zainteresovana* (26)] **Trade:** custom-free [*bescarinskom* (11)], **free** [*slobodnoj* (87)], **trade** [*trgovinska* (33), *trgovinske* (37), *trgovinskoj* (19)], **tourist** [*turistički* (17)]
Nouns	**General:** contractor [*izvođača* (11)], **economy** [*privreda* (32)], **stock exchange** [*berzi* (48)], **GDP** [*gdp* (11)], **Lira/Turkish currency** [*lira* (57)], **producer** [*proizvođač* (25)], **registry** [*registar* (12)] **Investment:** advancement [*unapređenju* (23)], **businessman** [*biznismen* (48), *biznismenima* (35), *biznismena* (102), *biznismene* (14), *privrednika* (272), *privrednici* (139), *privrednike* (43), *privrednicima* (98)], **firm** [*firma* (298)], **interim agreement** [*predugovor* (11)], **investor** [*investitor* (48), *investitori* (92), *investitora* (102), *investitore* (53), *investitorima* (56)], **chamber** [*komoru* (15)], **company** [*kompanija* (442), *kompanije* (372), *kompanijom* (64)], **factory** [*fabriku* (34)], **flow** [*priliv* (16)], **concern** [*koncern* (15)], **consortium** [*konzorcij* (27)], **buyer** [*kupac* (28)], **investment** [*investiranja* (29)], **partner** [*partner* (134)], **participation** [*ucešcu* (10)], **protokol** [*protokola* (29), *partnerom* (29), *partnerima* (53)], **signal** [*signal* (23)] **Trade:** exchange [*razmjena* (58)], **fair** [*sajam* (149)], **honey** *med* (30), walnut [*oraha* (27)], **textile** [*tekstil* (31), *tekstila* (38)], **importer** [*uvoznik* (10), *uvoznici* (10)], **import** [*uvozom* (20)], **purchase** [*nabavci* (10)] **Transport & travel:** airport [*aerodrome* (10)], **air company** [*aviokompanija* (28)], **air fleet** [*avijacija* (20)], **bus** [*autobusi* (11)], **railways** [*željeznicama* (15)], **summer vacation** [*ljetovanje* (21)], **Talgo** [*talgo* (27)], **train** [*vozovi* (10)], **transit** [*tranzit* (12)], **truck** [kamion (25)] **Illegal economy:** Acik Can [acik (31), *džanu* (19), *cana* (10)], **citizen** [*državljanin* (132), *državljaninu* (63), *državljanina* (132), *državljane* (71), *državljana* (186), *državljanima* (41), *državljani* (79)], **drugs** [*drogu* (48)], **Edin & Admir Džihić** [*džihic* (14)], **Hamdo Dačić** [*hamdi* (16), *dacicu* (17)], **heroin** [*heroin* (55)], **(im)migrant** [*migranata* (20), *migrante* (17), *imigrant* (11)], **smuggling** [*krijumčarenjem* (11)], **transfer** [*prebacivanje* (14), *prebacivanjem* (15)]

	Actors: Muzaffer Çilek [*cilek* (20)], Enka [*enka* (27)], Hayat Holding - Kastamonu Entegre [holding (46)], **MOL** [*mol* (13)], **PTT/** Turske pošte [*pošta* (46), *pošte* (33), *poštama* (10)], Şarik Tara [*tara* (11)], Şişecam Soda [*šišedžam* (15)], Seha Industrial [*seha* (42)], Takaşbank [*takasbank* (12)], **TOBB** [*tobb* (21)], Turkoil [*turkoil* (30), *turkoila* (15)]
Verbs	**Investment:** express [*iskazali* (16)], commit [*obavezala* (11)], invest [*investiraju* (30), *investirati* (40), *investira* (15), *ulaže* (30), *ulažu* (43)]
	Trade: export [*izvoziti* (23), *izvozi* (31), *izvozili* (11)], import [*uvozi* (35), *uvozimo* (11)], increase [*porastao* (27)], offer [*nudi* (169)], pay [*platila* (11)], procure [*nabavljali* (14)], transport [*prevozio* (13)]
	Illegal economy: run away [*pobjegao* (32)], transfer [*prebaciti* (11)], smuggle [*švercovali* (14)]

Turkish investment in Bosnia. The largest group of collocates related to Turco-Bosnian economic relations belonging to this discourse strand (see Table 2) were in most cases used as part of the discourse that supported Turkish foreign policy toward Bosnia. This discourse strand featured two distinct sub-topics:

a) reporting on visits by Turkish businessmen or Turkish officials, during which they met with Bosnian partners and officials, and issued statements expressing more or less serious and detailed interest in investing in the Bosnian economy; there were also cases when pledges to invest were made by Turks during visits by Bosnian businessmen and officials in Turkey;

b) reports on already started or finished investment projects. The frequent presence of media reporting on investments aroused in the Bosnian public a great deal of expectation, but the number of Turkish investments in the Bosnian economy has been relatively few.[26] Collocates with a meaning related to expressing intention ("interested in," "to express") appeared in the context of supposedly showing interest in investing in Bosnia:

Turska kompanija je zainteresirana za kupovinu vecinskog djela kapitala nekadašnjeg privrednog giganta sanske opcine i Bosanske krajine.

A Turkish company is interested in buying the majority capital of the former industrial giant of the Sana municipality and of the Bosnian Krajina.

(*Dnevni avaz*, 26 February 2007)

---

[26] Ibid.

> *Bičakčić je tada izjavio da su turski investitori „zainteresirani za oblast hidroenergetskog potencijala, ali su mogući i neki drugi projekti iz oblasti industrijske proizvodnje u branši kojom se bavi Calik Holding".*
>
> Bičakčić then said that Turkish investors "are interested in the field of hydropower potential, but some other projects in the field of industrial production are possible, in the field Calik Holding is working in".
>
> (*Slobodna Bosna*, 13 August 2009)

> *Turci iskazali interes za suradnju sa našim tvrtkama*
>
> Turks expressed interest in cooperation with our companies
>
> (title, *Dnevni list*, 8 October 2010)

Collocates semantically linked to the concept of investing ("to invest", "investment", "investor", "protocol", "to commit", "participation", "interim agreement") very often appeared as part of this discourse strand in texts reporting on investment activities of Turkish businessmen in Bosnia:

> *Turske investitore interesiraju mogućnosti ulaganja u BiH*
>
> Turkish investors are interested in investment opportunities in Bosnia and Herzegovina
>
> (title, *Dnevni avaz* 8 July 2005)

> *Imamo predugovor s partnerom iz Turske vrijedan 2,4 miliona eura"; kazao je Ademovic.*
>
> "We have an interim agreement with a partner from Turkey worth 2.4 million euros "; Ademović said
>
> (*Nezavisne novine*, 7 October 2010)

> *On je naveo da se kompanija iz Turske obavezala da ce u stalnom radnom odnosu zadržati svih 890 radnika ...*
>
> He said that the Turkish company pledged to keep all the 890 workers permanently employed ...
>
> (*Nezavisne novine*, 4 May 2005)

Very frequent collocates with common business-related meanings like ("businessman", "company", "concern", "consortium", "partner", "firm",) were also mostly used as part of the discourse strand of Turkish investments in Bosnia. They appeared in texts reporting statements by Turkish diplomats or activities of Turkish investors:

> ... delegacija Parlamenta BiH i od premijera i predsjednika te zemlje Redžepa Tajipa Erdoana i Ahmeta Nedždeta Sezera dobila je uvjeravanja da ce ubuduce turski *biznismeni* mnogo više investirati u BiH nego što je to bio slucaj do sada ...
>
> ... the delegation of the Bosnian Parliament received assurances also from the prime minister and the president of that country, Recep Tayyip Erdoğan and Ahmet Necdet Sezer respectively, that in future many more Turkish businessmen will invest in Bosnia than has been the case so far ....
>
> (*Dnevni avaz*, 30 April 2005)

> Najveci privredni gigant Natron nakon uspješne privatizacije osigurao je posao za 760 radnika, posao ce dobiti još 150 radnika. Turski *koncern* Hayat vec je uplatio 14 miliona maraka, cime su ispunjen uslovi za registraciju kompanije Natron-Hayat...
>
> After successful privatization, the largest economic giant Natron has provided employment for 760 workers, another 150 workers will be employed as well. Turkish Hayat Group has already paid 14 million marks, completing the requirements for the registration of the company Natron Hayat ...
>
> (*Oslobodenje*, 15 May 2005)

> Sljedece sedmice napuštam BiH, ali prije nego što odem, BiH ce posjetiti jedna znacajnija turska *kompanija* koja je zainteresovana za ulaganje kazala je Bajdur ne želeci precizirati detalje.
>
> Next week I am leaving Bosnia and Herzegovina, but before I go, one major Turkish company interested in investing will visit Bosnia and Herzegovina, said Bajdur avoiding specifying any details.
>
> (*Dnevni avaz*, 12 December 2005)

> Turski *partner* udvostrucio ulaganja.
>
> The Turkish partner doubled the investment.
>
> (the title, *Oslobodenje* 22 March 2007)

Collocates explicitly referring to Turkish companies and businessmen that invested or had plans to invest in Bosnia ("Hayat Holding-Kastamonu Entegre" , "Enka", "Seha Industrial" "PTT", "Muzaffer Çilek", "Şarik Tara" etc.) appeared exclusively in the context of this discourse strand:

> U novo zajednicko preduzece Natron Hayat, sa omjerom vlasništva 70:30 posto u korist kompanije *Kastamonu Entegre*, turski partner ce uz 14 miliona KM osnivackog kapitala osigurati investicije od minimalno 21 milion eura za sanaciju i modernizaciju proizvodnih kapaciteta ...
>
> With 14 million KM the Turkish partner will provide the initial capital investment of at least EUR 21 million for rehabilitation and modernization of the production capacities in the new joint venture Natron Hayat, where the ownership ratio of 70:30 percent is in favour of the company Kastamonu Entegre, ...
>
> (*Oslobodenje*, 4 February 2005)

> *Ponude su dostavili Konel iz Hrvatske, Integral iz Laktaša, Mirad iz Zenice te konzorcij koji cine turska Enka, slovenacki Gradis i ortacka grupa (menadžment i radnici).*
>
> Bids were submitted by Konel from Croatia, Integral from Laktaši, Mirad from Zenica and a consortium consisting of the Turkish Enka, Slovenian Gradis and partnership group (management and workers)
>
> (*Oslobođenje* 26 March 2007)

> *Šarik Tara je najbogatiji biznismen Turske ...*
>
> Šarik Tara is the richest businessman in Turkey ...
>
> (*Oslobođenje*, 20 May 2006)

Criticism. Critical discourse towards Turkish foreign policy in Bosnia within the macro-topic of Turco-Bosnian economic relations was not common. Only one collocate can to a larger degree be related to this discourse. The research corpus contained 23 collocates exclusively or mostly referring to the illegal economy, including the drug trade, stemming from Turkey. Nevertheless, these texts did not reveal that they held negative discourse prosody toward Turkey and they belong to routine reporting on crime. The most common topic of the critical discourse was pointing the negative side of Turco-Bosnian economic relations, such as the fact that Turkish economic investments were lagging behind those of Western or neighboring countries, or that the Bosnian trade with Turkey was continuously creating a deficit at the expense of the Bosnian side. This type of information was exposed in order to counter the claims that Turkey has some sort of special relations with Bosnia or a soft spot for her. The creators of such texts were juxtaposing economic data with the media hype over the supposed great interest in investing in Bosnia by Turkish companies. The other, less common, sub-topic was reporting on the problems and failures of actual Turkish economic investment in Bosnia. Collocates "to import" and "import" were occasionally used to raise the issue of the large Bosnian deficit in trade with Turkey or other problems related to the trade with that country:

> *Međutim, moramo reci da je u toj razmjeni BiH u velikom deficitu, buduci da jedan znacajan dio roba koje uvozimo iz Turske dolazi preko trecih zemalja" ...*
>
> However, we must say that within this exchange, Bosnia and Herzegovina is in a big deficit, given the important factor that a large part of the goods that we import from Turkey arrive through third countries
>
> (*Infokom*, 1 April 2008)

> *Jednostavnije, iz Turske uvozimo odjevne predmete i kucne uredaje koji su jeftiniji obicnom kupcu nego kvalitetnija roba iste vrste porijeklom iz susjednih ili zapadnih zemalja.*

> To simplify, from Turkey we import clothing and household devices that are cheaper to the ordinary customer, than the quality goods of the same type originating from neighboring or Western countries
>
> (*Dani*, 25 February 2012)

> ... *pokrivenost izvoza uvozom BiH iz Turske svake godine ide na štetu BiH* ...
>
> ...the coverage of imports by exports from Turkey to Bosnia is each year at the expense of Bosnia and Herzegovina ...
>
> (*Oslobođenje*, 26 March 2008)

While the collocate "investor" was exclusively associated with the pro-Turkish discourse, the collocate "buyer" was largely associated with the critical discourse, mostly in the context of reporting on problems with investments actually coming to fruition, even in some cases attempting to highlight the supposed dishonesty of Turkish businessmen in Bosnia:

> *Turski kupac sada pokušava kupiti vrijeme*
>
> The Turkish buyer is now trying to buy time
>
> (Title, *Dnevni Avaz* 18 April 2009)

> *Četrnaest mjeseci kasnije, ovih dana, neumoljive činjenice kažu: turski kupac nije povezao staž i obezbijedio uvjete za penzionisanje radnika koji ispunjavaju zakonske uvjete za to, nije uplatio zaostale poreze i doprinose za ostale radnike* ...
>
> Fourteen months later, these days, inexorable facts claim that the Turkish buyer did not connect the contribution record and did not provide the conditions for the retirement of workers who meet the legal requirements for it, did not pay the taxes and contributions for the rest of the workers ...
>
> (*Dnevni avaz*, 25 October 2008)

Other Macro-Topics

The contemporary Turco-Bosnian cultural relations were a major topic in the reporting on Turkey by the mainstream Bosnian newspaper media. Nevertheless, by and large, it was centered on very modern cultural developments, not related to the conservative cultural affinities of the AKP and its allies in the Turkish and Bosnian conservative scenes and therefore of no or only marginal use for the promotion of Turkish foreign policy. Consequently, the reporting on culture in Bosnian mainstream media was largely free of discourses on Turkish foreign policy. Topics on culture represented in this macro-topic included television (e.g. Turkish soap operas), art-house cinema (e.g. Nure Bilge Ceylan, Sarajevo Film Festival), and literature (Orhan Pamuk). As collocation analysis shows, Bosnian mainstream newspapers showed relatively little interest in invoking Ottoman history while referring to "Turkey" and "Turkish", even less to connect Turkey with religion. For example, collocates "Ottoman", "mosque," or "Islam" do not appear above the threshold used for this study. Other sources confirm that religion and the Ottoman heritage and Islam play an extremely important role as the communication medium between actors in conservative scenes in Turkey and Bosnia, but these topics seem to be underplayed in the mainstream. The collocate "empire" appears mostly in contexts that are not related to pro-Turkish discourse. Nevertheless, the discursive use of Ottoman history, as well as Islam, was present in the mainstream Bosnian printed media, albeit in an indirect fashion, mostly when reporting on the Turkish assistance for the renovation of the architectural heritage. Instances of such reporting belong to a previously analyzed discourse strand (*Turkey as a help provider*). The mainstream Bosnian newspapers also produced a great deal of material on Turkish politics in contexts that were not directly related to Bosnia, but such reporting cannot be associated with discursive support or criticism for Turkish foreign policy. The coverage of Turkey outside the context of Turco-Bosnian relations was largely rudimentary as well as neutral and dispassionate in the mainstream Bosnian printed media. The occasional reporting on the Turkish regional diplomatic initiatives involving Bosnia was the only notable exception. Coverage of sporting events, the largest group of collocates, was almost completely devoid of instances of discourses supporting or criticizing Turkish foreign policy.

Conclusion

The analysis showed that the representations of Turkey in Bosnian mainstream printed media between 2003 and 2014 were often used to influence public opinion about Turkish foreign policy toward Bosnia. Discourses on Turkish foreign policy toward Bosnia were present when reporting on two major topics related to Turkey: Turco-Bosnian diplomatic relations and Turco-Bosnian economic relations, which taken together represented roughly one-third of all collocates. The discourse *supporting* Turkish foreign policy dominated the reporting on both of these macro-topics, albeit with greater emphasis within the topic of Turco-Bosnian diplomatic relations. On the other hand, the discourse critical of Turkish foreign policy had a smaller impact on the reporting on Turkey within these two macro-topics. The discourse strand of special relations was a central discourse strand within the pro-Turkish discourse. These results also suggest the conclusion that Turkish foreign policy under AKP was successful in its public diplomacy efforts in Bosnia, which were focused around cultural and media projects, and they indirectly influenced media reporting. A large part of the Bosnian media, mostly from Sarajevo, but often from other parts of Bosnia as well, readily agreed to convey the message when reporting on Turco-Bosnian diplomatic and economic relations and in more cases than not supported Turkish foreign policy towards Bosnia.

Appendix: The list of top 100 collocates

Rank	Occurrence	Occurrence (Left side)	Occurrence (Right Side)	MI score	Collocate
1	20	1	19	10.91249	Vefahana
2	19	0	19	10.91249	Jatirmilar
3	31	5	26	10.86668	Bulentom
4	91	16	75	10.80557	Vefahan
5	13	4	9	10.80557	Rizespor
6	10	2	8	10.77498	Kamenoresci
7	10	8	2	10.77498	Dijaneta
8	14	1	13	10.71984	Vefahanom
9	45	27	18	10.67642	Konzulom
10	10	0	10	10.64945	Erbu
11	14	7	7	10.63238	Ankaragucu
12	45	25	20	10.62298	Pocasnim
13	21	5	16	10.60436	Recepom
14	24	4	20	10.59056	Tulunom
15	12	12	0	10.59056	Legalizirana
16	61	11	50	10.57644	Abdulahom
17	15	0	15	10.57145	Unmi
18	11	11	0	10.56456	Komunikacione
19	18	3	15	10.55885	Tayyipom
20	10	1	9	10.53397	Necdet
21	12	3	9	10.49745	Turguta
22	30	5	25	10.49745	Gormez
23	63	25	38	10.49745	Državljaninu
24	15	7	8	10.49745	Aksakal
25	14	5	9	10.47191	Davatoglu
26	130	8	122	10.45912	Tajip
27	81	13	68	10.45792	Melek

28	71	6	65	10.41838	Ahmetom
29	17	6	11	10.41499	Arinc
30	38	2	36	10.40553	Redžepom
31	34	7	27	10.38524	Babacan
32	20	5	15	10.37643	Nihat
33	31	2	29	10.37483	Tajipom
34	11	4	7	10.37192	Šiša
35	11	4	7	10.37192	Bescarinskom
36	57	5	52	10.37034	Lira
37	28	11	17	10.36229	Metin
38	17	2	15	10.35609	Tajipu
39	21	2	19	10.35061	Redžepu
40	100	25	75	10.34689	Bulent
41	212	106	106	10.33207	Moldavija
42	10	0	10	10.32752	Sadet
43	12	7	5	10.32752	Ozgur
44	10	3	7	10.32752	Hurijet
45	12	4	8	10.32752	Džam
46	32	2	30	10.32752	Bulenta
47	247	26	221	10.32169	Recep
48	77	11	66	10.32129	Perzijskom
49	23	4	19	10.30676	Ergin
50	15	2	13	10.29581	Lire
51	11	5	6	10.28445	Askin
52	75	15	60	10.28332	Gulom
53	19	5	14	10.25352	Botas
54	167	13	154	10.2518	Redžep
55	10	2	8	10.23441	Taipom
56	10	1	9	10.23441	Ocakom
57	15	15	0	10.23441	Nastupnu
58	15	0	15	10.23441	Aciku
59	99	42	57	10.22896	Armenija
60	18	1	17	10.22443	Saadet
61	18	18	0	10.22443	Novoimenovanog
62	26	7	19	10.22061	Nurullah
63	21	5	16	10.21734	Tobb
64	16	16	0	10.21205	Ambasadoricom
65	122	12	110	10.19937	Kastamonu
66	14	5	9	10.19628	Cihat
67	105	9	96	10.18379	Redžepa
68	12	7	5	10.17552	Takasbank
69	12	2	10	10.17552	Sezerom

70	82	14	68	10.17201	Ocak
71	22	18	4	10.16246	Mevlut
72	41	10	31	10.16151	Baydur
73	13	0	13	10.15349	Abdullahom
74	10	1	9	10.14695	Zula
75	10	4	6	10.14695	Sulejmaniju
76	10	6	4	10.14695	Mehter
77	10	3	7	10.14695	Inegola
78	24	5	19	10.1399	Davutoluom
79	42	6	36	10.13488	Recepa
80	14	0	14	10.13488	Bajsakom
81	92	10	82	10.12316	Tajipa
82	184	82	102	10.12316	Malta
83	218	91	127	10.11462	Estonija
84	16	9	7	10.10513	Industrijalaca
85	33	6	27	10.0989	Contingent
86	29	4	25	10.09804	Industrial
87	86	26	60	10.09082	Tulun
88	13	8	5	10.08936	Sanayii
89	67	14	53	10.08376	Bajdur
90	14	2	12	10.07598	Melih
91	15	15	0	10.06449	Prebacivanjem
92	10	9	1	10.06449	Burkine
93	43	8	35	10.05335	Erdoganom
94	77	9	68	10.03972	Entegre
95	12	0	12	10.03802	Ocaka
96	18	3	15	10.03802	Ciler
97	12	2	10	10.03802	Baysakom
98	12	12	0	10.03802	Ambasadoricu
99	26	13	13	10.02796	Tuncer
100	13	3	10	10.02796	Tofaš

A Literary Map of Turkey

Lisa Maria Teichmann and Franz-Benjamin Mocnik

Abstract

What are the most common places in Turkey appearing in Turkish literature? It is hardly possible to read all novels or articles published in the past 35 years and collect each place name into a comprehensive list. We, therefore, offer an approach featuring computer-assisted extraction of spatial elements from a collection of texts (corpus). Through an automated search, a set of simple rules determines whether a word is recognized as a place name (toponym) by matching the character strings. The matches are then filtered. With a wide range of sources from different genres, the METU Turkish Corpus served as the exemplary basis for this project, in which we demonstrate the extraction and filtering methods for a publicly available digital Turkish text corpus. A digital, interactive map (http://projects.mocnik-science.net/literary-map-of-turkey/) has been created as a product and tool for the evaluation. The "literary" map also provides the reader with an overview of how intrinsically toponyms and daily Turkish are connected.

Introduction

Istanbul in Demir Özlü: İthaka'ya Yolculuk
... *Bir fuhuş kentiydi* **İstanbul**

Ankara in Nazlı Eray: Uyku İstasyonu
...*emyeşil bir parktan* **Ankara**'*ya bakmak istiyordu*

İzmir in Fatih Atila: Alaturka Rapsodi
...*ri Kütahyalı, öbürü* **İzmirli**, *tam bir piç. İst...*

In his work *Conjectures about World Literature*, in which Franco Moretti coined the term "distant reading" as a quantitative approach in the study of literature opposed to close reading, he writes that "the more ambitious the project, the greater must the distance [to the text] be."[1] Our project investigates new – for the case of Turkish yet not existent – methodologies of what we call "very distant reading". By looking at a vast number of texts with no regard to their content, the interpretation and analysis process is shifted to a later stage. Imagining close and distant reading not as two separate methods but as two endpoints of a bar, on which research ought to position itself, this project aims at shifting the cursor towards distant reading at the very beginning of data analysis. It, therefore, allows further interpretation at a later stage.

---

[1] Franco Moretti, "Conjectures on World Literature", *New Left Review* 1 (2000): 48.

With the help of computers, automated extraction of spatial references offers the possibility to process a vast amount of texts: words and phrases from the texts are compared to toponyms collected from *OpenStreetMaps*, and matches are collected. The matches are filtered by heuristics rules to exclude erroneous matches, which exist e.g. due to homonyms. By using the example of METU Turkish Corpus, we evaluate the feasibility of the different filters (by en- or disabling them) for our specific research question. Our methodology is therefore open to scrutiny, any evaluation may be traced back and reconstructed in further research.

Since our approach remains outside the boundaries of corpus-linguistics, it is important to interpret the results in the context of the used methods. The evaluation of the results shows which information about spatial relations can successfully be extracted by a computer, the data quality of the extracted information, and which problems occur. Future research may further improve the quality of the results, discuss the context of the methodology in greater detail, and identify further applications.

In the first chapter, we review existing Turkish language corpora, while focusing on the METU Turkish corpus and why it is most suited for our research. The field of literary geography, its theoretical and methodological framework, and a review of the project *A Literary Atlas of Europe*, is the topic of the second chapter. Chapter three is dedicated to our vision, this project's implications – why we set out and what can be gained from it as well as its partially language-related challenges. In chapter four we discuss the data extraction using toponyms, and the visualization of spatial aspects of the texts by interactive maps. Finally, in "Evaluation and Outlook" we evaluate the results, their quality and viability, as well as possible applications in future research.

1. Textual corpora: a (p)review

To give an overview of existing Turkish language corpora is quite challenging for there is no comprehensive study on the past and current developments in computational linguistics and language resources. Additionally, most of the secondary sources about digital language corpora date back at least five years. This chapter then can be considered an attempt to summarize the state of the field and existing digital Turkish corpora. Since this study focuses on the representation of geographical places in Turkish fiction, this overview is restricted to written text corpora, which include a high quantity of works of fiction.

As shown here, fiction is not a major field in the design and construction of Turkish language corpora. Accordingly, research making use of corpora is mainly concerned with building and applying tools of corpus linguistics. Text technology (*Texttechnologie*), which is closely related to literary studies on the other hand is a field yet to be discovered in the Turkish context.

Nevertheless, over the past years the scientific interest in Turkish language resources has increased. While at the biennale International Conference on Language Resources and Evaluation (LREC) – a must for every scientist working in this field – 2010 in Malta only one paper[2] dealt with Turkish language resources, LREC 2012 took place in Istanbul, where the number of contributions related to Turkish was significantly higher, reaching 7 papers.[3]

Next to topics like natural language processing and parsing,[4] Turkish corpora were represented by a number of papers, which goes in alignment with the current trend pointed out by the conference chair Nicoletta Calzolari in her introductory message:

> Major trends, i.e. not the most crowded topics but those increasing with respect to last LREC: "Data", as normal in our conference, but I would say even more than before: data/corpora (in all the modalities and for many purposes: annotation, extraction, classification, translation, and so on) receive even more attention than last time.[5]

In this regard two major Turkish corpus projects – the Turkish National Corpus[6] and the METU Turkish Discourse Bank (METU-TDB)[7] – were presented, as well as the Turkish Paraphrase Corpus.[8] Two years later, at LREC in Reykjavik the papers on Turkish NLP and NER were predominant to Turkish corpora.[9]

---

[2] For full program see: *LREC 2010, Seventh International Conference on Language Resources and Evaluation*, http://www.lrec-conf.org/proceedings/lrec2010/index.html (accessed, January 26, 2020).
[3] *LREC 2012, Eighth International Conference on Language Resources and Evaluation*, http://www.lrec-conf.org/proceedings/lrec2012/index.html (accessed, January 28, 2020).
[4] Gülşen Eryiğit, "The Impact of Automatic Morphological Analysis & Disambiguation on Dependency Parsing of Turkish," *LREC Proceedings*, http://www.lrec-conf.org/proceedings/lrec2012/pdf/198_Paper.pdf (accessed, January 28, 2020).
[5] *The ELRA Newsletter* 16, no. 1 & 4 (2012), http://www.elra.info/media/filer_public/2013/09/06/vol16n1-4.pdf, (accessed, January 28, 2020).
[6] Yeşim Aksan, Mustafa Aksan, Ahmet Koltuksuz et.al., *LREC Proceedings*, "Construction of the Turkish National Corpus (TNC)" http://www.lrec-conf.org/proceedings/lrec2012/pdf/991_Paper.pdf, (accessed, January 28, 2020).
[7] Utku Şirin, Ruket Çakıcı and Deniz Zeyrek, "METU Turkish Discourse Bank Browser," *LREC Proceedings* http://www.lrec-conf.org/proceedings/lrec2012/pdf/788_Paper.pdf, (accessed, January 28, 2020).
[8] Seniz Demir, Ilknur Durgar, El-Kahlout et al., *LREC Proceedings*, http://www.lrec-conf.org/proceedings/lrec2012/pdf/968_Paper.pdf (accessed, January 28, 2020)..
[9] *LREC 2014, Ninth International Conference on Language Resources and Evaluation*, http://www.lrec-conf.org/proceedings/lrec2014/index.html (accessed, January 28, 2020).

This only stresses how the interest of the scientific community is shifting and what various purposes language corpora can serve. If we look at the papers based on the corpora mentioned above, one can observe an emphasis on the technicalities and challenges in building a corpus for Turkish as well as developing tools for and conducting linguistic analysis rather than on literary studies.[10] The use of language corpora to deal with questions of literary representations and language, translation and especially literary geography are fields yet to be explored. Therefore, we shall give a short overview of existing corpora before we look into why and how we made use of the METU Turkish Corpus.

Turkish National Corpus (TNC)

URL	http://www.tnc.org.tr/index.php/en/
Title	Turkish National Corpus (TNC)
Type of resource	text corpus, Browser
Target group	Researchers
Mono-, bi-, multilingual	Monolingual
Written/spoken	Written, spoken (2%)
Language(s)	Turkish
Dia-, synchronic	Synchronic
Historical	Yes
Media	Text
Size	50 million words
Source(s)	period of 20 years (1990-2009)
Availability	free resource for non-commercial use, registration required for use of Demo Version
Interface	Browser
Data	Samples from genres *imaginative and informative* (adapted from British National Corpus BNC)
Format	MySQL Database
Encoding	UTF-8
Annotation	Annotation tool NooJ TR
Publication of data	TNC-based publications will be submitted and announced through TNC web site
Literature	Y. Aksan et al., "Construction of the Turkish National Corpus (TNC)," in *Proceedings of the Eight International Conference on Language Resources and Evaluation (LREC 2012)*, http://www.lrec-conf.org/proceedings/lrec2012/papers.html (accessed January 29, 2020).

---

[10] See list of publications related to Turkish National Corpus, "TNC-based Publications," *Turkish National Corpus (TNC)*, http://www.tnc.org.tr/index.php/en/papers, (accessed, January 28, 2020).

| Duration | 2009 (first publication) ongoing |

The Turkish Corpus (TS)

URL	http://tscorpus.com/en
Title	TS Corpus-The Turkish Corpus
Type of resource	text corpus, Browser
Target group	researchers
Mono-, bi-, multilingual	monolingual
Written/ spoken	Written
Language(s)	Turkish
Dia-, synchronic	Diachronic
Historical	Yes
Media	Text
Size	491,360,398 Words
Source(s)	collected from the internet such as newspapers, meeting reports, instructions on the university pages, The Grand National Assembly of Turkey reports
Availability	only for research and/or academic studies, registration required
Interface	Browser
Data	491 million PoS tagged tokens (491,360,398 million)
Format	-
Encoding	-
Annotation	PoS tagging with tokenizer and PoS tool
Publication of data	If you use TS Corpus in your research, and want to cite it, please cite the following paper: B. Sezer, T. Sezer, "TS Corpus: Herkes için Türkçe Derlem," in *Proceedings of the 27th National Linguistics Conference* (Ankara: Hacettepe University, Linguistics Department, 2013), 217-225. Also add URL of the TS Corpus Project homepage
Literature	T. Sezer, "TS Corpus Project: An online Turkish Dictionary and TS DIY Corpus," *European Journal of Language and Literature* 9, no. 1(2017): 18-24.
Duration	From 2012, ongoing

METU Turkish Corpus

URL	http://ii.metu.edu.tr/corpus
Title	METU Turkish Corpus
Type of resource	text corpus, download

Target group	Researchers
Mono-, bi-, multilingual	Monolingual
Written/spoken	Written
Language(s)	Turkish
Dia-, synchronic	Synchronic
Historical	-
Media	Text
Size	2 million words
Source(s)	post-1990 written Turkish samples
Availability	free of charge for research purposes only, no direct corpus access, corpus can be downloaded by filling out and submitting a user agreement http://ii.metu.edu.tr/sites/ii.metu.edu.tr/files/metu_corpus_license_eng_v3_0.pdf
Interface	Zip file with single sample files, workbench
Data	2 samples from one source, each sample 2000 words
Format	Xces and xcs
Encoding	Unicode test format that contains Turkish characters (?)
Annotation	XML, adapted TEI standard
Publication of data	No distribution of the data in any original or modified form
Literature	Bilge Say, Deniz Zeyrek, Kemal Oflazer and Umut Özge "Development of a Corpus and a Treebank for Present-day Written Turkish," in İmer, Kamile and Gürkan Doğan, eds., *Proceedings of the Eleventh International Conference of Turkish Linguistics, August, 2002* (Famagusta: Eastern Mediterranean University Press, 2004), 183-192.
Duration	From 1999

METU-Sabanci Turkish Treebank

URL	http://ii.metu.edu.tr/corpus
Title	METU-Sabanci Turkish Treebank
Type of resource	subcorpus, linguistic language resource, download
Target group	Researchers
Mono-, bi-, multilingual	Monolingual
Written/spoken	Written
Language(s)	Turkish
Dia-, synchronic	Synchronic

Historical	-
Media	Text
Size	7262 grammatical sentences
Source(s)	post-1990 written Turkish samples
Availability	free of charge for research purposes only, no direct corpus access, corpus can be downloaded by filling out and submitting a user agreement http://ii.metu.edu.tr/sites/ii.metu.edu.tr/files/metu_sabanci_license_eng_v3.pdf
Interface	Zip file with single sample files, workbench
Data	Sample files from METU Turkish Corpus
Format	XML
Encoding	?
Annotation	XML, annotation tool
Publication of data	No distribution of the data in any original or modified form
Literature	Kemal Oflazer, Bilge Say, Dilek Zeynep Hakkani-Tür, Gökhan Tür, "Building a Turkish Treebank", in *Building and Exploiting Syntactically-annotated Corpora*, ed. Anne Abeille (Dordrecht: Kluwer Academic Publishers, 2003).
Duration	?

METU Turkish Discourse Bank (METU-TDB)

URL	http://ii.metu.edu.tr/corpus
Title	METU Turkish Discourse Bank
Type of resource	Annotated text corpus, download
Target group	Researchers
Mono-, bi-, multilingual	Monolingual
Written/spoken	Written
Language(s)	Turkish
Dia-, synchronic	Synchronic
Historical	-
Media	Text
Size	500,000 word
Source(s)	Subcorpus of METU Turkish corpus (post-1990 written Turkish samples)
Availability	free of charge for research purposes only, no direct corpus access, corpus can be downloaded by filling out and submitting a user agreement
Interface	Zip file with single sample files, Browser
Data	Sample files from METU Turkish Corpus

Format	XML
Encoding	UTF-8
Annotation	annotation tool (DATT - Discourse Annotation Tool for Turkish)
Publication of data	No distribution of the data in any original or modified form
Literature	See "Publications", *METU-TDB*. http://medid.ii.metu.edu.tr/publications.html (accessed January 29, 2020)
Duration	October 2007-February 2011

2. METU Turkish corpus

In order to describe how we use the METU Turkish corpus and why it is suited for our project, in this chapter we take a closer look at its features.

2.1. Description

The METU Turkish corpus is described as a "balanced" – meaning that it represents a variety of different textual sources from different genres – "written Turkish electronic Corpus".[11]

2.2. Size

The size is set by an agreement with the publishing houses on 2000 words/source (more if the last sentence is included). Depending on the source, three samples were taken. The aim was set to be 2 million words. By the time of the first publication the corpus had 1.200.000 words, 520 samples from 291 sources).[12] By 2011 the size has reached 2.000.000 words from 201 books, 87 journal issues and issues of 3 daily newspapers totalling 999 samples.[13]

2.3. Content

The METU corpus consists "of post-1990 written Turkish sampled from various genres." Therefore, it can be considered a collection of contemporary sources which is "rather synchronic than diachronic."[14] Furthermore, its representativeness plays an important role. Samples are

---

[11] Bilge Say, Deniz Zeyrek, Kemal Oflazer and Umut Özge "Development of a Corpus and a Treebank for Present-day Written Turkish," in *Proceedings of the Eleventh International Conference of Turkish Linguistics, August, 2002*, eds. İmer, Kamile and Gürkan Doğan (Famagusta: Eastern Mediterranean University Press, 2004), 4.
[12] Say, Zeyrek, Oflazer and Özge, "Development of a Corpus and a Treebank for Present-day Written Turkish," 5.
[13] Bilge Say, "Bilge Say PPT, July 2010", *METU OpenCourseWare*, http://ocw.metu.edu.tr/mod/resource/view.php?id=1641 (accessed, 15.05.2015).
[14] Say, Zeyrek, Oflazer and Özge, "Development of a Corpus and a Treebank for Present-day Written Turkish," 4-5.

randomly chosen and not according to statistical sampling for a specific period. The only restriction was that no more than five publications/author (10 samples) are included.

2.4. Genres

According to the query search menu in the workbench, the samples are organized in twelve genres:

Anlatı = narrative

Anı = memoir

Araştırma İnceleme = research-survey

Deneme = essay

Gezi = travel

Günce = diary

Haber = news

Köşe Yazısı = column

Makale = article

Öykü = short story

Roman = novel

Söyleşi = discourse (?)[15]

However, the metadata included in the text files lists additional genres, such as

Bugünün Kitapları = contemporary books

Gezi İzlenimleri = travel journals   Öykü Kitabı = short story book

Özyaşam Öyküsü = autobiography   Undefined

Even if there is no date of the following table, it clearly shows the emphasis on fiction within the METU corpus compared to other genres. The fact that the majority of samples are taken from novels was decisive for choosing this corpus for our analysis.

---

[15] If the English terms differ from or do not appear in the table of METU corpus cited above, they are the author's own translation.

Genre distribution of the METU Turkish Corpus[16]		
Genre tag	Category Count	%
Novel	123	15.63
Story	114	14.49
Research-Survey	49	6.23
Article	38	4.83
Travel	19	2.41
Interview	7	0.89
Memoir	18	2.29
News	419	53.24
TOTAL	787	100.00

All files are text files and no pictures or any data on graphic content is included.

2.5. Annotation/Tagging

Annotation of the corpus is based on TEI (Text Encoding Initiative) standards and makes use of XCES Corpus Encoding Standard, which have been adapted in order to specialise standards formulated by TEI. All files are in XML format, a standard markup-language for digital text corpora. The METU corpus is therefore both TEI and XCES conform; meaning that each file has header and body with several tags. Since the tagging is claimed to be revised by two annotators, it should contain a small amount of errors. Spelling mistakes are annotated separately. It is important to note that these standards conform to the time of building the first prototype of the corpus. Sources regarding this cited by Say date back to 1996-2002.[17]

Metadata tagged:

Monograph/analytical

Author, Year, Publisher Paragraphs, lists etc.

---

[16] "The Corpus", *METU Turkish Discourse Bank,* http://medid.ii.metu.edu.tr/theCorpus.html (accessed, 15.05.2015).
[17] Say, Zeyrek, Oflazer and Özge, "Development of a Corpus and a Treebank for Present-day Written Turkish," 183-192.

See tag-in use file in corpus ZIP

A richer morphosyntactical annotation has been undertaken in the sister project, a subcorpus of the METU Turkish Corpus, METU Turkish Treebank.

2.6. Tools

The corpus comes with a query-workbench. It is developed in JAVA and is therefore operation system independent. The query search serves the simple function of keyword search for which two types exist: Boolean (words and stems) and concordance (key-word-in-context) or regular expression queries. The search can be filtered according to author and genre and it is possible for the user to save and print a session. The workbench is described as "a user-friendly query engine for linguists".[18] However, statistical output is not possible in the current state and semantic searches could be an interesting future feature.

Hence, why is the METU Turkish corpus suited for our study? Firstly, it provides a wide range of sources from fiction with a number of contemporary "representative" authors and texts, such as Orhan Pamuk, Tezer Özlü, Ahmet Altan, etc. Secondly, it is freely available for research purposes and is the only Turkish language corpus from the list above, which can be downloaded as a complete version in text files.

What are the prior challenges in working with the METU corpus? As we have shown in the genres appearing within the files, inconsistent metadata asks for additional filters and query options. Turkish orthography brings with its own challenges when it comes to encoding, especially if there is no established standard for it. Because of copyright issues and the sample structure the corpus does not allow a comprehensive analysis or comparison of the complete texts or even works of one author. Since the corpus conforms to past standards, like XCES, tools used for TEI conform corpora are not applicable. The workbench did not provide the necessary requirements for our purposes, because it only allows simple query search and does not provide any statistical information.

---

[18] Say, "Bilge Say PPT".

3. Towards a Geography of Language: Theory and Methods

In the following chapter we briefly outline the theoretical framework of this project, namely distant reading and literary geography/cartography. As an example from this field, *A Literary Atlas of Europe* is briefly reviewed.

3.1. Distant Reading with Maps

Literary maps: what do they do? Franco Moretti asks in his book *Graphs, Maps, Trees*,[19] in which he introduces a different "reading" of literary texts by creating graphs, trees and maps. As in his work *An Atlas of the European Novel: 1800-1900*,[20] the author follows a strongly quantitative approach to fiction on the crossroad between literary studies and geography by looking at the form of the novel and its change over time by tracing themes like home-land, city images etc. The "challenge of quantity" Moretti mentions,[21] can nowadays be met with computer-assisted methods and different methodologies and dealing with a huge amount of spatial data in and beyond literary texts offers various possibilities in the field of geography and literary studies. To the question weather "maps *add* anything to our knowledge of literature?" in his Atlas[22] Moretti answers by describing maps as "analytical tools: that dissect the text in an unusual way".[23] Dissecting the text is indeed a tricky task, especially if we have to dissect a large number of texts. From a methodological point of view dissecting might as well mean to prepare the text for analysis by creating and applying the analytical tool which he calls a map.

But how do we prepare hundreds, thousands of texts for analysis? In one of his earlier works "Conjectures on World Literature,"[24] Moretti introduces "distant reading", a quantitative approach that aims at the analysis of "world literature" (opposed to the study of national literatures). He questions whether a field, which bases most of its research on a rough number of 200 books (the literary canon) can come to comprehensive conclusions about literature in general, for example the emergence of the novel in the Western world. He opposes this usual method of literary studies to his proposed anti-canonical study of world literature, looking at the "great unread", the 99% of texts excluded from the canon so far.

---

[19] Franco Moretti, *Graphs, Maps, Trees* (London, New York: Verso, 2005), 35.
[20] Franco Moretti, *An Atlas of the European Novel: 1800-1900* (London, New York: Verso, 2011).
[21] Moretti, *An Atlas of the European Novel*, 5.
[22] Moretti, *Graphs, Maps, Trees*, 35.
[23] Moretti, *An Atlas of the European Novel*, 3.
[24] Moretti, "Conjectures on World Literature ", 54-68.

Distant reading: where distance [...] *is a condition of knowledge*: it allows you to focus on units much smaller or much larger than the text: devices, themes, tropes – or genres and systems.[25]

By looking at questions about literary history, like the rise of novel in Europe, Moretti applies distant reading as a method to look at world literature in the form of an experiment. "You define a unit of analysis [...] and the follow its metamorphoses in a variety of environments – until, ideally, all of history becomes a long chain of related experiments [...]."[26] Looking at a large amount of texts by using toponyms as a unit of analysis in order to conduct experiments through the analytical tool of the map is the major methodology of this project. We describe this method as "very distant reading", because it relies solely on the computer-assisted extraction of toponyms and its language-related challenges. The question arises whether this approach suggests that our project can be classified as literary geography or literary cartography.

3.2. Literary Geography and Literary Cartography: A Literary Atlas of Europe

One of the most influential projects dealing with toponyms and fictional space is the project *A Literary Atlas of Europe*. Starting in 2004, this project, designed by cartographers and literary scholars at the ETH Zurich, investigates the possibilities maps offer for the analysis of fiction and clearly situates itself in the framework of literary geography.

The main focus of a future 'literary geography' are the manifold interactions between real and imaginary geographies in various literary genres. What happens when the 'literary world' and the real world meet or intersect?[27]

A Literary Atlas of Europe takes Literary Cartography then as the core method of literary geography. According to three thematic regions in Europe (Alpine: Vierwaldstättersee/Gotthard, coast- and border region: Nordfriesland, urban space: Prague), a corpus of related texts was designed. By filling out forms for each text, the literary space was categorized and mapped with GIS. Later, statistical information from this database was visualized in a single or a collection of maps. Due to the very detailed data about the fictional spaces available in the database, a variety

---

[25] Ibid., 57.
[26] Ibid., 61-62.
[27] Barbara Piatti, Hans Rudolf Bär, Anne-Kathrin Reuschel, Lorenz Hurni and William Cartwright, "Mapping Literature. Towards a Geography of Fiction," in *Cartography and Art*, eds. W. Cartwright et al. (Wiesbaden: Springer, 2009), 177-192; Barbara Piatti, Anne-Kathrin Reuschel and Lorenz Hurni, "Literary Geography – or how Cartographers open up a New Dimension for Literary Studies," https://icaci.org/files/documents/ICC_proceedings/ICC2009/html/nonref/24_1.pdf (accessed, January 28, 2020).

of visualizations was realized, like movements, fuzzy shapes, vague fictional places etc. Barbara Piatti describes the relation between literary geography and cartography in their project as follows:

> While literary geography is the overall *topic*, literary cartography provides one possible *method*, more precisely: *tools* in order to explore and analyse the particular geography of literature.[28]

Interestingly, language it seems is not a key factor in the design of literary maps in *A Literary Atlas of Europe*. Although this project deals with a big amount of data and text, each text still has to be manually evaluated and interpreted before it enters the database. Piatti argues:

> Of course, the complex spatial dimension in fiction can never be captured by such an automatic search machine. On the contrary, it depends on the educated, professional reader to analyse the text, who has to accept, among other restrictions, that some spatial aspects of literature will prove to be unmappable.[29]

Through the heuristically developed filters, in this project we modify the automatic search engine in order to (see chapter 5.2) decrease the number of erroneous matches. Although many spatial aspects remain unmappable, we rely on language-specific features to create what Piatti terms a "literary GIS".[30] Since we do not create a corpus for that matter but rely on available digitalized texts, which are except for their publishing date highly heterogeneous (thematically as well as genre-wise), toponyms remain uncategorized accept for their matchability with existing GIS data. Taking upon the methodological framework of *A Literary Atlas of Europe*, our project hopes to develop novel ways to extract spatial entities from texts through "a combination of theory and practical (trial and error) experiments."[31]

4. Vision

By "vision" we understand the original motivation and implication behind our project as well as what can be gained from it.

---

[28] Ibid.
[29] Ibid.
[30] Ibid.
[31] Ibid.

4.1. Implications

Why a Literary Map? Similar to *A Literary Atlas of Europe* this project set out to map geographical locations according to their name in a given collection of texts from different genres, although both projects use different methods (manual and computer-assisted recognition of toponyms). Turkey is an ideal example for a literary map because place and space play a significant role in Turkish literature, fictional and non-fictional. We might think of Orhan Pamuk's Istanbul, Yaşar Kemal's rural Turkey (Çukurova) or the significance of mapping for scholarly literature about the Armenian genocide etc.[32] However, besides a few very regionally or thematically defined publications,[33] a comprehensive study on the literary geography of Turkey does not yet exist, this project attempts to inspire interdisciplinary corpus-based research, which makes use of database resources. Not only shall this approach open doors to the investigation of literary history through distant reading, but also introduce user-friendly tools to a wide public that wishes to engage with Turkish language and literature.

The Language of Geography: While *A Literary Atlas of Europe* is concerned with the relation between fictional space and geospace, *A Literary Map of Turkey*'s focus clearly lies on the language of toponyms. It claims that geography has a language consisting of toponyms – an aspect widely overlooked in former studies on this topic – which is culturally, politically and historically formed and strongly linked to the everyday language spoken within and beyond the borders of the country, and therefore inherently discursive. As stated above, any interpretation of results has to be placed in a specific context. Each toponym therefore has to be interpreted according to the cultural and language-related context in which it occurs. **Homonymic** place names for example have to be looked at separately, while further interpretation might be based on concordances (the words surrounding the toponym = context) in order to determine the specific use(s) within the sentence.

The Geography of Language: Reversibly, the "literary rhetoric" of geography according to toponyms may be understood as crucial to the style of a text of an author. It might even indicate the genre (e.g. place names are expressed differently in travelogues than in a poem).

---

[32] See "Mapping Armenian Genocide," *The Armenian Genocide Museum*, http://www.genocide-museum.am/eng/mapping_armenian_genocide.php (accessed, January 28, 2020).
[33] See Catharina Dufft, *Orhan Pamuk's Istanbul* (Wiesbaden: Harrassowitz, 2008).

4.2. Challenges

The challenges for conducting this project were on the one hand technical and language-related to Turkish on the other.

Language resource: Of course, it is a question of time and financial resources to build a corpus for the specific purpose of the project. When relying on already existing digital text corpora, a number of obstacles appear to modify and make use of the data in order to approach the central research question. In the case of the METU corpus, encoding and annotation format constituted our first obstacles to overcome. Since the language encoding was not clearly identifiable, Turkish special characters had to be sorted out and replaced. The annotation format is a mixture of TEI conform XML tags and CES coding, a former version of the latest TEI P5 guidelines. In order to extract metadata, current tools for TEI conform texts, such as XPath or XQuery could not be applied, hence a parser in Javascript was specially developed for the project's challenges.

Language-related: When matching the place names with the data from the *OpenStreetMap*, the challenges of the Turkish language immediately became visible. The fact that many words in everyday Turkish are at the same time a place name – said differently: many place names are seemingly defined by words of everyday Turkish – raised a complicated challenge, which we attempted to overcome by creating filters and a blacklist of the most frequent words, which do not necessarily relate to a geographic location (see chapter 5.2.). These filters had to be developed according to the special needs of the Turkish language, being an agglutinative language

Content-related: Place names can change over time. When having a synchronic corpus from a specific (contemporary) period (post-1990), we can assume that place names appearing within the texts also appear on a modern database such as *OpenStreetMaps*. If we were to look at historical sources, an additional database could be consulted.[34] In the case of Turkey this aspect of a literary map is especially interesting, because an increased number of place names – mostly of Armenian, Greek, Arabic or Kurdish origin – have (been) changed after 1913 due to the Turkification and language cleansing first initiated by Enver Pasha.[35]

---

[34] Such as *Index Anatolicus*, http://www.nisanyanmap.com (accessed January 28, 2020), a VGI database which includes 42107 contemporary and 32951 historical name places.
[35] For a comprehensive study of this topic see: Sevan Nişanyan, *Hayali Coğrafyalar: Cumhuriyet Döneminde Türkiye'de Değiştirilen Yeradları* (Istanbul: Türkiye Ekonomik ve Sosyal Etüdler Vakfı, 2011).

5. Exploration of Spatial Aspects by Interactive Maps

"Then you make a map of the book and everything changes" Franco Moretti writes in his chapter on maps.[36] How do we approach a "very distant reading" in order to make way for a comprehensive study of Turkey's literary geography by using a digital text corpus?

In this section, we review data sources to conclude spatial aspects of text corpora by matching spatial entities and filtering the results. Additionally, we discuss how an interactive map can represent the gained data in a meaningful way.

5.1. Data Sources

Two data sources are needed for the exploration of the spatial aspects of a text corpus: the corpus itself whose texts contain references to spatial entities, as well as a collection of spatial entities to identify the references in the texts.

Text Corpus. A text is, as a collection of words, a formal representation of things. When a text is interpreted, the words take on meanings and refer, in consequence, to objects, processes, and relations between the objects and processes. The meaning of a word depends on the context in which the word occurs, i.e. on the surrounding words and the grammatical structure that integrates the word into the text, as well as on the context provided by the type of the text, the subject matter and many more aspects (metadata). We require a text corpus to contain the texts in machine readable form (which is true for digital text corpora) in order to facilitate computer-aided approaches. In addition, the corpus is required to contain metadata that can be used to correlate the spatial aspects.

The METU Turkish Corpus will be used in the scope of this text to evaluate which information about space can easily be extracted from Turkish text corpora. The METU corpus mostly meets the requirements for our method. With additional metadata from *OpenStreetMaps* toponyms could be easily matched. The corpus offers a wide range of different fictional and non-fictional texts, which provides us with a wide range of place names. Metadata for each text sample enabled us to create groups (genre, author) for a collection of toponyms allowing us to look at e.g. all toponyms appearing in Turkish novels within the corpus. However, since the corpus is constructed of samples from texts, it is not possible to list all toponyms appearing in e.g. the novel *The New Life* by Orhan Pamuk. Some of the samples appeared twice in the corpus, which can

---

[36] Moretti, *Graphs, Maps, Trees*, 36.

possibly misrepresent the number of matched toponyms. However, we could denote and delete some of the duplicates.

Collection of spatial entities. A collection of names of spatial entities is needed in order to identify words in the corpus that are related to space. The *OpenStreetMap* project[37] aims at creating a free and editable map of the world and maintains for this purpose a publicly accessible database which comprises data on a high number of spatial entities, such as streets, houses, and water bodies. The database contains names for many of these spatial entities and can thus be used to create the required collection. We decided to use the toponyms of cities, towns, suburbs, villages, seas, islands, bays, and beaches in Turkey, together with the location provided by the database.

The information of the *OpenStreetMap* project is collected by individuals as volunteered geographic information (VGI). It is, thus, of varying quality, and some regions are more completely mapped than other ones.[38]

Texts usually contain not only place names but also references to objects which are located in space, like a company or a fair. Collections of such well-known entities with a specific name can, in principle, be gained from Wikipedia. The *DBpedia* project[39] aims at providing data from Wikipedia as linked data, which is a representation of data that can express semantics and link entities, such as objects to locations in space. As the data in the Turkish Wikipedia is highly heterogeneous and of mixed data quality, we do not use it in our exploration. In particular, we were able to extract around 4,000 place names in Turkey from *DBpedia* in contrast to 22,328 place names from *OpenStreetMap*.[40]

The meaning of a word in a context is much harder to describe than the meaning of the word itself, and words representing entities without natural location in space can gain a location by the context.[41] The generic terms "car" and "bar" have, for example, no natural location in space

---

[37] *OpenStreetMaps*, https://www.openstreetmap.org/#map=17/41.09134/29.04739&layers=T (accessed 01.06.2015).
[38] Patrick Maué, Sven Schade, "Quality of geographic information patchworks", Paper presented at the 11th AGILE International Conference on Geographic Information Science, 2008, https://www.researchgate.net/publication/230606825_Quality_of_Geographic_Information_Patchworks (accessed January 28, 2020) ; Mordechai Haklay, "How good is volunteered geographical information? A comparative study of OpenStreetMap and Ordnance Survey datasets," *Environment and Planning B: Planning and Design* 37, no. 4 (2010): 682–703.
[39] *DBpedia*, http://dbpedia.org (accessed January 28, 2020).
[40] At the time of extraction: 01.06.2015.
[41] Katrin Erk and Sebastian Padó, "A structured vector space model for word meaning in context" in *Proceedings of the 2008 Conference on Empirical Methods in Natural Language Processing* (Association for Computational Linguistics, 2008), 897-906.

as they denote linguistic categories, but they can refer to certain instances of the category when they are interpreted in a spatial contexts, e.g. "Lisa's car" or "Franz-Benjamin's favourite bar". It is highly challenging to create a data set that allows us to determine the meaning of a word in the given context, or at least the spatial meaning. We have discussed why the METU Turkish Corpus and data from the *OpenStreetMap* project meet the requirements to tackle the questions of section 3 in a meaningful way. In the next section, we discuss how both data sources can be combined to study spatial aspects of the text corpus.

5.2. Data Mining

A text can contain references to space. In this section, we approach the question of how these references to space can be computationally detected.

Matching of Spatial Terms. References to space in a text can, in principle, be detected by comparing the meaning of the words and phrases to spatial concepts. When we discover that a spatial concept occurs in the text, we have found a reference of the text to a spatial concept. It is impossible to formally represent and compare meanings and concepts, because meanings potentially depend on context.[42] As a word can occur in many contexts, it can have numerous meanings.[43] The comparison of words in a text to names representing spatial entities is, in consequence, not sufficient. When the word "AĞRI",[44] for example, occurs in a text, we cannot infer from that occurrence that the town "AĞRI" rather than the feeling of pain is meant.

The comparison of words has a major advantage: it is simple and fast. When a word that denotes a spatial entity occurs in the text, we cannot conclude that the text refers to the spatial entity, but there is a good chance. In the case that a word of the text also denotes a spatial entity, we speak of a *match*, and the process of finding such matches will be called *matching* throughout the paper.

Excluding Erroneous Matches. The found matches, i.e. words of a text that also denote spatial entities, can suggest that the word in this context refers to the spatial entity. If the word refers to the spatial entity, we call the match *true*, otherwise *erroneous*. It cannot be decided whether a match is true, without concluding the meaning that the word gains from its context. We thus try

---

[42] Erk and Padó, "A structured vector space model for word meaning in context", 897–906.
[43] Adam Kilgarriff, "I don't believe in word senses", *Computers and the Humanities*, 31, no. 2(1997): 91–113.
[44] The word "ağrı" can mean "pain" or the toponym of a Turkish city.

to heuristically filter the matches to exclude the erroneous ones. As the filters are heuristic, they cannot be proven correct, true matches may be filtered out, and erroneous matches may not be filtered out. The filters are chosen so that a lower percentage of the remaining matches is erroneous. We use the following filters:

Filter 1: Words with less than 4 characters are not matched. The probability of finding matches is much higher for shorter words than for longer ones. For example, the probability of matching "a" in a text is much higher than matching "ankara". On the other hand, we expect the probability of matching a place name in a text to be, by and large, independent of the name's length. Filtering out matches of very short words may, thus, increase the percentage of true matches.

Filter 2a: Case sensitive matching. As in English, proper names in the Turkish language start with a capital letter whereas most other words do not. Place names are, in most cases, proper names and thus written with a capital first letter. "Ortada bir orta şekerli kahve var." (In the middle there is a medium sweet coffee.) Orta meaning both, a place and "sweet".

Filter 2b: A word at the beginning of a sentence is not matched, if it occurs with lower case first letter in the middle of a sentence. At the beginning of a sentence words usually start with a capital first letter. This is why Filter 2a cannot properly distinguish between proper names and other names. Based on the assumption that all matches of the same word are either true or erroneous, we can conclude whether a match of a word at the beginning of a sentence is true if the word also occurs in the middle of a sentence. "Ortada bir **orta** şekerli kahve var." (In the middle there is a medium sweet coffee.)

Filter 2c: A word at the beginning of a sentence is only matched, if it contains an apostrophe or if it occurs in the middle of a sentence (case sensitive). Similar to Filter 2b which *excludes* matches at the beginning of a sentence if it occurs in the middle of a sentence with a *lower case* first letter, we can *include* all matches of words at the beginning of a sentence that also *case sensitively* occur in the middle of a sentence. "**Orta'da** kahve var." (In Orta there is coffee.). "**Orta** güzel bir yer çünkü Orta'da çok park var." (Orta is a nice place because in Orta there are many Parks.)

Filter 3: Only matches at the beginning of a word are regarded as true. Place names occur, in many cases, at the beginning of a word. When a word occurs in the middle or at the end of a word, there is a great chance that it does so only by chance. "Orta'da güzel portakal aldım." (I bought some nice oranges in Orta).

Filter 4: Only longest matches. Place names often start with the same letters. Suburbs, for example, in many cases begin with the name of the town but contain additional letters or words. When the name of a suburb is matched, we may exclude the match of the name of the town because the suburb is referred to at first hand, and the town is only indirectly referred to. Kavaklı (town) - Kavaklıdere (metropolitan district).

Filter 5: Filter by blacklist. Places are mainly named after things and appear with different meanings. Therefore, the set of matches may still include some erroneous matches. When we identify some words that often lead to erroneous matches, we can exclude them. We excluded the following words due to their high number of occurrences in the corpus. Interestingly, an increased number of place names are – besides proper nouns, such as Atatürk or Erdoğan – very frequent words in daily Turkish, which leads to a misrepresentation of the data on our map if these very frequent words are not filtered out:

Sultan, Çocuklar (children), Çay (tea), Cumhuriyet (republic), Orta (middle), Yayla (highland), Süleyman, Türkler (Turks), Pınar (well), Erdoğan, Murat, Ocak (January), Aralık (December), Kasım (November), Yazı (writing), Güneş (sun), Büyük (big), Demokrasi (democracy), Mart (march), Osmanlı (Ottoman), Paşa, Atatürk, Yüksek (high), Ulaştı (he/she reached it), Doğan (born), Abdullah.

We have discussed how we can try to find place names in a text and filter the matches in order to gain a list of matches with a good ratio of true to erroneous matches. In the next section, we will discuss the meaning of such information and the resulting implications on how to visualize these matches.

5.3. Spatial Information and the Representation by Maps

Information that is related to space has specific properties, and maps are capable of visualizing these properties of spatial information. In this section, we discuss why maps are meaningful to visualize the matches of section 4.2 and which features of the map are important for this purpose.

Spatial Information. Information is called *spatial* if it refers to space. Such references can be provided by coordinates, by place names, or by other information which, in the given context, represents things or processes that are or happen in space. Spatial information can, in addition to spatial aspects, also contain information about other aspects. Such information is called *thematic information*. Many different concepts can be used to describe spatial information (Kuhn).[45]

Maps as a Representation. The analysis and the communication of information, in particular spatial information, requires many different abilities: the communicated data has to be set in context, i.e. it has to be related to reality to become information; ontologies that describe how these relations look like have to merged in order to understand the information if more than one ontology is provided (Frank, Fonseca);[46] information has, in many cases, to be aggregated in order to emphasize certain aspects of the information; etc.

The representation of data in a map emphasizes spatial aspects, amongst others the geometry of objects, the position in space, and the relative position of objects, because it represents the data in a two-dimensional space. Maps thus afford humans to grasp spatial aspects of the presented information, and we can thus explore the data much faster.[47] Thematic aspects, however, may become equally or even harder to grasp.

Maps can, in the context of places referred to in literature, be understood as a representation that highlights spatial aspects. The data mining process and the representation of the data in a map cannot be understood as an evaluation of the data which returns a complete analysis, because only the interpretation of the results gives the returned data a meaning. It can rather be understood as a change of the representation of the corpus into a representation that affords spatial analysis. The vagueness of the representation in a map, e.g. due to erroneous matchings, is not desired but can be understood as part of the representation which needs human interpretation.

Interactivity. The matches can be displayed in a map at the locations of the spatial entities they refer to. This allows us to grasp the distribution of spatial references to spatial entities. The matches can even be grouped, depending on the scale as well as the number and locations of the matches, in order to visualize a high number of matches without losing perceivability.

---

[45] Werner Kuhn, "Core concepts of spatial information for transdisciplinary research," *International Journal of Geographical Information Science* 26, no. 12(2012): 2267–2276.
[46] Andrew U. Frank, "Spatial ontology: a geographical point of view," in *Spatial and temporal reasoning*, ed. Oliviero Stock (Dordrecht: Kluwer Academic Publishers, 1997), 135-153; Frederico T. Fonseca, Max J. Egenhofer, Peggy Agouris, and Gilberto Camara, "Using ontologies for integrated geographic information systems," *Transitions in GIS* 6, no. 3 (2002), 231–257.
[47] Alan MacEachren, *How maps work* (New York: Guilford Press, 2004)

There are more aspects than spatial ones that can be represented in a digital map. In particular, a digital map affords to select/filter the data and to provide details on demand —two very convenient principles in information visualization.[48] The corpus contains many texts which can be categorized by different criteria, e.g. the type of the text. In our reference implementation, we offer to select all texts, texts by their types, and individual texts. The filters discussed in section 4.2 can be separately activated to filter the matches. This allows us to examine the effect of the filters on the resulting data, in particular on the data quality. More thematic information for each match, such as the author and the title of the text as well as a short excerpt, is provided when a match is selected in the map.

We have discussed which data sources can be used for a meaningful examination of spatial aspects of a text corpus; how the process of data mining, including the matching and filtering, can be conducted; and how the gained information can be interactively represented on a map. In the next section, we will evaluate the proposed methods by the use of a reference implementation.

6. Evaluation and Outlook

Spatial aspects of a text corpus are hard to grasp when the texts are directly accessed and not represented in a way that emphasizes spatial aspects. We discussed in sections 5.2 and 5.3 that matching of spatial terms, subsequent exclusion of erroneous matches by heuristic filtering and the representation of the gained data by an interactive map may serve for the purpose of emphasizing spatial aspects of texts contained in the corpus.

In a reference implementation, we combine data from the METU Turkish Corpus and the *OpenStreetMap* project with the methods discussed in section 5. In this section, we discuss the results gained by the reference implementation, as well as their quality and viability. At the end of the section, possible applications of the map representation are discussed.

6.1. Results

The reference implementation uses 519 texts (998 samples) from the METU Turkish Corpus which contain 2,005,873 words. This corpus is compared to a collection of 22,328 spatial

---

[48] Ben Shneiderman, "The eyes have it: a task by data type taxonomy for information visualizations," *Proceedings of the IEEE Symposium on Visual Languages* (IEEE, 1996), 336–343.

entities in Turkey from the *OpenStreetMap* project. There are 800,447 matches which corresponds to 39.9 percent of the number of words. This high number of matches suggests that many words are recognized by different matches (compare filter 4), and that many matches were erroneous. The application of the filters discussed in section 4.2 results in 55,702 matches, which corresponds to 2.8 percent of the number of words, i.e. the filters are excluding 93 percent of the matches. The distribution of the matches is non-uniform. In particular, the number of matches is higher for larger cities, e.g. Istanbul and Ankara, than for smaller towns. Detailed information is provided by table 1. Examples of erroneous matches that were not excluded by a filter as well as true matches that were excluded by a filter can be found in table 2.

Table 1: Number of matches after each filtering step

Filter	Description	Matches
Unfiltered matches		800,447
Filter 1	Words with less than 4 characters are not matched.	564,144
Filter 2a	Case sensitive matching.	79,103
Filter 2b	A word at the beginning of a sentence is not matched, if it occurs with lower case first letter in the middle of a sentence.	68,657
Filter 2c	A word at the beginning of a sentence is only matched, if it contains an apostrophe or if it occurs in the middle of a sentence (case sensitive).	64,782
Filter 3	Only matches at the beginning of a word are regarded as true.	62,448
Filter 4	Only longest matches.	55,702
Filter 5	Filter by blacklist.	51,550

Table 2: Examples of filters for different matchings

Filter	Erroneous match		True match
	Excluded	Included	Excluded
Filter 1	Çıplak	Kandilli	Karaköy
Filter 2a	Kalabalıkla	Kasaba	Tuzla'da
Filter 2b	Yangınlar	Manastır'da	-
Filter 2c	Esendal'ın	Ayangil'in	Kabakçı
Filter 3	Bosna-Hersek	Balığı	-Sinop'tan buraya

Filter 4	Kavaklıdere	Yalnızlıklar	Güdüllü
Filter 5	Sultan	Çocuklar	-

6.2. Quality of the Results

In the following, we evaluate the quality of the results that are gained after the filtering. Each filter aims at excluding erroneous results whilst keeping true results. The results of a filter depend on the input, which are the results of the previous filter, and the filters are thus not independent of each other. It is, hence, not meaningful to evaluate the quality of the gained data for each filter separately. Instead, the effect of combinations of filters will be evaluated.

Metadata: Words appearing in the metadata of the samples partially match with toponyms, such as Prof. Dr. Trugay Dalkara, a Turkish author and the toponym of a village.

Common names: Apparently many toponyms have been derived from popular surnames. The matches still include a high number of names, especially surnames such as "Süleyman" or "Nilüfer". (In addition, "Nilüfer" is the title of a novel as well as its main character, which leads to an increased number of matches.)

Same toponym for different places: In Turkey, many villages, suburbs or districts share the same name. "Aksaray" is both a city in central Anatolia and a district in Istanbul.

Water: *OpenStreetMaps* does not provide a large number of toponyms for seas and lakes in Turkey. "Boğaz" (the strait and waterway between the Asian and European continent) is not recognized as the waterway in Istanbul, but a village. Likewise, "Akdeniz" (Mediterranean Sea) is matched with a place in Antalya.

6.3. Viability of the Results and Possible Application

In section 6.1 and 6.2 we discussed the results and quality of our method. Hence, in this section we describe to what extent and to what purpose they can be applied and improved.

Linguistic filtering: Through the conceptual design of filters according to basic linguistic rules in the Turkish language and the matching with a list of toponyms, our approach nevertheless points towards the interconnectedness between language and toponyms. By filtering erroneous matches, we tried to reveal these two aspects of geography. Each filter may be disabled for each text in order to tune the matching to the specific features of the text and its language. For that matter, an additional linguistic evaluation (e.g. through linguistic filters) with the METU Turkish Treebank may be implemented for the corpus in the future. To come to more comprehensive and statistically supportable results, an additional or larger corpus may be added.

Named Entity Recognition (NER) filters: Another improvement would be to parse all words in the corpus with a named entity recognition tool. In that way only nouns could be extracted, classified and tagged as places.

Place categories: Similar to *A Literary Atlas of Europe of Europe*, further categorization may be applied to toponyms enable the visualization according to villages, towns, streets or cities. In that way, the question about the importance of city districts in newspapers compared to novels may be tackled. **Timeline:** Furthermore, time is not a defining category in the current version. Adding a timeline to allow further inquiries on literary history and to display how place names have changed in different periods could be developed. Such a timeline may serve as the starting point for building a (diachronic) database of place names in Turkey.[49] *A Literary Map of Turkey* may thus be combined with historical databases and maps, such as the *Index Anatolicus*.[50]

Comparativeness: Our method to build a database of toponyms appearing in a collection of texts from different genres could be applied to different languages as well, in order to facilitate comparative research studies. The database may also be extended beyond the borders of toponyms in Turkey to investigate which European or Asian place names appear in the Turkish text samples.

Fictional Space: How does the author make a place speak? How does he/she use place names to shape his/her writing? To what extent do place names form the language of a text? These questions are twofold and refer to both the literary and spatial aspect of toponyms: How can we evaluate whether toponyms are significant for the text/geography? Questions such as these may serve as a starting point for further investigations building on *A Literary Map of Turkey*. With our method assumptions about the appearance of significant places in Turkey, such as the capital Ankara or Istanbul, can be made easily. For each genre a general picture of the places mentioned can be drawn and it can be investigated why a certain place, like Konya does not appear even in one of the samples of the corpus.

---

[49] TEI offers a tag to date the timeframe when a certain place name was used.
[50] See footnote no. 34.

Conclusion

A Literary Map of Turkey aims at inspiring to engage with the topic of fictional place and space in the scope of literary geography, distant reading, vision, computer-aided approaches etc. by investigating under which circumstances it is possible to detect spatial references within a text corpus. As our evaluation depicts, our results are fruitful for additional possible features to refine our method and its application on the METU and/or other corpora.

In this project we offered a computer-assisted method to extract references of the texts to spatial entities by matching words and filtering the results. We discussed the challenges, adjusted our methods accordingly and problematized the complexity of mapping spatial entities in texts due to the specific difficulties the Turkish language is posing. As an example, we showed how a digital Turkish text corpus was used in a reference implementation. By modifying the filters and combining them, matching spatial data allows us to achieve a "very distant (spatial) reading" of the sources at hand. The possibility to select different genres and texts while en- and disabling the filters allows to look at the relation between spatial entities and text. The nature of this relation has yet to be explored. What are the most common places in Turkey appearing in literature then? The extracted data and our visualization give us an overview which places are matched. Therefore, our study hopes to be the basis for a more comprehensive research on the literary geography of Turkey.

The Patriarchy Index: A Comparative Study of Power Relations Within Southeastern Europe and Turkey

Siegfried Gruber

Abstract

The notion of "patriarchy" has pervaded the scholarly descriptions of peasant families in preindustrial Europe. In using the term, however, scholars have referred to many different elements (e.g. the dominance of patrilineal descent, domination of men over women and of the older generation over the younger generation). Combinations of these elements have been used in a manner that generally does not allow researchers to measure comparatively the "intensity" of patriarchy across time and space. In this paper, a tool for comparative studies of power relations in historical families is proposed. Approaches for measuring patriarchy are suggested, and a list of numerical variables are provided which are easily derived from census microdata that can be used for measurement purposes. To illustrate how these comparative studies can be conducted, we use information from census and census-like materials from the Mosaic Project (www.censusmosaic.org) for Albania (1918), Bulgaria (1877-1947), Croatia (1674), Hungary (1869), Romania (1838 and 1869), Serbia (1863 and 1884), and Istanbul (1885 and 1907). The Patriarchy Index allows us to identify regions with different degrees of patriarchy within one country and a map of patriarchy within Southeastern Europe. Why are we interested in patriarchy in Southeastern Europe? Southeastern Europe and Eastern Europe have often been portrayed as being more patriarchal than Western Europe and some regions (e.g. Northern Albania) have been depicted as being extremely patriarchal in pre-modern times. This index allows now to test these hypotheses based on quantifiable data. It is also possible to test whether Southeastern Europe was uniform in terms of patriarchy or whether there were major differences within this area and between rural and urban populations. First results[1] confirm that Eastern and Southeastern Europe were actually more patriarchal than Western Europe and that there were differences within this geographical region. This paper should provide more analyses within this area and compare the different regions with respect to different features of patriarchy: domination of men over women, domination of the older generation, patrilocality, and son preference.

Introduction[2]

The notion of patriarchy has pervaded the scholarly descriptions of peasant families in historical Eastern and South-Eastern Europe. The term has often included many different elements, such as the dominance of patrilineal descent, patrilocal or patrivirilocal residence after

---

[1] Siegfried Gruber and Mikołaj Szołtysek, "The patriarchy index: a comparative study of power relations across historical Europe," *The History of the Family* 21, no. 2 (2016): 133-174.
[2] The Patriarchy Index was developed together with Mikołaj Szołtysek and a more elaborated discussion of the theoretical path from analysing family systems and patriarchy to the development of the Patriarchy Index and a more detailed description of the variables used in this index can be read in Gruber and Szołtysek, "The patriarchy index," 133-174. The maps used in this publication are partly based on the following source: © EuroGeographics for the administrative boundaries.

marriage, power relations that favour the domination of men over women and of the older generation over the younger generation, customary laws that sanctioned these patterns, the absence of an interfering state that could mitigate their influence, and an inert traditional society that emanated from these conditions. Combinations of these elements have been used to explain the peculiarity of the residence patterns in the East and South-East of Europe relative to the West, but in a manner that generally does not allow researchers to measure comparatively the intensity of patriarchy across time and space and to clearly distinguish different kinds of patriarchy. In this paper it should be proved that patriarchy can be meaningfully measured in quantitative terms and that different variants or even systems of patriarchy can be distinguished not only within Europe but also within Southeastern Europe.

After discussing patriarchy, especially in Southeastern Europe, and its quantification, the elements of the Patriarchy Index are elaborated. The data used for this paper is presented and the results of the Patriarchy Index for Southeastern Europe within Europe is discussed. Afterwards the different elements of patriarchy are analysed for Southeastern Europe. Finally, it will be discussed whether we can speak of different variants of one kind of patriarchy within Southeastern Europe or of different kinds of patriarchy.

Patriarchy

Patriarchy was seen as a step in the development of mankind which replaced an older stage characterised by matriarchy.[3] A patriarchal regime was based on traditional power relations and personal relations between ruler and ruled.[4] In feminist studies this concept was used to analyse societies and patriarchy meant also a status of societies which should be changed. The establishment of civilization and first states was connected to the rise of patriarchy and the subordination of women according to Lerner.[5] In addition, in feminist theory it was concluded that patriarchy "has clearly existed in many different manifestations in many past societies".[6]

---

[3] Johann Jakob Bachofen, *Das Mutterrecht: eine Untersuchung über die Gynaikokratie der alten Welt nach ihrer religiösen und rechtlichen Natur* (Stuttgart: Krais & Hoffmann, 1861); Lewis Henry Morgan, *Ancient Society* (New York: MacMillan & Company 1877).

[4] Max Weber, *Wirtschaft und Gesellschaft* (Tübingen: Mohr, 1922).

[5] Gerda Lerner, *The Creation of Patriarchy* (New York and Oxford: Oxford University Press, 1986).

[6] Judith M. Bennett, Feminism and history," *Gender and History* 1, no. 3 (1989): 262.

Balkan patriarchy attracted quite some interest of researchers because of its assumed historical depth and strength – the Balkan area was seen as the most patriarchal within Europe with Northern Albania being the most patriarchal within this area. This region was inhabited by "extremely patriarchal groups",[7] living in a "fully fledged tribal society in the middle of Europe"[8], and practicing blood feuds and the tradition of "sworn virgins".[9] In the 1920s Cvijić described a cultural zone of a "patriarchal regime" in the Western Balkans. The patriarchal mentality was a feature of the mountain people there and was brought to the plains by migrations of these mountain people.[10] The male moral authority was reinforced by both traditional and state law.[11] Balkan patriarchy has been defined as

> a complex of hierarchal values embedded in a social structural system defined by both gender and age. This structuring is further linked to a system of values orienting both family life and broader social units. Balkan patriarchy achieves its historical form through the classically complex and interlocking systems of patrilinearity, patrilocality, and a patriarchally-oriented common law. Such supports not only divide and ascribe position by gender, but also allocate to males the predominant role in society. An obvious corollary to this defined structure is the formal subordination of women within the context of an overtly 'protective' family and household environment.[12]

This Balkan patriarchy (as patriarchy in general) has its roots in the familial organisation. Many functions of the family are connected to the level of patriarchy. A decrease in such functions (religious rituals, defence, economy, education) leads generally to a decrease in the level of patriarchy.[13] But this is no development, which knows only one direction, i.e. towards decreasing patriarchy. Kaser writes about a "patriarchal backlash" during the last two decades in his book

---

[7] Bernd J. Fischer, (1999) "Albanian Highland Tribal Society and Family Structure in the Process of Twentieth Century Transformation," *East European Quarterly* 33, no. 3 (1999): 281.
[8] Berit Backer, *Behind Stone Walls: Changing Household Organization among the Albanians of Kosova* (Peja: CreateSpace, 2003).
[9] Antonia Young, *Women Who Become Men: Albanian Sworn Virgins* (Oxford, New York: Berg, 2001); Christopher Boehm, *Blood Revenge. The Anthropology of Feuding in Montenegro and Other Tribal Societies* (Lawrence: University Press of Kansas, 1984).
[10] Jovan Cvijić, *Balkansko poluostrvo i južnoslovenske zemlje* (Zagreb: Hrvatski štamparski zavod, 1922), 154-160.
[11] Margaret Hasluck, *The Unwritten Law in Albania* (Cambridge: Cambridge University Press, 1954); *Kanuni i Lekë Dukagjinit*. Mbledhur dhe kodifikuar nga Shtjefën K. Gjeçovi (Tirana: 1989); Ian Whitaker, "Familial roles in the extended patrilineal kingroup in northern Albania," in John G. Peristiany, ed., *Mediterranean Family Structures* (Cambridge: Cambridge University Press, 1976), 195-203; Ian Whitaker, "'A Sack for carrying Things": the Traditional Role of Women in Northern Albanian Society,' *Anthropological Quarterly* 54, no. 3 (1981): 146-156.
[12] Joel M. Halpern, Karl Kaser and Richard A. Wagner, "Patriarchy in the Balkans: Temporal and Cross-Cultural Approaches," *The History of the Family* 1, no. 4 (1996): 427.
[13] Michael Mitterauer and Reinhard Sieder, *The European Family: Patriarchy to Partnership from the Middle Ages to the Present* (Chicago: University of Chicago Press, 1984).

about gender relations in Turkey and in the Balkans since 1500. He defines the main elements of the patriarchal pattern in this area as segmentary distance, genealogical distance, and generational distance.[14] Earlier, the core elements of the patriarchal ideology were defined as ancestor worship, warfare and vengeance, and agnatic dyadic relationships.[15] In addition the patriarchal system in Eastern and Southeastern Europe was connected to a system of equal male inheritance.[16]

Mitterauer used the term "patriarchalism" and referred especially to three phenomena: patrilineality, the principle of seniority and the priority of men.[17] According to Therborn, patriarchy "has two basic intrinsic dimensions. The rule of the father and the rule of the husband, in that order. In other words, patriarchy refers to generational and to conjugal family relations or, more clearly, to generational and to gender relations. ... the core of patriarchal power was, above all, that of father to daughter and of husband to wife".[18] This is in contrast to other people focusing on the patrilineal and patrilocal aspect and therefore the father-son-relationship.

In this paper the notion of patriarchy departs from the often value-laden, monolithic, and ideologically determined discourse of Western feminism.[19] Instead, the concept is simply treated as a useful descriptive tool for discussing social patterns in a comparative perspective. In line with a number of theorists, patriarchy is not seen as having a single form or site, but as encompassing a much wider realm.[20] Thus, the notion of patriarchy corresponds to "systems of sex- and age-related social inequality" in which individuals have differing levels of access to power, capabilities, prestige, and autonomy.[21]

---

[14] Karl Kaser, *Patriarchy after Patriarchy: Gender Relations in Turkey and in the Balkans, 1500 – 2000*. (Wien, Berlin: LIT Verlag, 2008), 9
[15] Halpern, Kaser, and Wagner, "Patriarchy in the Balkans," 429.
[16] Karl Kaser, *Macht und Erbe. Männerherrschaft, Besitz und Familie im östlichen Europa 1500-1900* (Wien, Köln, Weimar: Böhlau, 2000).
[17] Michael Mitterauer, "A Patriarchal Culture? Functions and Forms of Family in the Balkans," in *The Balkans: Traditional Patterns of Life* (Wien: Beiträge zur historischen Sozialkunde, Special issue 1999), 14.
[18] Göran Therborn, *Between Sex and Power: Family in the World, 1900-2000* (London, New York: Routledge, 2004), 13.
[19] See Sylvia Walby, *Theorizing patriarchy* (Oxford: Blackwell, 1990). cf. Deniz Kandiyoti, "Bargaining with patriarchy," *Gender & Society* 2, no. 3(1988): 274-290., 274-275.
[20] cf. Kandiyoti, "Bargaining with patriarchy." Suad Joseph, "Patriarchy and Development in the Arab World," *Gender and Development* 4, no. 2(1996): 14-19.
[21] Bhanu Niraula and S. Philip Morgan, "Marriage formation, post-marital contact with natal kin and the autonomy of women: Evidence from two Nepali settings," *Population Studies* 50, no 1(1996): 35-50.

Quantifying Patriarchy

However, even the most wide-ranging descriptions of Eastern and South-Eastern European patriarchy[22] are not very useful when the task is to measure and compare the intensity of patriarchy across time and space among historical societies. There are several reasons why measuring and comparing degrees of patriarchy may be useful. In an earlier study,[23] we showed that joint family societies with seemingly similar underlying concepts of kinship and descent may display significant differences in their household recruitment and domestic group organisational strategies, as well as in the life course patterns of individual members. We therefore recommended that researchers make a more conscious effort to systematise varying degrees of "jointness" and "apartness" across different complex family societies. This can now be done more effectively, as continuous improvements in the census microdata revolution have made it feasible to assemble for the first time a very large amount of comparable individual-level data for continental Europe in pre-industrial times (Mosaic project)[24] in addition to the data from Northwestern Europe (NAPP).[25]

This is not the first attempt to measure features of patriarchy in a quantitative way, there were already some previous attempts in this direction. Cain used the median age difference between once-married spouses as an indicator of patriarchal structure in a cross-national analysis of fertility in the developing world.[26] Erlich used quantitative methods to investigate changes in household structure in Yugoslavia during the 1930s. She used the term "patriarchal regime" to describe a complex set of traditional ways of living and customs with deep roots in the distant past. At the centre of this regime was "the extended family, called zadruga".[27] She calculated percentages

---

[22] E.g. Karl Kaser, "Serfdom in Eastern Europe," in *The history of the European family*, vol. 1., eds. David I. Kertzer and Marzio Barbagli (New Haven: Yale University Press, 2001), 25-62; Karl Kaser, "Power and inheritance: male domination, property and family in Eastern Europe, 1500-1900," *The History of the Family*, 7, 2002: 375-395; Halpern, Kaser, and Wagner, "Patriarchy in the Balkans", 425-442; Mitterauer, "A Patriarchal Culture? Functions and Forms of Family in the Balkans", 4-20. For Russia, see Christine D. Worobec, *Peasant Russia: Family and Community in the Post-Emancipation Period* (Princeton: Princeton University Press, 1991), 175-216.
[23] Mikołaj Szołtysek and Siegfried Gruber, "Stem Families, Joint Families, and the European Pattern: What kind of a Reconsideration Do We Need?,", *Journal of Family History* 37, no. 1 (2012), 105-125.
[24] See *Recovering Surviving Census Records to Reconstruct Population, Economic, and Cultural History*, www.censusmosaic.org (accessed, January 21, 2020) and Gruber and Szołtysek, "The patriarchy index: a comparative study of power relations across historical Europe," 133-174.
[25] see *International Census Data For Social Science Research*, www.nappdata.org/napp (accessed, January 21, 2020).
[26] Mead Cain, "Patriarchal structure and demographic change," in *Conference on Women's Position and Demographic Change in the Course of Development (1988: Oslo). Solicited papers* (Liège: International Union for the Scientific Study of Population, 1988), 19-41; Mead Cain, Syeda Rokeya Khanam, and Shamsun Nahar, "Class, Patriarchy, and Women's Work in Bangladesh," *Population and Development Review* 5, No. 3 (1979): 405-438; Ansley Coale and Paul Demeny, *Regional Model Life Tables and Stable Populations* (Princeton: Princeton University Press, 1983).
[27] Vera St. Erlich, *Family in Transition: A Study of 300 Yugoslav Villages* (Princeton: Princeton University Press, 1966), 32.

of villages for the period of break-up of these kinds of households by regions.[28] Halpern, Kaser, and Wagner focused on the father-son and brother-brother dyads, and measured both the frequency of these relationships and their time span. Among the measures proposed were the age at marriage, the age at childbirth, and the sex of the last child.[29]

A recent index, the "Social Institutions and Gender Index" (SIGI) measures discrimination against women for over 100 countries. This composite index is made up of 14 variables like age at marriage, discriminatory inheritance practices, son bias, etc. (genderindex.org). But SIGI is based on variables which are hardly available for historical times and is therefore restricted to contemporary times. All these measures capture one feature of patriarchy or a few of them, but not all of them (except SIGI). An index containing several different measures about different aspects of patriarchy would be better suited to analyse patriarchy in a comparative way (like SIGI), because not all aspects of patriarchy will render the same results: Some societies will be more patriarchal in one aspect and less patriarchal in another. Such combinations of different levels of patriarchy in various aspects of patriarchy could be used to design a system of different variants or even different systems of patriarchy in Europe for different regions or different social groups. This would be similar to Simon Szreter's conclusion that there was not one fertility decline in Britain, but multiple fertility declines. In analysing different occupational groups he could distinguish twenty or more distinct fertility régimes.[30]

Patriarchy Index

Research comparing different societies needs a clear definition about the analysed feature (e.g. patriarchy) and the measure used (even if not using quantitative methods). This is not always done, e.g. when patriarchy is only vaguely defined. The author believes that "similarities outweigh differences, and that it is possible to identify some common underlying transcultural and transhistorical continuities in the forms of male oppression of women".[31] The Patriarchy Index is made up of the four components representing different domains of patriarchy:

- domination of men over women,

---

[28] Erlich, *Family in Transition*, 46.
[29] Halpern, Kaser, and Wagner, "Patriarchy in the Balkans," 430-433
[30] Simon Szreter, *Fertility, Class and Gender in Britain, 1860-1940*. (Cambridge: Cambridge University Press: 1996).
[31] Pavla Miller, *Transformations of Patriarchy in the West, 1500-1900* (Bloomington and Indianapolis: University of Indiana Press, 1998), xii.

- domination of the older generation over the younger generation,
- patrilocality, and
- son preference.

Aspect 1: Domination of men over women

1.1 Proportion of female household heads

Patriarchal hypothesis: Only men can be household heads.

Description: This is the proportion of all female household heads among all adult (20+ years) household heads of family households. We use an age-standardized measure to account for different age structures in different societies at different points in time. This measure should be negatively correlated with patriarchy, as in truly patriarchal societies women would not be allowed to become household heads under most circumstances.

1.2 Proportion of young brides

Patriarchal hypothesis: A lower female age at marriage facilitates male domination.

Description: This is the proportion of ever-married women in the age group 15-19 years. This measure should be positively correlated with patriarchy because we assume that in truly patriarchal areas women would be married as soon as possible to insure their virginity at marriage.

1.3 Proportion of wives who are older than their husbands

Patriarchal hypothesis: The husband is always older than his wife.

Description: This is the proportion of all wives who are older than their husbands among all of the couples for whom the ages of both partners are known. If a husband is married to more than one wife, only the first wife is considered here. It is an age-standardized measure and should be negatively correlated with patriarchy, because we assume that in truly patriarchal areas men would not marry women older than themselves.

1.4 Proportion of young women living as non-kin

Patriarchal hypothesis: A woman cannot live outside the home of her or her husband's relatives.

Description: This is the proportion of women aged 20-34 years who live as non-kin, usually as lodgers or servants. It is an age-standardized measure and should be negatively correlated with patriarchy because we assume that in intensely patriarchal societies, young, unmarried women tend to be controlled by relatives, and are prevented from living with or working for non-relatives, especially before marriage.

Aspect 2: Domination of the older generation over the younger generation

2.1 Proportion of elderly men co-residing with a younger household head

Patriarchal hypothesis: The oldest man is always the household head.

Description: This is the proportion of elderly men (aged 65+ years) living in a household headed by a male household head of a younger generation. Only family households are considered here, and the elderly men must be relatives of the household head. This measure should be negatively correlated with patriarchy because we assume that in intensely patriarchal areas no younger man is permitted to become household head as long as an older male household member is alive.

2.2 Proportion of neolocal residence among young men

Patriarchal hypothesis: Sons are not allowed to establish their own household upon marriage.

Description: This is the proportion of household heads living without any relatives except spouse and children among ever-married men in the age group 20-29 years. This measure only applies to family households, and is age-standardized. This measure should be negatively correlated with patriarchy, because it is assumed that in strictly patriarchal societies sons with living fathers are not permitted to establish their own independent households.

2.3 Proportion of elderly people living with lateral relatives

Patriarchal hypothesis: Some sons tend to stay in the household even after the death of their father.

Description: This is the proportion of elderly people (aged 65+ years) living with at least one lateral relative in the household. Lateral relatives are defined as siblings, aunts/uncles, nephews/nieces, grand nephew/nieces, cousins, and other distant relatives (including in-laws). In addition, two married relatives of the same generation form a lateral extension (this applies to lineal relatives: children, parents, grandchildren, and grandparents; always including their in-laws). This measure only applies to family households. This measure should be positively correlated with patriarchy because we assume that in intensely patriarchal areas some men will not establish their own households at all, or will have to wait until late in life.

Aspect 3: Patrilocality

3.1 Proportion of elderly people living with married daughters

Patriarchal hypothesis: All daughters move into their husband's father's house.

Description: This is the proportion of elderly people (aged 65+ years) living with at least one married daughter in the same household among those elderly people who live with at least one married child in the same household. This measure only applies to family households. This measure should be negatively correlated with patriarchy because in intensely patriarchal areas it is expected that all daughters will leave their parental household upon marriage.

Aspect 4: Son preference

4.1 Proportion of boys among the last child

Patriarchal hypothesis: After the birth of a daughter parents will try to have another child.

Description: This is the proportion of boys among the last children.

The analysis is restricted to children of the household heads and the age group 10 to 14 years, because in the younger age groups we cannot know whether the last child really is the last child, and in the later age groups we cannot know whether one of the children has already left the parental household because of marriage or service. This measure only applies to family households.

This proportion has already been used in an analysis of the fertility decline in a Serbian village, which yielded a male surplus for almost all birth decades between 1850 and 1939. After 1879 the proportion was always 60 percent or more.[32] We would expect to find that this measure is positively correlated with patriarchy.

---

[32] Richard A. Wagner, *Children and Change in a Serbian Village, 1870-1975*. (Unpublished doctoral dissertation) (University of Massachusetts, Amherst., 1984), 232.

4.2 Sex ratio of youngest age group

Patriarchal hypothesis: Girls are treated worse or are considered to be of lesser importance.

Description: This is the sex ratio (boys to 100 girls) in the youngest age group (0-4 years old). We investigate the youngest age group because the effects should be most marked in this age group. This measure only applies to family households. This measure should be positively correlated with patriarchy because we assume that increasing patriarchy should lead to higher female mortality or the under-registration of females.

Age Standardization

Theoretically, the Patriarchy Index should be applicable to any kind of human society, as long as some basic requirements are met (sufficient population size, and the availability of microdata which cover the whole population and report each person's sex, age, marital status, and relationship to household head). Among the challenges we face in creating such an index is that the age structures of societies may differ, and these differences could heavily affect the results of the index for the given society under investigation. There are several ways we can control for the age distribution:

- restricting the analysis to one age group,
- age standardization, and
- regression.[33]

Some of our measures are restricted to a single age group, and some use age standardization. The standard population should not be based on only one historical population, but should cover the whole of Europe, because our data now cover the whole of Europe. As real populations are always affected by fertility or mortality crises and the migration flows of the preceding decades, a constructed population is better suited for our purposes. We have therefore chosen the age structure of a stable population: Model West, mortality level 6, rate of population growth 5 per 1,000.[34]

---

[33] Steven Ruggles, "The Future of Historical Family Demography," *Annual Review of Sociology* 38, 2012: 431
[34] Coale and Demeny, *Regional Model Life Tables and Stable Populations*, 60, 110.

Calculation of the Patriarchy Index

Each aspect of patriarchy represent a sub-index consisting of the variables described above within these domains of patriarchy. Each variable can have 0 to 10 patriarchy points, and all of the respective variables are summed up to obtain the patriarchy points of one feature of patriarchy. All of the variables except for the last two are turned into patriarchy points in the same way. A result of 0 points means a proportion of 0.00 of the respective variable. A result of 10 points represents the maximum that can be achieved for each variable.

The last two variables are calculated differently because they have a different range. As the minimum we assume the proportion which is seen is neutral. This is 0.51 for the proportion of boys among the group of last children, and 105 for the sex ratio of the youngest age group. All of the proportions below these values are set to these defined minimum values. The maximum value is again the maximum achieved for the respective variable.

The patriarchy points are rounded, which make the results easier to grasp for each variable. In this way we obtain 11 categories for each variable ranging from 0 to 10 patriarchy points. A score of 0 indicates the lowest degree of patriarchy, while a score of 10 indicates the highest degree of patriarchy.

Finally, the Patriarchy Index is calculated by summing up the four subindices, but each sub-index is reduced to a maximum of 10 patriarchy points. The Patriarchy Index can therefore have a minimum of 0 and a maximum of 40 patriarchy points.

The analysed regions or societies are categorised into five different levels of intensity of patriarchy:

- very low patriarchy   0 – 10 points,
- low patriarchy   11 – 16 points,
- medium patriarchy   17 – 23 points,
- high patriarchy   24 – 29 points,
- very high patriarchy   30 – 40 points.

Data Used

The data used for the analysis in the paper are provided by the Mosaic project, which identifies, gathers, harmonizes, and distributes surviving historical census microdata for Europe. It aims at building a comprehensive and detailed resource for the historic study of populations by historians, demographers, economists, and other researchers. The Mosaic project builds on historical integrated census microdata projects such as the Integrated Public Use Microdata Series (IPUMS) and the North Atlantic Population Project (NAPP). Records are distributed in the same integrated format, so that historical comparisons can be made across time and space. Data for the Mosaic project is provided by its partners, which include an international set of institutions in Europe and beyond. Every interested researcher can download data for his/her own research free of charge. The only conditions are that you register as a user with the Mosaic project and that you cite the data properly. A detailed description of the Mosaic project, its main issues, data structure and coverage has been published recently.[35]

Table 1: Data used for analysis

Census	Rural regions	Population	Cities	Population
Albania 1918	8	82,646	6	57,965
Dubrovnik region 1674	1	1,880	-	-
Hungary 1869	6	22,996	-	-
Istanbul 1885 and 1907	-	-	2 censuses	8,354
Rhodope region 1877-1947 (Bulgaria)	1	6,590	1	1,783
Serbia 1863	1	7,128	1	2,618
Serbia 1884	1	9,434	-	-
Wallachia 1838	4	21,546	-	-
Overall	22	152,220	10	70,720

Patriarchy in Southeastern Europe Within Europe

There were differences in levels of patriarchy in Europe around 1900: moving further to the south and east of the continent, the more rigid patriarchal rules one could find.[36] This is based on Therborn's analysis of existing surveys and publications. First published results of the

---

[35] Mikołaj Szołtysek and Siegfried Gruber, "Mosaic: recovering surviving census records and reconstructing the familial history of Europe," *The History of the Family* 21, no.1 (2016): 38-60.
[36] Therborn, *Between Sex and Power*, 71.

Patriarchy Index display a rather smooth continuum from very low to very high levels of patriarchy. There are no clear-cut groupings of regions with high or low patriarchy across historical Europe, but certain patterns do emerge. Western Europe tended to be much less patriarchal than Eastern Europe. In Southeastern Europe we found the largest concentration of regions with very high patriarchy intensities, only some regions in Eastern Europe scored equally high. In Southeastern Europe regions with lower patriarchy did exist, too, being located in Hungary and Romania.[37]

All regions with very high patriarchy are located in Southeastern Europe, at the level of high patriarchy 75 percent of the regions are from Southeastern Europe. At the level of medium patriarchy almost 40 percent of the regions are from Southeastern Europe, while at the levels of low and very low patriarchy no Southeastern European regions have been found yet (see table 2). These results are generally in line with scholarly research and well-known stereotypes, but the Patriarchy Index allows to analyse different regions within countries and different aspects of patriarchy. Therefore it is justified to take a closer look at this part of Europe and at different aspects of patriarchy separately.

Table 2: Patriarchy Index for Southeastern European regions compared with other European regions[38]

Patriarchy level	Other European regions	Southeastern European regions	Percentage
Very low	48	0	0.0
Low	119	0	0.0
Medium	24	15	38.5
High	4	12	75.0
Very high	0	5	100.0
Overall	195	32	14.1

Domination of Men over Women

The first variable in this aspect of patriarchy to be analysed is the proportion of female household heads. Three quarters of the regions yield a share of less than 10 percent. Among the

---

[37] Gruber and Szołtysek, "The patriarchy index," 133-174.
[38] Data for other European regions from Mikołaj Szołtysek and Siegfried Gruber, "Quantifying Patriarchy: Living Arrangements and Power Relations in Historic Europe," Paper presented at the European Society of Historical Demography Conference, Alghero, September 2014.

eight regions with a higher proportion are four cities (especially both Istanbul censuses have quite high shares) and four regions of the Austro-Hungarian census of 1867 (three in present day-Hungary and one in present-day Romania). Proportions below 5 percent were to be found especially in Albanian regions of 1918 (including two cities), rural Serbia, two Wallachian regions, and the villages around Dubrovnik. There was a general tendency towards higher proportions of female household heads in cities, but especially Kruja and Kavaja in Albania had very low proportions, too.

Female ages at marriage were generally low in these societies and in half of the analysed regions 30 percent or more of women were already married in the age group of 15 to 19 years. The highest shares were reported for the rural Albanian regions, followed by Istanbul, and the rural Wallachian regions. The lowest proportions were reported for the Dubrovnik area, the cities of Kruševac (Serbia), Shkodra (Albania), and Čepelare (Bulgaria).

Husbands were generally older than their wives, only in a third of the regions of analysis more than ten percent of the wives were older than their husbands. The highest share with more than 20 percent was recorded for the villages in the Dubrovnik area. High shares were also reported for Istanbul and some Hungarian regions. Extremely low percentages were to be found for the Wallachian and some of the Albanian regions (including some cities).

Almost all young women lived in the household of their parents or husbands: in half of the regions of analysis less than one percent of them lived outside of these households. These regions include Wallachia in 1838, the Serbian regions, the Rhodope region, and some Albanian regions. More than five percent of these young women lived outside these households only in five regions: both Istanbul censuses and three Hungarian regions.

The male domination sub-index yields 30 or more points out of a maximum of 40 points for half of the regions of analysis and no region has less than 20 points. The highest levels of male domination are calculated for Albanian regions and Wallachia in 1838. The lowest levels of male domination are to be found in Hungarian regions in 1867, both Istanbul censuses, and the villages of the Dubrovnik area.

Domination of the Older Generation over the Younger Generation

Generally, the older male generation headed the household, only in ten regions more than 10 percent of the households were headed by a member of the younger generation. These regions were predominantly Albanian and Hungarian. The lowest proportions of household heads of the younger generation were reported for Albanian cities and the villages of the Dubrovnik area.

In half of the regions of analysis less than 20 percent of young married men lived in a neolocal household arrangement. These were predominantly Albanian rural regions, but included also the rural Serbian, Bulgarian, and Croatian regions. In contrast to this more than half of these men lived neolocally in eight regions: Wallachia in 1838, the Serbian city of Kruševac, and some Hungarian regions.

In seven regions more than half of the elderly persons coresided with at least one lateral relative. These regions were all located in rural Albania in 1918. In contrast to this in nine regions less than ten percent of the elderly population coresided with at least one lateral relative. These regions were located in Wallachia in 1838, in Hungary in 1867, and in the city of Čepelare.

The sub-index of domination of the older generation over the younger generation yields more than 20 points (out of a maximum of 30 points) for half of the regions of analysis. The highest levels are calculated for rural Albanian regions while the lowest levels are calculated for the four Wallachian regions.

Patrilocality

The proportions of married daughters among married children were generally low: two thirds of the regions of analysis had a share of ten percent or less. Especially low were the shares in the rural Albanian, Serbian, and Bulgarian regions. Only in five regions more than a quarter of the households containing married children included a married daughter. These regions included both Istanbul censuses and three Hungarian regions.

Son Preference

The son preference among the youngest child was pronounced only in some regions. Boys constituted 60 percent or more of the last children in only four regions: in Istanbul in 1885, the

Rhodope region, the Albanian city of Kruja and the rural Albanian region of Puka, where the proportion was even more than 80 percent.

The sex ratio of the youngest age group was higher than 110 (i.e. 110 boys for 100 girls) in eleven regions of analysis. These were all Albanian regions including one Hungarian region.

The sub-index of son preference yields therefore more than five points only in six regions: all of them in Albania with the exception of this Hungarian region.

Table 3: Descriptive statistics of the variables used in the Patriarchy Index

	Mean	Standard deviation	Minimum	Maximum
Female household heads	0.07	0.04	0.01	0.19
Young brides	0.27	0.14	0.05	0.56
Older wives	0.08	0.05	0.01	0.22
Female non-kin	0.03	0.04	0.00	0.15
Younger household head	0.07	0.05	0.00	0.17
Neolocality	0.33	0.25	0.05	0.88
Lateral extension of households	0.30	0.22	0.02	0.71
Married daughter	0.11	0.12	0.00	0.49
Boy as last child	0.53	0.08	0.45	0.81
Sex ratio	107.2	13.9	88.1	136.2

Patriarchy Index for SEE

The patriarchy index for these Southeastern European regions yielded very high patriarchy for five regions (all of them in rural Albanian in 1918), 12 regions with high patriarchy (Albanian rural regions and cities, rural Serbia, the Rhodope region), and 15 regions with medium patriarchy (Hungarian and Romanian regions, both Istanbul censuses, the Serbian city of Kruševac, the villages of the Dubrovnik area, and the city of Čepelare in the Rhodope mountains). This clearly shows a spatial pattern: very high patriarchy in the core of rural Albania, high patriarchy in the bordering regions of Northern Albania, the Albanian cities, and two neighbouring regions (Serbia and Bulgaria), and medium patriarchy in the other regions of Southeastern Europe analysed here (see map 2). This spatial pattern has some similarity with maps depicting the distribution of joint family households in Southeastern Europe.[39] The correlation between living in joint family households and patriarchal living arrangements is confirmed by these maps.

Variants of Patriarchy or Different Systems of Patriarchy?

In a final stage we want to analyse whether we can differentiate between different variants of patriarchy or even different systems of patriarchy in Southeastern Europe based on the Patriarchy Index. A cluster analysis[40] based on the 9 variables used for the Patriarchy Index yields six clusters:

1. 4 regions in Northern Albania
2. 3 regions in Central Albania
3. 6 Albanian cities, 2 rural Serbian regions, and the Albanian region of Gora
4. 6 regions in different areas
5. 4 Hungarian regions and both censuses of Istanbul
6. 4 Wallachian regions

We can see a quite clear spatial pattern in these clusters: most of the regions are very similar to the neighbouring ones, only cluster 4 is completely mixed (see map 3).

Table 4: Mean values of 6 clusters

	Cluster 1	Cluster 2	Cluster 3	Cluster 4	Cluster 5	Cluster 6
Regions	Puka, Kruja, Shkodra, Zhuri	Berati, Tirana North, Tirana South	6 Albania cities, rural Serbia, Gora	Partium 1867, Transylvania 1867, Rhodope region, Kruševac, Dubrovnik area	4 Hungarian regions, Istanbul	Wallachia
Female household heads	0.04	0.04	0.06	0.08	0.13	0.04

---

[39] Maria Todorova, *Balkan Family Structure and the European Pattern. Demographic Developments in Ottoman Bulgaria* (Washington: 1993): 148; Karl Kaser, *Familie und Verwandtschaft auf dem Balkan. Analyse einer untergehenden Kultur* (Wien, Köln, Weimar: Böhlau, 1995), 268.
[40] Hierarchical cluster analysis, using Ward's method of agglomeration and squared Euclidian distance.

Young brides	0.47	0.36	0.24	0.14	0.26	0.32
Older wives	0.06	0.04	0.06	0.11	0.14	0.02
Female non-kin	0.00	0.01	0.02	0.02	0.09	0.00
Younger household head	0.15	0.04	0.04	0.07	0.09	0.08
Neolocality	0.07	0.15	0.19	0.39	0.44	0.79
Lateral extension of households	0.66	0.47	0.41	0.11	0.18	0.05
Married daughter	0.01	0.02	0.06	0.10	0.30	0.14
Boy as last child	0.62	0.48	0.54	0.53	0.54	0.46
Sex ratio	116	136	109	100	102	91
Patriarchy Index	31	31	26	22	19	20

Cluster 1 is characterised by high levels of patriarchy in all variables except that it has the highest share of households headed by a member of the younger generation. Half of the regions belong to very high patriarchy and half of the regions to high patriarchy. Cluster 2 is even more patriarchal in the sense that no variable has low levels of patriarchy. All the regions in this cluster belong to the very high patriarchy level. Cluster 3 has rather medium values in all variables, but the lateral extension of households is high, young women do not live outside the household of relatives, and there are almost no household heads of the younger generation. All regions belong to the group of high-level patriarchy. Cluster 4 is characterised by the lowest level of early female marriage, high levels of wives older than their husbands, and high levels of neolocality. Five regions belong to medium patriarchy and one region to high patriarchy. Cluster 5 is characterised by high levels of female household heads, wives older than their husbands, young women living as non-kin outside the households of relatives, neolocal living arrangements of young married men, and a high share of married daughters in the households of elderly people. Cluster 6 is characterised by high levels of young brides and the highest level of neolocality among young married men, the lowest proportion of wives being older than their husbands and the lowest level of lateral extension of households. In addition there is no sign of son preference, but on the contrary it seems that in Wallachia in the 1838 census sons are missing.

Whether these are variants of a common Southeastern European pattern of patriarchy or whether these are different systems of patriarchy, cannot be answered using only these regions. Comparative data from other European regions and neighbouring regions in Asia will be needed to see which other combinations of patriarchal features did exist. The cluster analysis suggests that the major dividing line in the Southeastern European area (according to the data used here) was between the rural Albanian regions (the most patriarchal ones according to the Patriarchy Index) and the other regions.

References

Data files

Ulf Brunnbauer. *Household registers of Rhodope region, Version 1.0* [Mosaic Historical Microdata File]. www.censusmosaic.org, 2014.

Alan Duben. *1885 Census of Istanbul, Version 1.0* [Mosaic Historical Microdata File]. www.censusmosaic.org, 2014.

Alan Duben. *1907 Census of Istanbul, Version 1.0* [Mosaic Historical Microdata File]. www.censusmosaic.org, 2014.

Joel M. Halpern and Siegfried Gruber. *1863 Census of Jasenički srez and the city of Kruševac, Serbia, Version 1.2* [Mosaic Historical Microdata File]. www.censusmosaic.org, 2015.

Joel M. Halpern and Siegfried Gruber. *1884 Census of Jasenički srez, Serbia, Version 1.1* [Mosaic Historical Microdata File]. www.censusmosaic.org, 2012.

Karl Kaser, Siegfried Gruber, Gentiana Kera, Enriketa Pandelejmoni. *1918 census of Albania, Version 0.1* [SPSS file]. Graz, 2011.

Laboratory of Historical Demography (MPIDR). *1838 Census of Wallachia, Version 1.0* [Mosaic Historical Microdata File]. www.censusmosaic.org, 2014.

Laboratory of Historical Demography (MPIDR). *1869 Census of Hungary, Version 1.0* [Mosaic Historical Microdata File]. www.censusmosaic.org, 2014.

Laboratory of Historical Demography (MPIDR). *Status Animarum for Lisac and Pridvorje, Version 1.0* [Mosaic Historical Microdata File]. www.censusmosaic.org, 2015.

Map

MPIDR [Max Planck Institute for Demographic Research] and CGG [Chair for Geodesy and Geoinformatics, University of Rostock] 2013: MPIDR Population History GIS Collection – Europe (partly based on © EuroGeographics for the administrative boundaries). Rostock.

Description of data files

Albania 1918:

The Albanian data consist of the population census conducted by the Austro-Hungarian army in 1918 in Albania.[41] The Austro-Hungarian army occupied the majority of the territory of the newly created independent Albanian state, and established a new administration in 1916. Officers of the Austro-Hungarian army collected the data with the assistance of Albanian officers.[42] This Albanian census is the first for which the original data are still available on the level of the persons recorded, and it is of high quality given the circumstances under which it was taken.[43]

The research project, "The 1918 Albanian Population Census: Data Entry and Basic Analyses," based at the University of Graz and funded by the Austrian Science Fund (2000-2003), sought to convert the data from the 1918 census into machine-readable form.[44] Up to now, the data of 309 villages and cities with a total of 140,611 persons have been transcribed into a database. The database contains a 10-percent sample of villages which covers the whole of the area of surviving census data, and a 100-percent sample of settlements of special interest (including all of the cities). The data of the 10-percent-sample are weighted to account for the population size of administrative units according to the published results.[45]

The analysis will be done by comparing the different regions in the area covered by the Albanian census of 1918. This area was divided into seven prefectures at that time, and the six cities of this area are separated based on the assumption that the behavioral patterns of the urban and the rural populations differed. The subprefecture of Gora has been separated from the

---

[41] For an evaluation see Beryl Nicholson, *The census of the Austro-Hungarian occupied districts of Albania in spring 1918. A preliminary note on the manuscript* (Newcastle upon Tyne: 1999).
[42] Franz Seiner, *Ergebnisse der Volkszählung in Albanien in dem von der österr.-ungar. Truppen 1916-1918 besetzten Gebiete* (Wien-Leipzig: Hölder-Pichler-Tempsky 1922), 3
[43] Siegfried Gruber (2007) „Die albanische Volkszählung von 1918 und ihre Bedeutung für die Wissenschaft," in Helga Kostka, ed., *Seiner Zeit. Redakteur Franz Seiner und seine Zeit (1874 bis 1929)* (Graz: Academic Publishers, 2007), 257.
[44] *The Albanian Census of 1918*, http://www-gewi.uni-graz.at/suedost/seiner/index.html (accessed, January 22, 2020).
[45] Seiner, *Ergebnisse der Volkszählung in Albanien*.

prefecture of Zhuri because this region was known for having a large number of male migrant workers, which makes it distinct from the neighboring regions.

Bulgaria 1877-1947:

This is a sample of household registers of villages of the Rhodope region in Bulgaria. The sources are civil and church registers, and cover Orthodox Bulgarians and Pomaks (Bulgarian-speaking Muslims) in a mountainous region bordering to Greece. The data were transcribed by Ulf Brunnbauer and additional information about this data is available.[46]

Dubrovnik region 1674:

These are soul listings (*status animarum*) for two Roman Catholic parishes near Dubrovnik (Croatia) in the year 1674. The archival material can be found in the *Historijski arhiv Dubrovnik*, call number Acta S. Mariae Maioris, saec. XVII. No. 1809/4 and 21.

Hungary 1869:

This is a sample of the 1869 census of Austria-Hungary (conducted on 31 December 1869), which was compiled by Péter Öri and Levente Pakot for the Max Planck Institute for Demographic Research. The surviving materials of the 1869 census are very unevenly distributed within the borders of the Kingdom of Hungary in 1869. The data cover the territories of present-day Hungary, Slovakia and north-western Romania. The sampling is based on nine regions: four in Hungary, three in Slovakia and two in Romania. The data cover the villages of all religious confessions within the Kingdom of Hungary: Roman and Greek Catholics, Lutheran, Reformed and Unitarian Protestants, Orthodox Christians and Jews. Information on mother tongue or ethnicity was not recorded in the census and could therefore not be used for sampling. The data for Slovakia is not used in this analysis.

Ottoman Empire/Istanbul 1885 and 1907:

The 1885 (1300 h.) and 1907 (1322 h.) censuses were the first Empire-wide censuses undertaken for purposes other than either taxation or military conscription. They were the first censuses to include information about women. The 1907 census is generally the more reliable of the two. The samples cover only five percent of the permanent Muslim population of five central

---

[46] Ulf Brunnbauer, "Families and mountains in the Balkans: Christian and Muslim household structures in the Rhodopes, 19th-20th century," *The History of the Family* 7, 2002: 327-350; Ulf Brunnbauer, *Gebirgsgesellschaften auf dem Balkan: Wirtschaft und Familienstrukturen im Rhodopengebirge (19./20. Jahrhundert)* (Wien, Köln, Weimar: Böhlau, 2004).

districts of Istanbul. As occupations were recorded for only a small percentage of the respondents, those with non-manual occupations were over-represented. The data have already been used for analyzing household structures in Istanbul.[47] This publication provides additional information about these sources.

Serbia 1863 and 1884:

The 1863 and 1884 population censuses of Serbia were drawn from the Serbian State Archives (*Arhiv Srbije*) in Belgrade. These data were provided after an official request was made by Prof. Joel M. Halpern to the archive; the data were delivered to him directly by archive personnel. No restrictions were imposed. Data for the city of Kruševac is based on published material.[48] In the 1960s digitization was carried out under grants to Joel M. Halpern at the University of Massachusetts, Department of Anthropology, with funding from the National Science Foundation, the National Institutes of Health (National Institute of Mental Health), and research grants from the University of Massachusetts. Subsequent work was done during the 1990s and 2000s at the University of Graz, Austria, beginning in 1993 with funding from the Austrian Science Fund (FWF). Detailed information is available in the Joel Martin Halpern collection at the University of Massachusetts at Amherst/Special collections & University archives.

The rural data cover the same nine villages in Central Serbia (Jasenički srez) at two points in time. These data have already been used for research about household structures and historical demography.[49]

Wallachia 1838:

This is a sample of the Wallachian census of 1838, and covers the southern part of present-day Romania. It is a representative sample of the rural population created by Bogdan Mateescu for the Max Planck Institute for Demographic Research. The sampling is based on four regional strata (east, north, south, southwest).

---

[47] Alan Duben and Cem Behar, *Istanbul households: Marriage, family and fertility, 1880-1940* (Cambridge: Cambridge University Press, 1991).
[48] Branko Peruničić, *Kruševac u jednom veku 1815-1915* (Kruševac: Istorijski Arhiv Kruševac, 1971).
[49] E.g., Joel M. Halpern, *A Serbian Village* (New York: Harper & Row 1958); Joel M. Halpern, "Town and countryside in Serbia in the nineteenth-century, social and household structure as reflected in the census of 1863," in *Household and Family in Past Time: Comparative studies in the size and structure of the domestic group over the last three centuries in England, France, Serbia, Japan and colonial North America, with further materials from Western Europe,* eds. Peter Laslett and Richard Wall (Cambridge: 1974), 401-427; Siegfried Gruber, *Lebensläufe und Haushaltsformen auf dem Balkan: das serbische Jasenica im 19. Jahrhundert* (Unpublished doctoral dissertation) (University of Graz, Graz, 2004).

Maps

Map 1: Data used for analysis

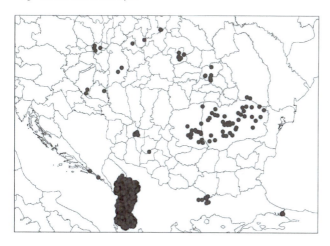

Note: Administrative boundaries of 1900.

Map 2: Level of patriarchy according to Patriarchy Index

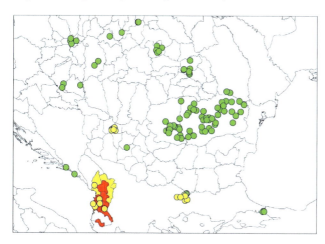

Note:
green: medium patriarchy
yellow: high patriarchy
red: very high patriarchy

Map 3: Clusters of patriarchal feature

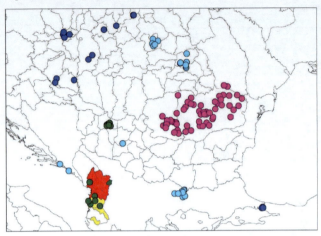

Table 5: Patriarchy Index

Region	Cluster	Female household heads	Young brides	Older wives	Female_nonkin	Male domination	Younger household heads	Neolocality	Lateral extension	Older generation domination	Patrilocality	Boys as last child	Sex ratio	Son preference	Patriarchy Index
Puka	1	8	8	8	10	34	8	9	10	27	10	10	4	14	35
Kruja	1	9	8	9	10	36	8	9	9	26	10	2	3	5	30
Shkodra	1	8	6	9	10	33	8	10	9	27	10	2	2	4	29
Zhuri	1	10	6	8	10	34	7	9	9	25	10	1	4	5	29
Berati	2	8	8	9	10	35	9	9	8	26	10	0	9	9	32
Tirana North	2	8	6	8	10	32	10	9	8	27	10	0	10	10	32
Tirana South	2	10	2	9	10	31	10	7	5	22	10	0	10	10	30
Kruja city	3	9	3	10	10	32	10	9	6	25	10	6	0	6	29

Patriarchy Index

Kavaja city	3	9	6	9	10	34	10	8	5	23	9	1	4	5	28
Jasenica 1884	3	9	2	7	10	28	9	9	7	25	10	0	1	1	26
Tirana city	3	7	6	7	10	30	9	9	5	23	9	0	4	4	26
Jasenica 1863	3	9	3	8	10	30	8	8	5	21	10	0	0	0	25
Gora	3	9	2	9	10	30	9	9	7	25	9	1	0	1	25
Elbasan city	3	6	5	9	9	29	10	8	5	23	9	2	1	3	25
Durres city	3	7	4	7	9	27	10	6	6	22	9	0	4	4	25
Shkodra city	3	6	2	9	9	26	9	6	5	20	9	2	1	3	24
Rhodope	4	8	3	8	10	29	8	8	2	18	10	4	0	4	25
Dubrovnik	4	9	1	4	9	23	10	8	3	21	9	0	0	0	22
Čepelare city	4	8	2	8	10	28	9	6	1	16	9	1	0	1	22
Partium	4	6	3	7	9	25	9	6	1	16	9	1	0	1	21
Kruševac city	4	7	1	9	10	27	8	3	2	13	9	1	0	1	21
Transylvania	4	7	2	6	10	25	9	5	0	14	7	0	0	0	18
NE Hungary	5	6	5	7	9	27	9	3	1	13	8	1	7	8	23
Istanbul 1885	5	4	5	6	7	22	10	6	6	22	6	3	0	3	20
Istanbul 1907	5	6	5	6	8	25	9	7	4	20	6	1	0	1	19
S Transdanubia	5	7	2	6	8	23	8	7	2	17	7	0	0	0	18
N Transdanubia	5	5	3	6	7	21	8	6	1	15	7	0	0	0	17
Great Plain	5	7	3	7	9	26	9	4	1	14	4	3	0	3	17
SW Wallachia	6	8	5	10	10	33	8	3	1	12	9	0	0	0	21
S Wallachia	6	9	5	9	10	33	9	1	0	10	8	0	0	0	20
N Wallachia	6	8	5	9	10	32	9	2	0	11	8	0	0	0	20
E Wallachia	6	9	4	9	10	32	9	2	1	12	8	0	0	0	20

Reading and Mapping Mid-Nineteenth Century Ottoman Tax Registers: An Early Attempt toward Building a Digital Research Infrastructure for Ottoman Economic and Social History

Murat Güvenç and M. Erdem Kabadayı

Abstract

This proposed paper would use advanced methods of cluster analysis and multiple correspondence analysis (MCA). It will present some outcomes of a three-year research project An Introduction to the Occupational History of Turkey via New Methods and New Approaches (1840–1940), funded by the Scientific and Technological Research Council of Turkey (TUBITAK) (Nr. 112K271), which will be completed in September 2015. Kabadayı is the principal investigator and Güvenç is the advisor of this project. Especially in recent years, MCA has gained popularity among social scientists, but to the best of our knowledge, it has not yet been used in economic or social history in the international literature in English. We will present the preliminary results of our application of MCA to the 1845 Ottoman tax registers (temettuat) focusing on Bursa. For this city, we have been able to locate 126 of the 145 neighbourhoods listed in the records. 7,914 individuals were recorded. 5,662 identified as household heads and 2,252 not. An important aspect of this work involves identifying patterns connected to ethno-religious affiliations.

Introduction

This paper is an early attempt to work on an unconventionally large dataset on urban earnings, occupations and ethno-religious affiliations of the entire households of Bursa, a large Ottoman city in West Anatolia in 1845, via emerging methods of data gathering, curation and analysis. Our approach and method went through stages of source collection, manual reading of the entire available collection of a tax survey for Bursa in the Ottoman archives,[1] and then data entry, coding occupations, bracketing economic indicators such as household income, occupational income and taxes, running a Multiple Correspondence Analysis (MCA), interpreting, mapping and reinterpreting our results.

Preliminary results are methodologically and substantively encouraging. The same digital research infrastructure based on state-of-art methods of pattern recognition will in all likelihood allow students of Ottoman urban social and economic history to decipher local specificities of different provinces of the Ottoman Empire. The empirical problem is moreover reduced to an issue of digitisation of Ottoman surveys and censuses, such as *temetuat* registers.

Mid-nineteenth Century Ottoman Tax Survey as an Empire-wide Databank?

The main archival source for this paper is a detailed Ottoman tax survey, *temettuat*,[1] conducted in the years 1844 and 1845.[2] We would like to summarize the political and financial background within which this empire-wide survey was conducted. The reforms and/or reform attempts (*Tanzimat*) of the Ottoman state reaches a culmination point in 1839 with an imperial reform decree. 1839 has far-reaching effects on state administration on various levels. The major financial turning point is that the centuries-old tax-farming practice (*iltizam*) was abolished. Instead of the indirect and communal taxation of *iltizam*, the central state administration tries to establish a direct and individual taxation system based upon income levels of individual households. However, due to the tax-farming practice, which relied on intermediaries, the Ottoman authorities did not have sufficient information on the tax base. The 1845 tax survey is the result of an attempt to extract income levels of Ottoman households. Taxation has been a contested domain between taxpayers and the states. The nineteenth-century Ottoman Empire is not an exception. The varying success of negotiations among the central state, local power holders and individual households determined the geographical scope as well as the quality of data extraction of the survey. Since the Ottoman territories had a huge diversity regarding both powers of local governances and concomitant limitations on the implementation of Ottoman central governmentality the taxation geography of the mid-nineteenth century empire is in itself a manifestation of regional and local power relations.

Arab and Kurdish lands, Bosnia, Montenegro were not covered by the survey. Similarly, Anatolian regions in the North East and South West are also not included. Major islands in the Mediterranean, Cyprus, Crete, Rhodes, Kos and Chios are covered yet numerous others not. Istanbul was exempted from the planned direct income-based tax therefore no survey was conducted in Istanbul. Tax registers of Izmir did not survive to today. It has been assumed that the survey registered in total more than 1,000,000 households. For the individual researcher, the structural and until now insurmountable problem with this survey has been that neither the

---

[1] For a detailed evaluation of these sources in English see Kayoko Hayashi and Mahir Aydın, eds., *The Ottoman state and societies in change: a study of the nineteenth century Temettuat registers* (London: Kegan Paul, 2004). For a review on literature based on *temettuat* see Said Öztürk "The use of Temettuat registers in Ottoman Studies," *Türkiye Araştırmaları Literatür Dergisi* 1, no. 1 (2003): 287-304.

[2] Since the Ottoman administration used the Islamic lunar calendar the year of the register is given as 1844/45. For the sake of simplicity only 1845 will be used in this paper.

Ottoman administration nor social scientists working on its successor states have published aggregate data or created datasets to analyse the information conveyed from it.

MAP 1: Geographical Coverage of the 1845 Tax Survey

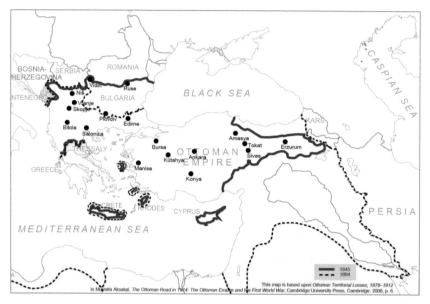

In spite of its limited areal coverage and its variables, the *temettuat* survey conveys the most extensive occupational data for Ottoman economic and social history. Male[3] bread-winning household members constitute the unit of observation. For each registered individual household member, the *temettuat* allows to extract names, titles related to social status, occupations, ethno-religious affiliations, household and occupational income and tax liability. Prior to this study, the same data have been treated in the context of a large research project.[4] Enumerators registered occupational and social titles as expressed without consulting an enumerator's code book as it was the case in the UK. The absence of an *a priori* would constitute a methodological problem in the absence of a comprehensive and extensive coding scheme such as the PST system, developed by

---

[3] In rare occasions the *temettuat* registers cover female household members.
[4] An Introduction to the Occupational History of Turkey via New Methods and New Approaches (1840 - 1940). Project Nr. 112K271, funded by the Scientific and Technological Research Council of Turkey (TUBITAK). Güvenç is the advisor and Kabadayı is the principal investigator of this research project. We would especially like to thank our research assistant Berkay Küçükbaşlar for his tedious work in data gathering and help in analysis. Berkay Küçükbaşlar also created all of the maps used in this paper.

the Cambridge Group for the History of Population and Social Structure.[5] It also enables students to bypass the rigidity of ready-made, outdated bureaucratic classifications and to assess the relevancy of different classificatory schemes depending on the nature of the research question.

Ethno-religious Division of Labour, a Prevalent Research Question in the Ottoman Social and Economic History

Historical demography is an extremely underdeveloped field both for the Ottoman Empire and for the Turkish Republic, which can be explained by a form of methodological nationalism and the concomitant limited availability of sources. The earliest modern individual-based population censuses of the late Ottoman Empire with extensive information on marital status, age, fertility and occupational information for the entire empire was conducted in 1881 and then in 1905. Earlier less comprehensive population registers based upon households and enumerating only the male population were conducted in the Ottoman Empire between the 1830s and 1881. These registers have been digitised as jpeg files and made available for research at the Ottoman state archives in Istanbul since 2011. The unavailability of historical demographic and occupational data in machine-readable format would account for the underdeveloped state of the art in Ottoman historical demography.[6] In the absence of reliable empirical data infrastructure, the Ottoman historiography related to the ethnic division of labour and economic performance of religious communities oscillated between narratives emphasizing an imagined harmonious and peaceful coexistence, and inter-communal tensions and rivalries.[7] The existing state of the art, which is to some extent "long on facts, short on insight", has passed the point of diminishing marginal returns.

---

[5] The Cambridge Group for the History of Population and Social Structure, http://www.geog.cam.ac.uk/research/projects/occupations/britain19c/pst.html (accessed 16 January 2020).
[6] The most cited work on Ottoman population is Kemal H. Karpat, *Ottoman Population, 1830-1914: Demographic and Social Characteristics* (Madison, Wisconsin: University of Wisconsin Press, 1985), yet its shortcomings have been heavily criticised by historical demographers immediately after its publication: Cem Behar, "Review of Ottoman Population 1830-1914. Demographic and Social Characteristics by Kemal H. Karpat," *Population Studies* 40, no. 2 (July 1, 1986): 322–23. In a similar vein and due to the limited data availability even the most authoritative compilation has major deficiencies. See Cem Behar, *The Population of the Ottoman Empire and Turkey* (Ankara: State Statistical Institute, 1996).
[7] Although there have been some studies of the role of ethno-religious affiliations of Ottoman subjects in their employment opportunities and labour relations we still lack the data to conduct comprehensive and extensive research projects. Kabadayı's article coming out from his PhD dissertation is one of such limited case studies, Mustafa Erdem Kabadayı, "Working in a Fez Factory in Istanbul in the Late Nineteenth Century: Division of Labour and Networks of Migration Formed Along Ethno-Religious Lines," *International Review of Social History* 54, no. Supplement S17 (2009): 69–90.

New Historical Perspectives on Mid-nineteenth Century Bursa in the Digitised Era

Bursa, a former capital and an economic centre has been taken up in numerous case studies[8] and is endowed with rich archival sources and other contemporary sources especially court registers including probate inventories, European consular reports and travelogues. The social and economic history of the city has been studied from different perspectives focusing mostly on its urban morphology and its industrial production base.[9] Yet we do not have at our disposal a comprehensive study producing an overall account on the patterns and transformation processes of its economic history. The present paper can of course not address this challenging issue for the urban economic history of the city. Nonetheless, we will try to show that the use of understudied archival sources such as *temettuat* would eventually open up new perspectives on the city's social and economic history. This paper is a first attempt to process the *temettuat* registers via new techniques of data analysis, to provide new insights and to develop new research questions for subsequent studies. If successful, such an endeavour would start a new interest and contribute to the scholarship on the city's urban history.

Facts and Figures on Bursa *Temettuat* Data

Presently the Bursa *temettuat* kept in Ottoman State Archives is compiled in some 148 registers and covers some 7,914 household members, 5,662 of which are household heads. It is highly representative as the population register of 1839, covering urban male population including infants gives the total number of households[10] as 6,335 and the males as 13,211. The higher coverage of the tax register leaves no doubt about its representativity. It is evident that it is impossible to describe and to account for the contributions stemming from female household members as they are not registered at all. But we know from other sources that compared to more industrialised parts of Eurasia female labour market participation was particularly low in mid-nineteenth century Bursa. Hence gender blindness of the data though regrettable should not pose significant issues of representation. Furthermore, the tax registers' occupational data information

---

[8] For a recent and extensive bibliography on Bursa see Nezaket Özdemir, *Bursa Kaynakçası* (Bursa: Bursa Kültür A.Ş, 2011).
[9] For an early and yet very well conducted study see, Leila Erder, "The Making of Industrial Bursa: Economic Activity and Population in a Turkish City 1835-1975" (unpublished PhD, Princeton, 1976). For the latest contribution from a similar perspective see Sevilay Kaygalak, *Kapitalizmin Taşrası: 16. Yüzyıldan 19. Yüzyıla Bursa'da Toplumsal Süreçler ve Mekansal Değişim* (İstanbul : İletişim Yayınları, 2008).
[10] Ottoman State Archives NFS.d. 1396 and 1398.

is insensitive to multiple occupations and hence may underrepresent urban economic activity. In spite of these otherwise important handicaps, the 5,662 household heads covered in the *temettuat* can, for all practical purposes, be taken up as a fairly reliable representation of an urban economy.

First, we assume that 5.662 household heads represent the entire city. This is a gender-blind perspective as we know. Surely the female members of Ottoman urban households also participated in the household economy. Furthermore, the tax registers' occupational data give very little information on the by-employment. These are major shortcomings of our data. Nevertheless, we are convinced that the registered household heads provided their primary occupations to the surveyors. Therefore, throughout this paper we will use the terms observations, residents and population almost interchangeably for the sake of our argument, that 5.662 household heads' ethno-religious affiliations, income levels and occupations can be used as proxies for the population of Bursa in 1845. This assumption is further backed by the very close coverage of the tax survey to the population register from 1839. 5662 observations technically still build a sample. This is indisputable yet we argue that our sample size is very close to the total number of households in Bursa in 1845 and this sample is representative to a very high and unprecedented level. In other words, our approach is that we are working with a very large sample without sampling.

Another important assumption is related to unit and venue of registration. *Temettuat* registers were conducted in neighbourhoods in urban locations and in villages in rural settings throughout the empire. The unit of register is, therefore, neighbourhoods for the towns. Individual registers were produced for neighbourhoods. In ethno-religiously mixed neighbourhoods separate registers for each community in the neighbourhood were created.

MCA's Possible Contribution to the Emerging Digital History of Southeast Europe and Turkey

Our survey is based on a pattern recognition procedure developed by L. Lebart stipulating the joint use of cluster and Multiple Correspondence Analysis (hereafter MCA), which is a generalization of its earlier predecessor Simple Correspondence Analysis. The Simple Correspondence Analysis, as its name implies[11] in French, is a method of data visualisation and of

---

[11] Correspondence Analysis is abbreviated as AFC which stands for *Analyse Factorielle des Correspondences*. Karl M. van Meter et al., "Correspondence Analysis: A History and French Sociological Perspective." in *Correspondence Analysis in*

factor analysis for categorical and ordinal variables devised for simple cross-tables. This method was popularized by Pierre Bourdieu in his famous contribution *Distinction* and in its earlier applications the proposed model has time and again proved its efficiency in deciphering multi-dimensional surveys. Yet for reasons beyond the scope of this paper the model did not have noticeable impact in English speaking countries.[13] Yet in practice, Simple Correspondence (CA) and MCA have been particularly helpful as unsupervised pattern recognition devices. The conceptual model proposed by Lebart can be operationalised through different procedures and is particularly useful in analysing historical archive data for the following reasons:

- It is fully *data-driven* hence prevents quasi obligatory use of *a priori* sociological and political concepts and categories which more often than not constitute a nightmare of students who work in archives.

- It does not have stringent conditions on data quality, quantity and the allure of data. It does not have prerequisites on the shapes and the allure of distributions. Albeit with some loss of precision, continuous, ordinal and qualitative attributes can be treated simultaneously.[12] This allows students to sidestep major and chronicle problems of data analysis.

- It is fully relational and helps students avoid the unavoidable reductionism of functional approaches[13.]

- It is fully relevant for the description of local contingent formations and may generate useful hints and insights regarding generative mechanisms and monitoring phenomenal or structural changes in time[14.]

---

the Social Sciences: Recent Developments and Applications, eds. Michael J. Greenacre & Jörg Blasius (San Diego: Academic Press, 1994), 128- 137.

[12] Notice that continuous data can easily be transformed and recoded as ordinal or nominal attributes but that the reverse is not true! Hence while statistical tools devised for continuous or ordinal variables cannot treat categorical data, flexible data analysis techniques developed for factor analysis of qualitative or ordinal variables can be used for recoding and accommodate all types of attributes regardless of their unit of measurement.

[13] For a thorough critique of substantivism and the ways in which it differs from relationism see Mustafa Emirbayer, "Manifesto for a Relational Sociology", *The American Journal of Sociology* 103, No. 2. (Sep., 1997): 281-317 and for a critique of functionalism see Peter Gould, "Letting the data speak for themselves," *Annals of the Association of American Geographers*, 71, issue 2 (1981): 166-176; David Byrne, *Interpreting Quantitative Data* (London, Thousand Oaks: SAGE, 2002).

[14] Michael Greenacre, "Correspondence Analysis and its Interpretation," and Thomas Müller-Schneider, "The Visualization of Structural Change by Means of Correspondence," in Greenacre & Blaisius, *Correspondence Analysis in the Social Sciences*. For the history of CA also in the same volume see Van Meter et al., "Correspondence Analysis. A History and French Sociological Perspective."

- The sensitivity of the descriptive tool to detect and depict local contingent conditions and its data-driven nature make it particularly useful for historical enquiry in general and for archival work in particular.
- Besides, the presence of outliers and/or missing data do not pose any major problems
- Results are to a large extent insensitive to the addition or subscription of attributes.
- As it is the case with conventional factor analysis CA or MCA detect and depict the structural properties of the context as well as the positions of different actors within these multi-dimensional structure formations. Hence, we must acknowledge that the latter are not unique to CA and/or MCA. But while conventional Factor Analysis (i.e. the Principal Component Analysis) is applicable exclusively to continuous variables, the CA can process counted data and the MCA can –subsequent to recoding – treat both counted and nominal data. One important advantage of the MCA is that it can treat individuals as they are (i.e. without having to regroup them into categories).
- CA and the MCA are particularly useful tools for historical studies as students have no control over their data and since a major part of the available data are nominal and consist of enumerations counts, which can hardly be treated through conventional tools.
- We must explicitly emphasize the exploratory nature of the technique and its inadequacies for confirmatory studies. This is a major disadvantage for those who consider the only approach possible and imaginable in social sciences. Yet if one considers the serious challenges to mainstream approaches stemming from structuration theory, critical realism, genetic structuralism of Bourdieu, Actor-Network Theory or assemblage theories, this need not be a serious flaw of the approach. Whether explicitly acknowledged or not, results derived from such exploratory studies may decipher a pattern invisible to the naked eye and in so doing contribute significantly to the formulation of original research questions and in so doing enhance the quality and relevancy of conventional approaches that circumvent the structure-agency, and try to detect agency as a consequence of human-non human associations.

The graphical user interface by Güvenç and Yıldırım suggests this approach. The interface operates in four steps:

Step 1: Detection of the positions of individuals and modalities in multi-dimensional space, through MCA.

Step 2: Clustering individuals and modalities with respect to their positions in the multidimensional space.

Step 3: Identification of individuals with congruent modality patterns.

Step 4: Clustering of modalities depicting similar deployment patterns in the population.

A typical application of the proposed model yields two related but irreducible results. First, it identifies the modality assemblages, which constitute the building blocks of social and economic formations. The identification of modality assemblages can be likened to the loading of variables in conventional factor analysis and would illustrate the distinctive substantive components of the context under scrutiny. The identification of individuals with congruent modality patterns can be likened to Q mode Factor Analysis, which identifies individuals with similar attribute endowments. The results of this second phase of the survey are particularly important for historians as they illustrate the ways in which the structural components project themselves on concrete individuals of the study. These distinctive properties of the methodology make it a particularly relevant tool for the analysis of social structures as well as of agents or actors.

To the best of our knowledge the MCA, in spite of its obvious advantages, has surprisingly not yet been used extensively in analysing the economic and social history of Southeast Europe in general and that of Turkey in particular.

Temettuat Registers and Records: an Overview

In this first round of examination we can group 5662 observations in 143 neighbourhoods into 6 clusters. In doing this, the total observations were classified, categorised and analysed according to the modalities of each individual observation.

These modalities are:

1- Ethno-religious affiliation (ER)
2- Location and unit of registry (neighbourhood: N)
3- Occupation (coded in PST)
4- Occupational income (OCC_I)
5- Total household income (HH_I)
6- Total tax to be paid (TAX)

Ethno-religious affiliations are grouped into 6 categories:[15]

1- Muslim (m)
2- Orthodox Christian (oc)
3- Armenian (a)
4- Catholic[16] (c)
5- Jewish (j)
6- Kıpti (Roma) (k)

Location and Unit of Registry

Few exceptions set aside *temettuat* records indicate for each household the name of the neighbourhoods. Households with unidentified locations are, more often than not, clustered in a single group. In this survey it was possible for us to identify 126 out of a total of 143 neighbourhoods mentioned in the Bursa *temettuat*. In disaggregate analyses, where individuals constitute the units of observations, neighbourhoods codes are taken up as attributes expressing the deployment pattern of households. In this regard ambiguities related to boundaries of the neighbourhood codes are particularly useful as they constitute the empirical basis of socio-spatial differentiation in Ottoman cities.

Occupations in PST 4 digit

Temettuat registers convey occupational information in the form of individual occupational titles. In order to be able to make sense of these titles and to reach a deeper understanding of the functioning of the urban economy, they have to be coded into occupational schemes. The PST

---

[15] Throughout this paper the abbreviations in parentheses will be used. These categories stem from Ottoman administrative units (*millet*). They are ethno-religious, since Muslim as a category includes various ethnicities such as Turks, Kurds, and Arabs; similarly Orthodox Christians also include ethnicities such as Greeks, and Bulgarians. Therefore these categories should be understood within the administrative logic of the mid-nineteenth century Ottoman state.

[16] The catholic community of Bursa was constituted mainly of inter-confessional converts from the Apostolic Armenians. For more information on the spread of Catholicism among Ottoman Armenians, see Kemal Beydilli et al., *Recognition of the Armenian Catholic community and the church in the reign of Mahmud II (1830)* (Cambridge, Mass: Harvard University, 1995). In our sample, Catholic Armenians are a small part of the entire Armenian community.

system we opted for enables us to detect occupational concentrations in the sectors and respective sub-sectors of the urban economy.

Occupational Income

Occupational incomes of the observations vary between zero and 15.000 *kuruş*. They are divided into six categories using K-Means clustering system:

0: No income (occ_i_0)

1-520: Low income (occ_i_1)

521-1300: Low-medium income (occ_i_2)

1301-2500: High-medium income (occ_i_3)

2501-4000: High income (occ_i_4)

>4000: Highest (occ_i_5)

Detailed documentation on price and wage levels of the Ottoman economy is not available.[17] Earning less than 500 *kuruş* in a year would definitely place a resident of Bursa into the category of low-income. Following brackets are set keeping in mind the price level of the 1860s in Bursa.

Household Income

The total incomes of households vary between zero and 90.000 *kuruş*. They are also divided into six categories using K-Means clustering system:

0: No income (hh_i_0)

1-1045: Low income (hh_i_1)

1046-2720: Low-medium income (hh_i_2)

2721-5130: High-medium income (hh_i_3)

---

[17] Pamuk's work is one of the few examples providing wage data: Şevket Pamuk, *İstanbul ve diğer kentlerde 500 yıllık fiyatlar ve ücretler [500 years of prices and wages in İstanbul and other cities]* (Ankara: T.C. Başbakanlık Devlet İstatistik Enstitüsü, 2000). However, it does not rely on nineteenth-century urban observations. Most reliable contemporaneous data on the relative levels of earnings and purchasing power can be found in the compilation of British consular reports in the 1860s: "Position of the Artisan and Industrial Classes in Foreign Countries," National Archives of U.K., FO 83/334. We will base our brackets of occupational and household income data in accord with this detailed collection.

5131-8440: High income (hh_i_4)

>8440: Highest (hh_i_5)

Slightly different than the occupational income brackets, variants of the household income have been clustered to differentiate the relative economic standings of the households.

Total Tax to be Paid

Calculated tax for the observations vary between zero and 1210 *kuruş*. They are also divided into six categories using K-Means clustering system:

0: No tax (tax_0)

1-83: Low tax (tax_1)

84-225: Low-medium tax (tax_2)

226-435: High-medium tax (tax_3)

436-750: High tax (tax_4)

>750: Highest (tax_5)

Modality Assemblages: An Overview

For the clarity of exposition, the six modality assemblages are extracted via Lebart's model. The results of the application suggest **an ethnic and economic differentiation** of the urban tax base.

Muslims constitute the largest group of taxpayers and form two distinct groups based on their labour market participation. The **first group** patronized jobs related to agriculture, forestry, gardening, food production, textiles and clothing, leather and leather goods, social services and administration. In spite of their presence, in some branches they were to a large extent underrepresented in trades and artisanal production. This group distinguished itself by low household and low occupational incomes and as expected, low tax assessments. It follows that a **typical** Muslim household head, if he had a remunerative job, was more likely to participate in the urban economy through these channels and trades, with no or very low barriers of entry, and have distinctively **low occupational or household incomes** and **low tax liabilities**.

The **second group** covers those with no qualifications, no permanent jobs and therefore no regular incomes. A large majority (90%) of them were classified as bachelors (*bikar*), beggars, students. They definitely had no remunerative jobs or operated in tedious irregular jobs like grave digging, recycling nails, repair of copper goods, services and entertainment, as gatekeepers and dancers (*köçek*) with little or no regular income at all. The tiny *Roma* community (*kıptiyan*) was spatially and functionally integrated into this lowest echelon (if not the underclass of urban society). This group, which accounted for only 3.4 % of *temettuat* was spread throughout the city. Yet two thirds of this group were significantly overrepresented in neighbourhoods listed in, with striking concentrations in *Sinanbey* (100%), *Veziri* (29.4%), *Sarı Abdullah* (23%), *Süzen Kefen* 19.4%, *Şerafettin Paşa* and *Mantıcı* (16%). *Sinan Bey*, which houses exclusively this group can be taken up as a perfect place to study the characteristics of the underclass in Bursa in 1845.

Orthodox Christian and Armenian household heads are particularly overrepresented in the **third category.** The former account for 10.6% and the latter 15.2% and in all 26% of household heads. This category has clear domination in certain trades while being underrepresented or totally absent in others. The ones dominated by them are listed below. Urban trades and jobs are highly represented in this category.

pst_4_18	miller
pst_4_19	cereal processing, other
Food Production	5% (48 Cases)
pst_4_30	clothing manufacture
pst_4_31	tailor
pst_4_32	maker of outdoor clothing
pst_4_49	cotton manufacturer
pst_4_51	cotton fabric maker
pst_4_53	linener
pst_4_55	silk fabric maker
pst_4_69	net maker
Textiles & Clothing	31% (279 Cases)
pst_4_71	potter
pst_4_101	tile maker
pst_4_75	watch maker
pst_4_83	bucket maker

pst_4_87	others, mixed metals
pst_4_124	jewellery, precious metals dealer
pst_4_94	locksmith
pst_4_96	sieve maker
Crafts-Manufacture	10% (90 Cases)
pst_4_102	builder
pst_4_104	joiner
pst_4_105	plasterer
pst_4_107	glazier
pst_4_108	paviour
Construction	17% (148 Cases)
pst_4_129	seller of bakery products
pst_4_137	innkeeper
pst_4_142	musician
pst_4_146	laundry work
pst_4_150	concierge
Services (1)	3 % (31 Cases)
pst_4_152	servant
pst_4_153	footman
pst_4_165	surgeon
pst_4_177	verger
pst_4_188	Home service, other
Services (2)	11 % (98 Cases)
pst_4_199	coachman
pst_4_200	boatman
Transportation	18% (160 Cases)
pst_4_204	labourer
Wage labour	5% (42 Cases)

One can easily read off this group which accounted for 16% of those liable to taxation had an undeniable domination in the field of transportation, construction, crafts, textiles and clothing. This employment profile is associated with **lower middle** occupational incomes and constitutes the modal category.

Armenian and Orthodox households lived in highly segregated neighbourhoods and could be easily detected in the urban space. *Ahmedbey Fenari, Molla Arab, Bucak, Şangur Şungur* neighbourhoods had exclusively Armenian and/or Orthodox residents. The latter (Armenian and/or Orthodox residents) accounted for 97% to 81% in *Hacı Yakub, Veled-i Harrat, Bulgarlar, Çelebi Sultan, Hoca Cafer, Koca Naip, Mesud Makramavi, Kırkmerdiban*, and *Ahmet Bey, Kayabaşı, Eşrafi, Attar Hüssam Kayganzade, Kale-i Umurbey*, and finally between 73% to 64% in *Hacı Baba, Hacı İskender, İshakşah*. Approximately two-thirds of *İç Odalar* (an accommodation facility) residents were Armenian.

The **fourth category** comprises some 1138 household heads accounting for 20% of entries of Bursa *temettuat*. Its religious-ethnic structure is distinctively diversified: Muslims and Jews are visibly under, Orthodox Christians, Armenians are significantly overrepresented. Out of a total of 66 Catholic Armenian no less than sixty are positioned in this category. This is a clear sign of economic specialization and income disparity within the Armenian Community with respect to religious affiliation. Catholic Armenians distinguish themselves with significantly higher incomes and are specialized in a significantly different set of economic activities. That is the reason why Catholic Armenians – in spite of the fact that they are not the modal category – end up being the ethno-religious sub-culture that characterises this particular assemblage.

Economic areas of activity are quite distinct than those observed in the previous group. Notice the absence of agriculture, transportation, construction, administrative jobs and labourers as well as the comparatively high presence of non-manual service jobs in retail and wholesale and public services.

- Food producers account for 12% (136 cases)
- Leather production and shoemaking 30% (336 cases)
- Textiles production processes and sales 18% (207 cases)
- Crafts and manufactures 9% (103 cases)
- Retail and wholesale, public services 31% (350 cases)

The category relates predominantly to middle and upper middle-income household heads. Lower middle annual tax liabilities and household incomes, – (83 to 225 *kuruş*) and (1045 and 2720 *kuruş*) respectively – and intermediary occupational incomes (between 1300 to 2500 *kuruş*) are **distinctively overrepresented and constitute distinctive modalities.**

Household heads assigned to this category depict significant concentrations in the following neighbourhoods and registration units: We start to get a clear sign pertaining to socio-economic differentiation of Bursa neighbourhoods.

Mehmed Karamani
Katolik milleti
Balıkcık
Ebu Şahme
Bakırhane
Hoca Alizade
Veled-i Enbiya
Köseler
Cami-i Kebir
Veli Şemseddin
Karakavi
Şükrü Hoca
Selçuk Sultan
Darphane
Veled-i Saray
Hayreddin Paşa
Hoca Tayyib
Bazar-ı Mahi
Başçı İbrahim
Karaağaç
Hoca Mehmed Karamani
Anarlı
Veled-i Kurt
Büyükbahçelerde Ermeniler
Bedreddin

Perakende Müslim/Gayrimüslim
Selçuk Hatun

The 148 Jewish household heads (approximately 75% of the Jewish community) are clustered in the **fifth category**. The employment categories listed here can be taken up as almost perfect examples of ethnic division of labour as they are fully patronized by the Jewish community, which accounts for only 3.6% of entire household heads. Observed ethnic division of labour is fascinating and invites for further in depth inquiry. We do not, for instance, have any hint to explain the reasons why the Jewish community has an impressive patronage among slaughtermen (23%) or porters (30%) or among silk workers (48%). Though we have no clues to solve these puzzles,[18] one should acknowledge that the unexpectedly high concentrations just discovered pose new and important questions for further historical inquiry.

The rest, assigned to other assemblages, distinguish themselves with comparatively higher and lower incomes and different employment profiles. A comparison with the intra-urban distribution of this group suggests that the Jewish community is the most particularly segregated, and that the *Kuruçeşme* neighbourhood is the *Jewish ghetto* of Bursa. Hence, we start to see that in spite of its highly diversified economic structure the Jewish community was most probably one of the most socially segregated and religiously cohesive.

The **sixth** and the last group covers major industrialists, producers and dealers of commodities such as cloth, candle and clothing accessories, coffee and silk, including financiers and stockbrokers, with high and highest occupational and household incomes and tax assessments. None of the religious and/or ethnic groups is predominant. **Though** non-Muslims are slightly overrepresented, and the well-off Muslim community has a non-negligible presence.

Notice however that this group is technically invisible in the space as none of the neighbourhoods emerges as an enclave where the well-off or the upper strata is predominant. As opposed to previous clusters with distinctive religious profiles and/spatial deployment patterns, this small, albeit strategically important component of Bursa's social structure, is to a large extent *invisible* to the naked eye, and would have not been detected at all, through conventional research methodologies.

---

[18] Preparing kosher food is an indicator to be further followed.

The principal engine behind Lebart's MCA model is an extremely powerful descriptive tool capable to detect, decipher and re-assemble the multi-faceted and to a large extent imperceptible traces of archive data in general and those in tax registers in particular. Although we have not referred to any a priori model mechanism or category, the above-mentioned six principal components of strata players in mid-century Bursa tax-base were successfully identified.

Concluding Comments of the First Round of Analysis

This brief exploratory survey illustrated the relevancy of the methodology by depicting Bursa's tax-base assemblage of six heterogeneous components or sub-groups with highly distinctive properties. To recapitulate our observation: ethnic division labour is undeniably important yet it should not be referred to as a master key capable to account for all subtleties.

- The first group of taxpayers constitutes the largest group of taxable household heads 41%. They are almost exclusively Muslim and highly overrepresented in manual works in agriculture, construction, certain branches of petty production, trade and in administrative jobs. Yet they have an undeniable presence in petty production services and trade and other branches of economic activity. The historical specificity of the urban economy can hardly be explained by limiting the contribution of Muslim households to agriculture and administrative jobs.

- The analysis of tax register detects that no less than 15.6% of the taxable household heads (885 cases) had no remunerative income at all. The tiny Roma community specialized in minor artisanal works and re-cycling operations was an integral part of this group where the *unemployed, bachelors without income, students, privately paid teachers, gatekeepers, pensioners, retired soldiers, gravediggers* were predominant. The unemployed bachelors, which constitute the bulk of this group (68%) can be interpreted as a potential reserve labour force dependent upon irregular informal employment and/or upon charity. This group too was predominantly though not exclusively Muslim.

- The third component comprises 19.5% of taxable household heads specialized in manual jobs[19] and low-ranking routine service jobs and transportation. Orthodox

---

[19] In food production, textiles and clothing, petty production, construction, transportation and services.

Christians and Armenians and lower-middle occupational income earners are distinctively overrepresented. In this cluster, the bulk of petty producers are concentrated in a distinctive set of neighbourhoods.

- In spite of the obvious underrepresentation of Muslims the fourth component covering 20% of potential taxpayers[20] has a diversified ethno-religious composition. This component could easily be identified with comparatively higher occupational incomes, over-representation of services, trades and other non-manual jobs and a distinctive spatial deployment pattern.

- The bulk of employment in the fifth category was concentrated in those who worked in tedious and most probably unattractive jobs like porters, or slaughtermen. This component related to the lower rank of the urban labour market was patronized by the Jewish community and to a lesser degree by a definite stratum of Muslim taxpayers.

- The ethnic division of labour and communitarian patronage and social segregation is most visible in lower and unattractive ranks of the urban labour market and that it gradually fades away towards higher levels of income. The structure of the sixth component where the bulk of the *well-off* of Bursa is concentrated constitutes an undeniable evidence of this very interesting property. This last category is identifiable with an overrepresentation of taxpayers with high and highest occupational and household incomes, hence highest tax assessments, is to a large extent invisible in urban space with hardly any noticeable concentration in neighbourhoods and with no clear ethno-religious identity.

These are important and relevant conclusions capable to give a new impetus to comparative urban economic history. We are more than ready to admit that they are too general. But this is not a drawback of the applied methodology. The re-interpretation of the same data this time with respect to the stratification of individuals will surely alleviate this problem. This constitutes the second round of the study undertaken for this paper.

---

[20] In this paper the term we would in fact prefer is *contributable* instead of taxpayer, since we cannot know whether the assessed taxes have been collected or paid. Yet for the sake of simplicity we will use taxpayer.

A Second Look into Inhabitants of Bursa in 1845 via their Corresponding Modalities

In the following part, we will comment on 8 of 12 **groups** of observations. The MCA that we run created 12 sequential groups positioned along their economic indicators starting from the have-nots and the haves. In this part, our focus will be again on economic indicators and ethno-religious affiliations of the residents of Bursa. First, we would like to map ethno-religious belongings of our 5662 observations on neighbourhood level for Bursa.

MAP 2: Ethno-religious affiliations of Bursa residents in Neighbourhoods in 1845

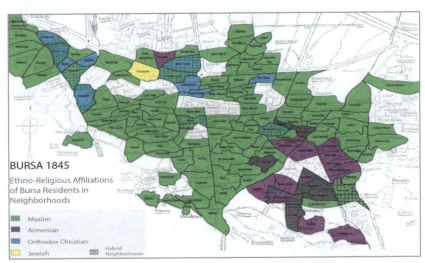

Since the registers are from 1845 and earliest detailed modern maps and plans of Ottoman cities are also from the second half of the nineteenth century it is also possible to map the information the *temettuat* registers convey on the occupational structure and ethno-religious composition of the neighbourhoods in Bursa.[21]

The earliest detailed cadastral plan of Bursa is from 1855 and there is also a detailed insurance map of the city with neighbourhoods from the 1880s. We used these two maps and

---

[21] A note is necessary for the blank spaces on the maps. Those are neighbourhoods, which do not correspond to the list of neighbourhoods in 1845 registers. All maps are works in progress and we would like to increase the quality and efficiency of the visualization of the information that the 1845 registers contain.

were able to locate 129 neighbourhoods of 142 listed in the *temettuat* registers of Bursa.[22] It can be seen that Bursa was a dominantly Muslim city with some mixed neighbourhoods. Those mixed ones were either Muslim-Orthodox Christian or Muslim-Armenian. The two Christian communities did not live together in any of the neighbourhoods and Jews had their own neighbourhood. If we leave aside one Armenian neighbourhood in the northwest all of the Armenian neighbourhoods are located in the southeast of the city. Of course, one should take into consideration that 13 neighbourhoods of Bursa could not be located on the map. Yet none of these neighbourhoods has mixed Armenian and Orthodox Christian inhabitants and no single Jewish household is registered there. Therefore, we can assume that if and when the missing neighbourhoods will be located the maps of ethno-religious distribution of neighbourhoods in urban space will not change drastically.

In the following, we will comment on the characteristics and locations of the members of 8 groups in the urban space of Bursa.

Group 1 (11x): *Lowest of the Low*/Roma of Bursa

Group 1 comprises 202 observations which makes 3.5% of Bursa. Although only 11.4% of the observations are Roma (k) in this group, all of the Roma of Bursa are included. This is one of the decisive modalities building this group in combination with zero household and occupational income as well as zero tax.

Table 1: Lowest of the Low/Roma of Bursa

Modalities (coded)	Modalities	PST 4digit	Cluster Membership	Counts of Modalities in Real Number in Group	% of the Group in Modality Total in Bursa	% of the Modality in Group	TOTAL in Bursa
er_6	Kıptiyan		3	23	100	11,4	23
er_1	Muslim		1	174	4,5	86,1	3905
hh_i_0	0		3	178	33,9	88,1	525
occ_i_0	0		3	200	14,3	99	1396
tax_0	0		3	155	13,9	76,7	1112
pst_4_206	no stated occupation or condition	99, 1, 0, 0	3	162	28,7	80,2	582
pst_4_209	beggar	99, 3, 2, 3	3	6	100	3	6

---

[22] We would like to thank Raif Kaplanoğlu for his generous support. His numerous publications and especially Raif Kaplanoğlu, *Bursa Yer Adları Ansiklopedisi* (Bursa: Bursa Ticaret Borsası Kültür Yayınları, 1996) and the maps therein were extremely helpful in preparing our map.

Not surprisingly, all of the 6 observations registered as beggars in Bursa are in this group. Similarly the entire population of the Roma neighbourhood (*Sinanbey*) falls in this group. Nevertheless residents from other neighbourhoods (*Veziri* and *Sarıabdullah*) are also included in this group. In the following map we have mapped the neighbourhoods, residents of which are also included in the group. We will map 5 groups or in other words neighbourhoods of these groups with 20% as the threshold of significance. Only the neighbourhoods with 20% or more of their residents included in the groups will be highlighted in the maps.

MAP 3: Lowest of the low / Roma of Bursa

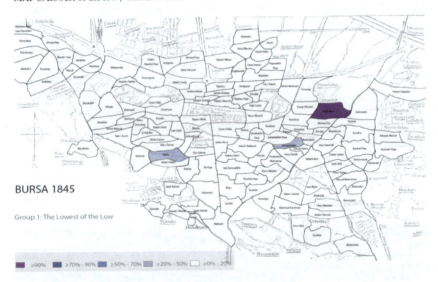

The map above shows both the location and the concentration of the poorest of the poor in Bursa. Although small in its size 99% of the occupational income of the observations in this group falls into the category of no income. 88.1% of the household income entries of the observations is also in no income category. All of the Roma (k) of Bursa are living in *Sinanbey* neighbourhood and all of the residents of this neighbourhood are Roma and all of them belong to the lowest of economic indicator categories. In addition to the Roma residents of *Sinanbey* 174 Muslim residents of two neighbourhoods (*Veziri* and *Sarıabdullah*) are also in this group of the lowest of the low, which show a high spatial concentration of extreme poverty in Bursa in 1845.

Group 2 (6x): Non-working, Non-earning Muslims

Group 2 comprises 614 observations which makes 10.8% of Bursa. The observations in this group are from a similar economic profile like the first one above. The decisive difference is that less than half of the observations fall into the category of zero household income. The observations are residents of 61 neighbourhoods and do not show a level of geographical concentration as Group 1. The similarity with Group 1 is that almost entire observations in Group 2 (99.8% of a larger set) have not stated that they are receiving any occupational income.

TABLE 2: Non-working, non-earning Muslims

Modalities (coded)	Modalities	PST 4digit	Cluster Membership	Counts of Modalities in Real Number in Group	% of the Group in Modality Total in Bursa	% of the Modality in Group	TOTAL in Bursa
er_1	Muslim		1	558	14,3	90,9	3905
hh_i_0	0		3	281	53,5	45,8	525
occ_i_0	0		3	613	43,9	99,8	1396
tax_0	0		3	198	17,8	32,2	1112
pst_4_206	no stated occupation or condition	99, 1, 0, 0	3	340	58,4	55,4	582
pst_4_209	Religion	5, 35, 3, 0	3	25	37,9	4,1	66
pst_4_207	Age, sickness, poverty	99, 3, 2, 0	3	15	38,5	2,4	39

If we map the neighbourhoods whose residents are included in Group 2 we see that all of the neighbourhoods in the group are in the range of 20 to 50%. In none of the neighbourhoods more than half of the residents fall into Group 2.

Although around 9% of the observations in this group are non-Muslims, we can still argue that this group comprises mainly of Muslims without any stated occupational income. They are Muslims because Muslims make 91% of this group, whereas around 70% of the observations are Muslim in the city. They are without any occupational income because no stated occupational income in Bursa is around 25% and in this there is only 1 observation out of 614 with a stated occupational income. It is obvious that stating no occupational income in a tax survey does not mean that people were not making any income in their occupations. However, such a high concentration (99.8%) is surely significant to group these observations into one category. What we can say about the distribution of these residents is twofold. They are not concentrated in limited numbers of neighbourhoods. They are not concentrated in any part of the city. Their relative absence in the southeast can be explained by the higher share of Armenians in that part of the city.

MAP 4 Non-working, non-earning Muslims[23]

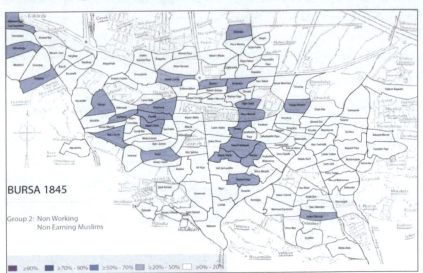

Group 3 (8x): Low-earning, Low-income Muslims

Group 3 comprises 1687 observations which makes 29.7% of Bursa. The one-third of city residents falling into this group can be identified as Muslims (99.2% of the 1687 observations are Muslims. There are only 2 oc and 11 a in this group). In a similar level of significance 99.3% of the observations in this group belongs to the low household income bracket. Not as close to 100% yet with 93.5% still remarkably high is the concentration of low-income occupations in the group. Similarly, 90.2% of the observations in this group falls to the lowest tax bracket.

---

[23] As mentioned before not all of the neighbourhoods included in the tax survey could be located. One such neighbourhood is *Semerci*. Furthermore, there is also a separate register, which covers Armenian agricultural workers. The observations in this register can also not be located yet all other 23 neighbourhoods having more than half of their residents are on the map above.

TABLE 3: Low-earning, low-income Muslims

Modalities (coded)	Modalities	PST 4digit	Cluster Membership	Counts of Modalities in Real Number in Group	% of the Group in Modality Total in Bursa	% of the Modality in Group	TOTAL in Bursa
er_1	Muslim		1	1674	42,9	99,2	3905
hh_i_1	0-1045		1	1675	39,1	99,3	4284
occ_i_1	0-520		1	1577	50,7	93,5	3110
tax_1	0-83		1	1521	40,7	90,2	3740
pst_4_58	textile fabric maker	2, 20, 0, 15	1	199	79	11,8	252
pst_4_3	minor, crops, labourer	1, 1, 1, 30	1	204	50,9	12,1	401
pst_4_12	wood cutter	1, 3, 0, 1	1	71	58,2	4,2	122
pst_4_80	blacksmith	2, 61, 0, 1	1	41	68,3	2,4	60
pst_4_143	barber	5, 20, 1, 1	1	71	53,4	4,2	133

Therefore, we can safely claim that one-third of Bursa residents are Muslims with low paid occupations having a low level of household income and paying low taxes. If we focus on these occupations, we can state that the category of fabric makers (*dolapçı*), blacksmiths, woodcutters, barbers and agricultural labourers is heavily overrepresented. There are 252 *dolapçı* in Bursa and 199 of them are in this group. Similarly, 41 of 60 ironsmiths and 71 of 122 woodcutters and 71 of 133 barbers are in this group. These four occupations are low paid occupations held by Muslims in Bursa.

The distribution of observations in Group 3, which constitutes around 30% of the residents in the city, shows that this Low earning Muslims are spread in the city. Only *Hoca Menteş* neighbourhood stands apart with having more than 90% of its residents in this group. All other neighbourhoods can have varying shares. Again, the relative absence of these neighbourhoods in the southeast, where Armenian neighbourhoods are concentrated, can be observed similar to the group of non-working, non-earning Muslims.

MAP 5: Low earning, low income Muslims[24]

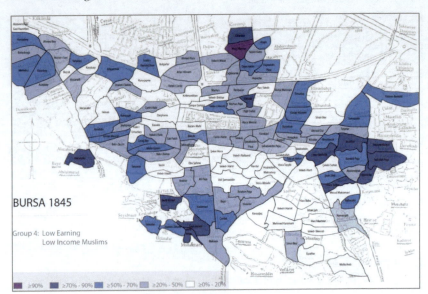

Group 4 (4x): Low-earning, Low-income Christians

This group comprises 875 observations 15.4% of the city population. Around 99% of the observations in this group are non-Muslims (48.5 Orthodox Christian and 50.4 Armenian). The occupations, which are heavily overrepresented in the group, are boatman, builder, tailor and general labourers. Taking into joint consideration with the previous group low-earning, low-income Christians we can claim that religion but not the ethnicity is a constituting element of occupational choices in Bursa for some occupations. Muslims dominated the occupations listed in that group and non-Muslims the ones in this group. Due to the 99% Muslim concentration in Group 3 and 99% non-Muslim concentration in this group we can safely assume that for the listed occupations being Muslim or not were decisive. This does not mean that all of the Bursa residents in those occupations were from the corresponding religious affiliation, however, an important part of the practitioners were either Muslim or non-Muslim. Almost all of 140 boatmen in Bursa were either Orthodox Christian or Armenian (123). In a similar manner the vast majority of 141

---

[24] There are only two neighbourhoods (*Abbas Bey Fenari* and *Semerci*) missing on this map. 89 neighbourhoods could be located.

tailors were Christians too (97). Nevertheless, if we compare Group 3 to 4 we can also suggest that for the observations in this groups religion mattered for concentrations in certain occupations but not for the levels of income. Observations in these two categories stated low-occupational and household incomes, around to 90% in both of the groups. The fact that our MCA built this half Orthodox Christian half Armenian group is a strong indicator that these two religious affiliations did go hand in hand with similar modalities.

TABLE 4: Low-earning, low-income Christians

Modalities (coded)	Modalities	PST 4digit	Cluster Membership	Counts of Modalities in Real Number in Group	% of the Group in Modality Total in Bursa	% of the Modality in Group	TOTAL in Bursa
er_2	Orthodox Christian		2	424	70,5	48,5	601
er_3	Armenian		2	441	51,2	50,4	862
hh_i_1	0-1045		1	817	19,1	93,4	4284
occ_i_1	0-520		1	771	24,8	88,1	3110
tax_1	0-83		1	712	19	81,4	3740
pst_4_200	boatmen	6, 3, 0, 1	2	123	87,9	14,1	140
pst_4_102	builder	2, 80, 1, 1	2	71	86,6	8,1	82
pst_4_31	tailor	2, 10, 1, 1	2	97	68,8	11,1	141
pst_4_204	labourer	90, 0 ,0 ,30	2	32	76,2	3,7	141

If we compare the map below with MAP 3 the total number of neighbourhoods having more than 20% of their residents in this group is lower. However, this is natural according to the Muslim, non-Muslims share of the population shares in the entire city. Group 4 is around half of Group 3. Regarding the concentration of neighbourhoods related to this group we can argue that they are close to the parts of the city where non-Muslims used to live, which is not surprising. What is important here is that they do not concentrate in few neighbourhoods but in many. There are two Armenian neighbourhoods *Molla Arab* and *Çelebi Sultan* and two Orthodox Christian one *Buçuk* and *Hacı Yakup* which were not in close proximity but having more than 90% of their residents in this group. This aspect is the visualization of our comments to the Table 4 that not being Orthodox Christian or Armenian but being Muslim or non-Muslim is a constituting element for this group.

MAP 6 Low earning, low income Christians[25]

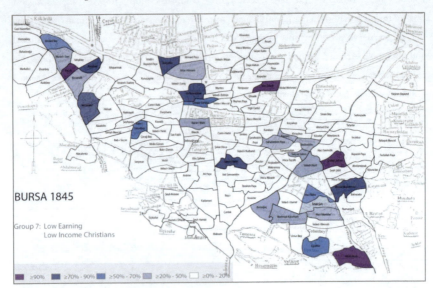

Group 5 (1x): Porters and Slaughter-men

This group is a relatively small one having 149 observations and 2.6% of the city population. Its significance comes from the occupational specialization, especially of porters and of slaughter-men. In spite of its very limited size this group compromises around the 60% of the porters and half of the slaughter-men of the entire city. With around 87% Muslims are also overrepresented in this group.

TABLE 5: Porters and slaughter-men

Modalities (coded)	Modalities	PST 4digit	Cluster Membership	Counts of Modalities in Real Number in Group	% of the Group in Modality Total in Bursa	% of the Modality in Group	TOTAL in Bursa
er_1	Muslim		1	129	3,3	86,6	3905
hh_i_1	0-1045		1	139	3,2	93,3	4284
tax_1	0-83		1	114	3	76,5	3740
pst_4_196	porter	6, 0, 0, 10	5	43	60,6	28,9	71

[25] We could locate 28 neighbourhoods contributing to this group with more than 20% of their residents. Locations of 4 registers could not be mapped: *Ahmed Bey Fenari*, Armenian agricultural workers, Armenian tenants, miscellaneous Non-Muslims.

| pst_4_23 | slaughter-man | 2, 1, 4, 1 | 5 | 32 | 48,5 | 21,5 | 66 |

The observations in this group are not concentrated in any neighbourhood. Therefore, we will not map the distribution of this group. Being not spatially but occupationally concentrated is rather a curious result for porters and slaughter-man. Case studies on these occupations in Bursa can reveal the dynamics behind this concentration.

Group 6 (10x): Jewish Silk Manufacturers, Small Traders and Commercial Agents of Bursa in *Kuruçeşme*

This group is the only mono-religious and simultaneously the only mono-neighbourhood one. It comprises 202 of 205 Jews in Bursa. It has only those Jews and no one else in it. It has 202 residents of 203 residents of Kuruçeşme neighbourhood. With 202 observations it corresponds to 3.6% of the city population.

TABLE 6: Jewish silk manufacturers, small traders and commercial agents of Bursa in Kuruçeşme

Modalities (coded)	Modalities	PST 4digit	Cluster Membership	Counts of Modalities in Real Number in Group	% of the Group in Modality Total in Bursa	% of the Modality in Group	TOTAL in Bursa
er_5	Jewish		5	202	98,5	100	205
hh_i_1	0-1045		1	176	4,1	87,1	4284
occ_i_1	0-520		1	153	4,9	75,7	3110
occ_i_4	2500-4000		6	3	6,5	1,5	46
tax_1	0-83		1	157	4,2	77,7	3740
tax_3	225-435		6	8	5,8	4	137
pst_4_135	peddler	4, 90, 1, 1	5	31	68,9	15,3	45
pst_4_54	silk manu-facturer	2, 20, 7, 0	5	30	48,4	14,9	62
pst_4_89	tinsmith	2, 62, 3, 0	5	9	100	4,5	9
pst_4_163	commercial agent	5, 31, 4, 60	5	23	40,4	11,4	57
pst_4_196	porter	6, 0, 0, 10	5	21	29,6	10,4	71

The confessional and spatial concentration of 4 occupations is worth reporting in detail. Although *Kuruçeşme* is only one neighbourhood and in this group, we have around one-third of 1% of city residents, we have all of the tinsmiths, around 70% of all peddlers, 50% of all silk manufacturers, 40% of all commercial agents and 30% of all porters in Bursa. Bursa was the capital of Ottoman silk production. Now we can clearly state Jews of Bursa living in only one neighbourhood and constituting a minuscule part of the city population were engaged in silk production so heavily that around half of the silk manufacturers were Jewish. Alongside and in fact parallel to this their extreme over-representation in commercial agents clearly argues for Jewish success in occupying these prestigious occupations. We clearly see an ethno-religious division of labour here. However, this does not mean that the Jewish community was the richest in Bursa. To contrary there is only 1 Jew in Group 8 with the highest earners and 2 in the first group with no income at all. In the above main group of Jews 153 of 202 stated that they had the lowest occupational income.[26]

MAP 7: Jewish silk manufacturers, small traders and commercial agents of Bursa in Kuruçeşme

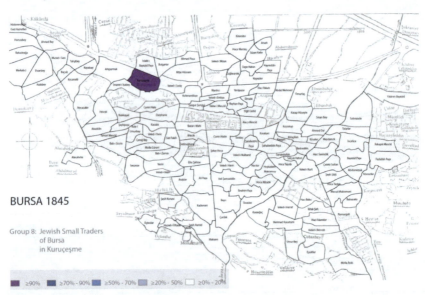

Although it superfluous to map one neighbourhood we still wanted to do this do locate the Jewish neighbourhood, i.e. Group 6 which is so distinct in its composition of modalities that *Kuruçeşme* neighbourhood will not be included by any other group.

---

[26] These observations are in accord with the findings of Dilek Akyalçın Kaya who is building her expertise on mid-nineteenth century Salonica and Jews of Salonica. See Dilek Akyalçın Kaya, "'Living off Others' Aid': The Socioeconomic Structure of Salonica's Jews in the Mid-Nineteenth Century," *Jewish History*, no. 3–4 (2014): 313.

Group 7 (7x): Christian Medium income Dealers of Textiles

In this group we see that a relatively small group of observations (with 293 observations, around 5% of total residents) was almost exclusively non-Muslim and concentrating on medium household incomes.

TABLE 7: Christian medium income dealers of textiles

Modalities (coded)	Modalities	PST 4digit	Cluster Membership	Counts of Modalities in Real Number in Group	% of the Group in Modality Total in Bursa	% of the Modality in Group	TOTAL in Bursa
er_3	Armenian		2	189	21,9	64,5	862
er_2	Orthodox Christian		2	93	15,5	31,7	601
hh_i_2	1045-2720		4	155	22,1	52,9	701
occ_i_2	520-1300		2	182	21,3	62,1	853
occ_i_3	1300-2500		4	49	21,5	16,7	228
tax_2	83-225		4	166	26,6	56,7	625
tax_3	225-435		6	13	9,5	4,4	137
pst_4_122	cloth dealer	3, 20, 0, 1	4	58	69	19,8	84
pst_4_133	sellers of clothing	4, 10, 1, 0	4	26	68,4	8,9	38
pst_4_21	baker	2, 1, 2, 1	4	28	57,1	9,6	49
pst_4_72	jeweller	2, 50, 0, 0	4	19	46,3	6,5	41
pst_4_46	cloth maker	2, 20, 0, 15	6	19	41,3	6,5	46

Few observations in this minute group of Orthodox-Christians and Armenians managed to establish themselves in few occupations. They made around 70% of all cloth dealers in the city. Similarly and logically in terms of vertical integration they also made the same percentage of sellers of clothing and around 40% of occupations in cloth-making. The other occupations where they had their strong presence were bakers and jewellers. This small group of Armenians and Orthodox Christians had the control of dealing in cloths and clothing. However, although these occupations secured them medium income levels they were not among the highest earners in the city.

The map shows the predominance of Christians and especially Armenians in this group. Only Bazar-ı Mahi is a Muslim neighbourhood. Hoca Tayyib, Karaağaç, Selçuk, Veled-i Kurt are Armenian, Mehmet Karamani an Armenian/Muslim and Şangur Şungur an Orthodox-Christian neighbourhood.

MAP 8: Christian medium income dealers of textiles[27]

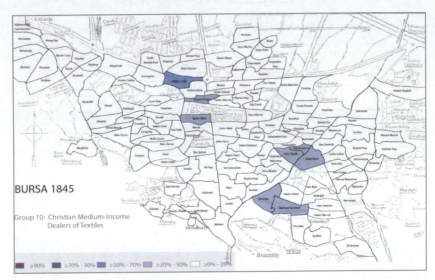

Group 8 (12x): The Highest Earners

This last group is the smallest of all, with only 42 observations it is less than 1%. These observations are rich and the elite of the city. Their income levels cover the highest brackets. 28 of 29 highest occupational income and 11 of 15 highest household income holders are in this tiny group. Their wealth is also reflected in the tax levels. Half of the second highest and all of the highest taxpayers of the entire city are among them.

TABLE 8: The highest earners

Modalities (coded)	Modalities	PST 4digit	Cluster Membership	Counts of Modalities in Real Number in Group	% of the Group in Modality Total in Bursa	% of the Modality in Group	TOTAL in Bursa
er_2	Orthodox Christian		2	10	1,7	23,8	601
er_4	Catholic		4	2	3	4,8	66
er_3	Armenian		2	11	1,3	26,2	862
hh_i_4	5130-8440		6	17	68	40,5	25
hh_i_5	>8440		6	11	73,3	26,2	15
hh_i_3	2720-5130		6	14	12,5	33,3	112
occ_i_5	>4000		6	28	96,6	66,7	29

[27] There is only one neighbourhood (*Balıkcık*) which we could not locate.

occ_i_4	2500-4000		6	12	26,1	28,6	46
tax_4	435-750		6	22	51,2	52,4	43
tax_5	750-1210		6	5	100	11,9	5
pst_4_123	silk dealer	3, 20, 7, 1	6	7	38,9	16,7	18
pst_4_46	cloth maker	2, 20, 0, 15	6	9	19,6	21,4	46
pst_4_113	Merchant	3, 0, 0, 3	4	6	14	14,3	43
pst_4_117	coffee dealer	3, 2, 3, 3	6	1	50	2,4	2
pst_4_155	stock broker	5, 30, 2, 2	6	1	50	2,4	2
pst_4_78	candle maker	2, 55, 8, 2,	6	1	50	2,4	2
pst_4_21	Baker	2, 1, 2, 1	4	4	8,2	9,5	49

The observations in this group are also heavily represented in high earning trading activities and services. 1 of 2 stockbrokers, 1 of 2 coffee dealers, and 1 of 2 candle makers of the city are in this group. Similarly, 6 of 18 silk dealers are among them.

Their ethno-religious make up is striking as well. The richest residents of Bursa have members of almost every ethno-religious group. Not surprisingly there are no Roma among them, since all of the Roma are in the first group, which we called the lowest of the low. In the richest group we have 18 Muslims, 11 Armenians, 10 Orthodox Christians, 2 Catholics and 1 Jew. At least for the mid-nineteenth century Bursa we can say that ethno-religious affiliation was not a very strong barrier of entry if one was not Roma, who were discriminated severely from all strata of economic and social life.

Conclusion

As mentioned above in our conclusion we will focus on the ethno-religious division of labour debate and also in a related manner the old, conventional yet not empirically tested claims that non-Muslim communities were the agents and beneficiaries of economic and social modernization in the late Ottoman Empire. This thesis has been formulated in several epochs of Ottoman historiography and came to fore with the Wallersteinian incorporation argument, which can be summarized as the integration of the Ottoman lands into the world system as a semi-periphery. Ottoman historians have closely followed Wallerstein and his theory in the 1990s. This academic opening created both new productive perspectives as well as hastily reached conclusions with claims of empire-wide validity. The thesis of the enrichment or take-off of non-Muslims is still a disputed topic.[28] Thanks to the analytical capabilities of MCA for the very first time the entire household-heads of a major Ottoman city could be analysed by taking into consideration various variables including their ethno-religious affiliations, economic indicators, occupations and the neighbourhoods under which they were registered. Our conclusions on the role of ethnicity and religion on economic well-being are too complex and from our perspective too sophisticated to approve or disapprove of simplified claims in the literature. We would like to stress that our results stem from and therefore could only be valid for mid-nineteenth century Bursa. Ethnicity mattered a lot for the Roma of Bursa. They were as a community entirely trapped in poverty just being lumped together with the poorest of the poor. Roma were not on a lower status then the poorest Muslims in Group 1. However, there was no single exception to their discrimination. No Roma could go beyond the lowest level of economic class in Bursa.

In Group 2 (Non-working, non-earning Muslims), Group 3 (Low-earning, low-income Muslims), and 4 (Low-earning, low-income Christians) we saw that religion played a role in bringing residents of Bursa together or apart as one of the factors. However, being Muslim or Christian did not result in different levels of earnings. These three groups comprise in total 56% of Bursa's population (3176 of 5662), which were mainly low earning first and belonging to Muslim or Christian confessions as of secondary importance. On the other hand, being Jewish was a completely different matter in the mid-nineteenth century Bursa. It did not bring along that the relatively small Jewish community was better off. Being Jewish in Bursa meant to live in one neighbourhood and having an occupation chosen from a smaller set than the one available for others. Yet those occupations could be prestigious or ordinary.

For a small group of Christians (Group 8 with 293 observations) being Orthodox Christian or Armenian was evidently related to being active in medium earning tertiary sector professions especially in trading textiles in Bursa. As an industrial and specifically textile city being able to sell those products was surely advantageous to make a better living than the average. For this group we can claim that being a Christian was probably not a hindrance but maybe a facilitator. However, the fact that we are only talking about around 5% of the residents with medium income does not

---

[28] Kasaba is one of the early introducers of the topic into the literature. Reşat Kasaba, "Was there a Comprador Bourgeoisie in mid-19th c. Western Anatolia?", *Review* 11, no. 2 (1988): 215–30. One of the most recent contributors to this debate is Timur Kuran, *The Long Divergence: How Islamic Law Held Back the Middle East* (Princeton, Oxford: Princeton University Press, 2011), especially chapter 10 "The Ascent of the Middle East's Religious Minorities" therein.

support the argument that non-Muslims were better off in Anatolia due to their cultural and linguistic connections to the *West*.

The smallest but most powerful group (Group 8) was comprised of a real mix of ethno-religious communities with two missing ones. We have already mentioned the position of the Roma. There was only one Jewish resident who could be one of the 42 wealthiest. Regarding the small share of the Jewish community this is not so surprising. What we would like to highlight here is that to be among the richest religion and ethnicity was surely important yet within the interaction of other factors and not as sole determinants. Reaching the highest echelons of socio-economic classes in Bursa was definitely not a religious neutral process but also not segregated along ethno-religious affiliations.

Lastly, on ethno-religious division of labour or the importance of ethno-religious affiliations for occupational choices we can say the conventional argument has taken ethnicity and religion as points of departure and main determinants of occupational chances and choices. We argue that historians should enlarge their data and mind-sets. Only after a thorough analysis of a given urban economy or a regional economy one can reach to conclusions about the role of ethnicity and religion in occupations. In Bursa for a very small number of occupations we could verify the importance of ethno-religious affiliations. Yet our results only hint at the importance of these factors for those occupations in Bursa in 1845. It would be ahistorical and wrong to overgeneralize the findings coming out of this set of variables to other locations in the Ottoman Empire even just for the year 1845.

Archival Documents

Temettuat registers of Bursa from the Ottoman State Archives in Istanbul:
ML. VRD. TMT. d. 7362, 7363, 7364, 7365, 7367, 7368, 7369, 7370, 7371, 7373, 7375, 7376, 7381, 7382, 7383, 7386, 7387, 7391, 7392, 7393, 7394, 7395, 7399, 7400, 7402, 7405, 7407, 7408, 7409, 7410, 7411, 7412, 7414, 7415, 7416, 7418, 7420, 7422, 7423, 7426, 7427, 7428, 7429, 7430, 7431, 7432, 7438, 7439, 7441, 7442, 7443, 7444, 7445, 7447, 7448, 7449, 7450, 7451, 7453, 7454, 7455, 7457, 7459, 7461, 7462, 7464, 7465, 7466, 7467, 7468, 7469, 7470, 7471, 7472, 7473, 7475, 7476, 7477, 7479, 7481, 7484, 7485, 7486, 7490, 7491, 7492, 7495, 7496, 7497, 7498, 7499, 7500, 7501, 7502, 7503, 7504, 7505, 7506, 7508, 7509, 7515, 7516, 7517, 7518, 7519, 7520, 7521, 7522, 7523, 7524, 7525, 7526, 7528, 7530, 7532, 7533, 7534, 7535, 7538, 7539, 7540, 7541, 7546, 7547, 7548, 7550, 7551, 7553, 7554, 7555, 7556, 7559, 7561, 7562, 7563, 7564, 7565, 7566, 7567, 7569, 7570, 7571, 7572, 16039, 16040, 16041, 16042, 17605, 17608.

Population registers of Bursa from the Ottoman State Archives in Istanbul:
NFS. d. 1396, 1398.

Archaeological Perspectives for Climate Change and Human Impacts on the Environment: An Agent-Based Modeling Approach

Bülent Arıkan

Abstract

While scholars have been discussing the impact of human societies on the environment since the Industrial Revolution, the body of literature on the history of ancient human impacts in different parts of the world continues to grow. In these discussions, the emerging consensus is that the wide range of anthropogenic impacts relates to the level of social organization, which defines the scale of human land and resource use. Using computational modeling methods, it is now possible to simulate complex, dynamic, and non-linear processes in a given environment at a given time that occur naturally or are due to anthropogenic influence. In the broadest sense, it is possible to divide models into two groups: (1) stochastic models only focus on one variable (e.g., change in precipitation) and apply random variations to estimate the end result with other variables and (2) agent-based models (ABMs) that are capable of estimating changes in a multitude of social, economic and environmental variables across time and space. The latter can simulate the dynamic and recursive real-world processes. Models, both ABMs and stochastic models, represent new approaches in interpreting multifaceted, interdisciplinary data in archaeology. The use of models and the mindset behind modeling not only allow researchers to display the long-term interactions among numerous variables but they also enable us to examine the emergent properties, which only surface in time and as a result of interaction between variables. Observing these qualities, experimenting with the variables that have greater significance for humans, socio-ecological research advances by developing a better and more complete understanding about how human societies made decisions and how the results of these decisions impacted them in the long-term. Consequently, it is possible to discuss the sustainability of ancient economic and social practices in specific spatial and temporal contexts.

1. Introduction

1.1. Models in Archaeology

While scholars have been discussing the impact of human societies on the environment since the Industrial Revolution, the body of literature on the history of ancient human impacts in different parts of the world continues to grow.[1] In these discussions, the emerging consensus is that the wide range of anthropogenic impacts relates to the level of social organization, which defines the scale of human land and resource use.[2]

---

[1] C. Michael Barton, Isaac I. Ullah and Sean Bergin, 2010. "Land Use, water and Mediterranean landscapes: Modeling long-term dynamics of complex socio-ecological systems," *Philosophical Transactions of Royal Society A* 368, no. 1931(2010): 5275-5297; C. T. Fisher, J. B. Hill and G. M. Feinman, eds., *The Archaeology of Environmental Change. Socionatural Legacies of Degradation and Resilience* (Tucson: University of Arizona Press, 2009); Sander Van der Leeuw, amd J. McGlade, *Archaeology: Time, Process and Structural Transformations* (London: Routledge, 1998); Sander Van der Leeuw, Charles L. Redman, "Placing archaeology at the center of socio-natural studies," *American Antiquity* 67, no. 4(2002): 597-605.

[2] Fisher, Hill and Feinman, *The Archaeology of Environmental Change*; J. B. Hill, *Human Ecology in the Wadi al-Hasa. Land*

Using computational modeling methods, it is now possible to simulate complex, dynamic, and non-linear processes in a given environment at a given time that occur naturally or are due to anthropogenic influence. In the broadest sense, it is possible to divide models into two groups: (1) stochastic models only focus on one variable (e.g., change in precipitation) and apply random variations to estimate the end result with other variables and (2) agent-based models (ABMs) that are capable of estimating changes in a multitude of social, economic and environmental variables across time and space. The latter can simulate the dynamic and recursive real-world processes.

1.2. What Models Are and Are not

Modeling of human-environment relationships is complex due to the multidimensional nature of the processes involved in it. In socio-natural systems, there is a whole suite of dynamic variables, mechanisms, and relationships that change spatio-temporally. Although representing all these in a single model is not possible and it is harder to verify the results of a model, computational models are especially useful in exploring the parameters and relationships in prehistory where we lack a better understanding of the results of such interactions. Coupled human-natural systems have non-linear relationships and models allow us to observe emergent properties: phenomena, which cannot be predicted at the start of the model and develop within the system over time. ABMs simulate these social and natural emergent behaviors at the local scale.

Modeling is an iterative process and it allows us to test the scale and intensity of the impact of a wide variety of parameters (e.g., population, subsistence, climate, etc.). Relying on the model results, it is possible to draw explicit interconnections with the past. Consequently, ABMs also provide a connection with the distant past at a conceptual level, which enables us to better understand decisions and limitations the ancient cultures had to face. Modeling is a powerful tool and models must function as hypothetical scenarios. The model results should be compared against the archaeological data and it is possible to falsify the implications of the model through such comparisons. Verifying a model is not possible in general due to the incomplete nature of the archaeological record.

1.3. The Benefits of Models in Archaeology

Based on the basic description of what models are and how they can be used in archaeology, it becomes apparent that this method represents a new approach in interpreting the

---

Use and Abandonment through the Holocene (Tucson: University of Arizona Press, 2006).

archaeological data. Three outstanding benefits of modeling in archaeology will be reiterated here. First, through the application of conceptual modeling, researchers can develop a connection with prehistoric societies where their relationships with the environment, decision-making processes, and strengths/limitations can be understood in their natural and social setting. Second, models allow researchers to observe emergent behaviors at a local scale, something that is not common in archaeology due to the incomplete nature of data. Additional data from models help us develop a more complete interpretation of data. Third, modeling gives researchers an opportunity to experiment with a wide variety of parameters in order to observe their wider impacts in socio-natural systems. Consequently, archaeological research gains an experimental nature where human-environment interactions are assessed using controlled experiments.

1.4. The Goals and Foci This Paper

This paper focuses on the agent-based modeling that is used for the research of the dynamic interactions among the climate, population, and land cover during the Early Bronze Age-I (ca. 5000–4750 cal. BP) at the site of Arslantepe, in the Malatya Plain of eastern Anatolia.

Through ABM, this research aims to answer two basic but interrelated questions: first, to what degree the Malatya Plain might have changed due to natural factors (e.g. changes in surface processes due to fluctuations in precipitation) during the Early Bronze Age-I. The second research question assesses the impacts of extensive agropastoralism on the biodiversity of Arslantepe's immediate environment during the Early Bronze Age-I. For this research, biodiversity is defined as the number of land cover classes (see Research Method) and the amount of area (in square meters) they cover at the end of each simulation: the higher the number of classes, the higher the biodiversity. ABMs will be run for the whole duration of the Early Bronze Age-I (i.e., 250 years).

Modeling results enable us to critically assess two important issues directly affecting the sociopolitical evolution of human societies. First, it is possible to quantify the rate of change in surface processes under different climatic conditions.[3] Significantly different climatic conditions

---

[3] C. Alvaro, "Architecture and the organization of space," in *Economic Centralization in Formative States. The Archaeological Reconstruction of the Economic System in 4th millennium Arslantepe*, ed. M. Frangipane (Roma: Sapienza Università di Roma, 2010), 45-71.; L. Bartosiewicz, "Herding in Period VI A. Development and changes from Period VII," in Ibid., 119-148.; C. Kuzucuoğlu and C. Marro, eds., *Sociétés Humaines Et Changement Climatique A La Fin Du Troisième Millénaire: Une Crise A-t-Elle Eu Lieu En Haute Mesopotamie?* (Istanbul: Institut Français d'Études Anatoliennes-Georges Dumézil, 2007); Neil Roberts, Warren J. Eastwood, Catherine Kuzucuoğlu, Girolamo Fiorentino, and Valentina Caracuta, "Climatic, vegetation and cultural change in the eastern Mediterranean during the mid-Holocene environmental transition," *Holocene* 21, no. 1(2011): 147-162.

directly affect hydrology, which then causes surface processes like *erdep* to adjust to new circumstances. Under arid conditions, the drop in the water table causes increased channeling in rivers, and *erdep* rates thus increase. In the Near East, multiproxy paleoenvironmental reconstructions suggest major periods of drought since the start of the Holocene, one of which is known as the 4.2 kyr BP event.[4] Although it has been suggested that this event was widespread,[5] recent research focusing on local climate histories in Mesopotamia reveals a more complex picture.[6]

The paleoclimate and landscape evolution models during the Bronze Age allow us to test the presence of this event in these parts of the Near East as well as assess the impacts of such climatic events on different landscapes (i.e. woodland, grassland, and shrub) through changes in *erdep* rates. Second, using results of the extensive agropastoral land use simulations, it is possible to model the environmental impacts of EBA human societies under different climatic conditions, at different population densities, and in various environmental settings (i.e., types of land cover).

2. The Regional Context

2.1. Topography and Land Cover

The Malatya Plain is a well-watered karstic formation in the northern extremity of northern Mesopotamia. The Plain provides access to central Anatolia, northern Mesopotamia, and the Caucasus through valleys in multiple directions. Consequently, the Malatya Plain became a hub for long-distance trade and cultural interactions from different regions of southwest Asia in antiquity.[7]

Even after thousands of years of human impact, biodiversity in the Malatya Plain remains high. This is mainly because the Plain is in a transition zone between the forested northern Mesopotamia to the steppe of the Caucasus. Additionally, the significant range of elevation within the Plain makes it ideal for a wide variety of plants and animals. This situation has been well-

---

[4] H. Weiss, M.-A. Courty, W. Wetterstrom, F. Guichard, L. Senior, R. Meadow and A. Curnow, "The genesis and collapse of Third Millennium north Mesopotamian civilization," *Science* 261, no. 5124 (August 1993): 995-1004.
[5] Ibid.
[6] Kuzucuoğlu and Marro, *Sociétés Humaines Et Changement Climatique A La Fin Du Troisième Millénaire*.
[7] M. Frangipane, "Arslantepe. Growth and collapse of an early centralized system: the archaeological evidence, in *Economic Centralization in Formative States. The Archaeological Reconstruction of the Economic System in 4th millennium Arslantepe*, ed. M. Frangipane (Rome: Sapienza Università di Roma, 2010), 23–42; Francesca Balossi Restelli, L. Sandori and Alessia Masi, "Agriculture at the end of 4th Millennium BC. Did the centralized political institutions have an influence on farming practices?" in Ibid., 103–118.

documented for the period of interest through multiproxy-based paleoenvironmental reconstructions.[8] Results also suggest that the middle Holocene climatic changes from warm and wet to warm and dry led to a significant change in the land cover.[9] The semi-open coniferous forest of the early Late Chalcolithic (5750 cal. BP) was replaced by open grassland by the end of this period (ca. 5000 cal. BP).[10] Due to a combination of natural and anthropogenic factors, this was replaced by woodland steppe during the EBA.[11]

3. Research Method

The agent-based model used in this research has been developed by a group of anthropological archaeologists, historians, ecologists, geologists, and computer scientists at Arizona State University with grants from the National Science Foundation. The MedLanD Modeling Library (MML) uses geographical information systems (GIS) in order to map changes in the mean annual precipitation and temperature (with the help of a paleoclimate model), soil fertility, mean annual agropastoral production, population, land cover, and rates of erosion-deposition. The main sources of data in simulating these complex and dynamic relationships among natural and anthropogenic interactions are archaeology, paleoproxies (i.e., palynology, geoarchaeology, stable isotope), paleoethnobotany, zooarchaeology, and ethnoarchaeology.

The MedLanD Modeling Library attempts to simulate three main variables. The first one is the economic variable. In this context, MML focuses on simulating the decision-making processes for land and other types of resource use, the impacts of agropastoralism on the land cover, and both intended and unintended consequences of decisions.[12] The temporal changes in

---

[8] Alvaro, "Architecture and the organization of space," 45-71; A. Masi, L. Sadori, I. Baneschi, A. M. Siani and G. Zanchetta, "Stable isotope analysis of archaeological oak charcoal from eastern Anatolia as a marker of mid-Holocene climate changes," *Plant Biology* 15, supplement 1 (2012): 1-10.; A. Masi, L. Sadori, G. Zanchetta, I. Baneschi and M. Giardini, "Climatic interpretation of carbon isotope content of mid-Holocene archaeological charcoals from eastern Anatolia," *Quaternary International* 303(July 2013): 64-72; L. Sadori and A. Masi, "Archaeobotanical research at Arslantepe: Traditional approach and new challenges," *Origini* 34 (2012): 433-446.
[9] Sadori and Masi, "Archaeobotanical research at Arslantepe: Traditional approach and new challenges," 433-446.
[10] Masi, Sadori, Zanchetta, Baneschi and Giardini, "Climatic interpretation of carbon isotope content of mid-Holocene archaeological charcoals from eastern Anatolia," 64-72; Sadori and A. Masi, "Archaeobotanical research at Arslantepe: Traditional approach and new challenges," *Origini* 34 (2012): 433-446.
[11] Masi, Sadori, Baneschi, Siani and Zanchetta, "Stable isotope analysis of archaeological oak charcoal from eastern Anatolia as a marker of mid-Holocene climate changes," 1-10; Sadori and A. Masi, "Archaeobotanical research at Arslantepe: Traditional approach and new challenges," *Origini* 34 (2012): 433-446.
[12] I. I. T. Ullah, *The Consequences of Human Land Use Strategies During the PPHN-B-LN Transition in Northern Jordan: A Simulation Modeling Approach*. Doctoral Dissertation, (School of Human Evolution and Social Change, Arizona State University, 2013).

agropastoral practices constitute the first quantifiable dimension in modeling to assess the environmental impacts of farming, grazing, and other types of natural resource use. In terms of agricultural practices, agents aim to produce surplus from a typical plot within the agricultural catchment of the site. The agricultural return depends on the type of grain, precipitation, soil depth, and the fertility of soil. On the other hand, grazing activities focus on producing a high amount of fodder near the village. The critical variables in calculating the grazing returns are the type of vegetation, the area of the grazing plot, and the edible biomass. In terms of other types of resource use, gathering firewood is considered to be a significant economic activity in MML.[13] The agents gather firewood by clearing plots for agriculture and they target patches with dense woody material. The environmental impacts of the above-mentioned economic activities are translated into an amount of cereals grown and an amount of biomass removed from plots, which are expressed in caloric values.

The second variable simulated in MML is the population dynamics. MML focuses on simulating the impact of anthropogenic activities on the productivity of land under human use (e.g., soil quality, erosion-deposition) and how anthropogenic activities affect the sustainability of population in the long-term. Since the caloric requirement for an average male and female are known, MML uses the results of the simulations that focus on the economy and convert them into annual caloric calculations.[14] Based on these calculations, birth becomes more likely in the case of overproduction and death becomes more likely in the case of underproduction while a steady state exists if there is no significant change in the annual caloric gain.

The third variable that MML simulates is the changes in the surface processes within the immediate research area, which mainly focuses on the erosion-deposition rates. Using precipitation (R-factor), soil erodibility (K-factor), and land cover (C-factor) as a measure of how well the vegetation may keep soil in place, the model calculates slope and curvature at a given spot and then erodes-deposits sediment in cells.[15] These calculations are based on the unique hydrology of each area that would result in reconstructing the local histories of surface processes through time.

---

[13] Ibid.
[14] Ibid.
[15] Ibid.

4. Conclusion

The models, both ABMs and stochastic models, represent new approaches in interpreting multifaceted, interdisciplinary data in archaeology. The use of models and the mind-set behind modeling not only allow researchers to display the long-term interactions among numerous variables but they also enable us to examine the emergent properties, which only surface in time and as a result of interaction between variables. Observing these qualities, experimenting with the variables that have greater significance for humans, socio-ecological research advances by developing a better and more complete understanding about how human societies made decisions and how the results of these decisions impacted them in the long-term. Consequently, it is possible to discuss the sustainability of ancient economic and social practices in specific spatial and temporal contexts.

A Keyword Search Engine for Historical Ottoman Documents

Pınar Duygulu and Damla Arifoğlu

Abstract

In this study, a keyword search system is presented for the easy indexing and retrieval of historical Ottoman documents by matching the visual shapes of words. With the help of this system, one would be able to search any keyword through thousands of documents in a fully automatic manner. Firstly, given a document collection, it is pre-processed by a binarization method, and small noises are cleaned by removing connected components smaller than a predefined threshold. Then, the pages are segmented into lines by a run-length smoothing algorithm. Words are then manually extracted and represented by patch-based and column-based features. The similarity between words is calculated by the Euclidean distance of feature vectors and words are ready to be matched based on a threshold of their similarity. An indexing and retrieval schema is provided for all words in the collection so that a user can search keywords like a search engine and retrieve all documents related to that keyword. Our experiments on an Ottoman collection show promising results for both intra- and cross-document word retrieval schemes.

1. Introduction

The Ottoman Empire, which lasted for more than 6 centuries (1299-1922) and spread over 3 continents, was one of the most powerful states of its time. More than 150 million historical documents produced constitute a large heritage and attract the interest of scholars from many disciplines such as history, literary studies, sociology and from many different countries. Although Ottoman is not a currently spoken language, many researchers are interested in accessing the archived material since the Ottomans shaped the history of the old world for several countries and left a remarkable legacy behind. In this marvelous heritage, there are huge collections of documents that are currently preserved in the archives, libraries, museums and private collections of almost forty nations, constituting an important part of the world's memory.

While the Ottoman Empire is known as one of the most powerful and significant forces in its era, the Ottoman literature is almost invisible to the world[1] and until recently, access to historical documents was provided only by manual indexing which can be considered costly because an excessive amount of human effort is required. Recently, digital environments have become available for keeping historical documents in image format. On the other hand, access to these historical texts is severely limited. The increasing demand to access these archives makes automatic retrieval and recognition of these documents crucial.

---

[1] Walter G. Andrews, Najaat Black and Mehmet Kalpaklı, *Ottoman lyric poetry: An anthology* (Seattle: University of Washington Press, 2006).

Recent attempts in the digitization of the archival material are important for the preservation and electronic access of these documents; however, there is a lack of resources for analysis and translation except a few recent attempts.[2] As stated by Walter G. Andrews, "Achieving a statistically accurate picture of the vocabulary of the Ottoman lyrics would demand a vast recording, sorting and counting project, which, although far from impossible using modern computer techniques, would require resources beyond what is currently available".[3] Most of the Ottoman documents not only contain text, but also drawings, miniatures, portraits, signs and ink smears which have also historical value and relation with the corresponding text, so most of the historical documents are kept in image format. Unfortunately, many documents are in poor condition due to age or being recorded in manuscript format. Thus, accessing these documents by their visual content is important. In recent years, as an alternative to Optical Character Recognition (OCR) techniques, word spotting methods have been proposed for the easy access and navigation of these documents; and this is the starting point of our study.

2. Challenges

However, it is challenging to work on Ottoman documents, because a word may be composed of one or more sub-words, a sub-word is a connected group of characters or letters, which may be meaningful individually or only meaningful when it comes together with other sub-words. This means there are inter-word gaps as well as intra-word gaps, and it is not easy to decide

---

[2] Esra Ataer and Pinar Duygulu, "Retrieval of ottoman documents," in *Proceedings of the 8th ACM International workshop on Multimedia Information retrieval* (New York: NY ACM, 2006), 155–162; Esra Ataer and Pinar Duygulu, "Matching ottoman words: An image retrieval approach to historical document indexing," in *Proceedings of the 6th ACM International conference on Image and Video Retrieval* (New York: NY ACM, 2007), 341–347; Ethem Fatih Can, Pinar Duygulu, Fazli Can and Mehmet Kalpakli, "Redif extraction in handwritten Ottoman literary texts," in *Proceedings of the 20th International Conference on Pattern Recognition* (Istabul: Curran, 2010); Ethem Fatih Can and Pinar Duygulu, "A line-based representation for matching words in historical manuscripts," *Pattern Recognition Letters* 32, no. 8(2011): 1126–1138; Damla Arifoglu, Pinar Duygulu, Mehmet Kalpakli, "Segmentation of Historical Documents using Cross Document Word Matching", *Pattern Analysis and Applications* 19 (2016): 647–663.; Damla Arifoglu, *Historical Document Analysis based on Word Matching Idea*, M.Sc. Thesis (Bilkent University, Ankara, 2011); Damla Arifoglu and Pinar Duygulu, "Word Retrieval in Ottoman Documents," in *2011 IEEE 19th Signal Processing and Communications Applications Conference (SIU)* (IEEE, 2011), 526-529; Ismet Yalniz, Ismail Altingovde, U. Gudukbay, Ozgur Ulusoy, "Integrated segmentation and recognition of connected Ottoman script," *Optical Engineering* 48, no. 11(2009): 1–12; Ismet Yalniz, Ismail Altingovde, U. Gudukbay, Ozgur Ulusoy, "Ottoman archives explorer: a retrieval system for digital Ottoman archives," *Journal on Computing and Cultural Heritage* 2, no. 3(2009): 1–20; Hande Adiguzel, Emre Sahin, and Pinar Duygulu, (2012), "A Hybrid for Line Segmentation in Handwritten Documents,", in *2012 International Conference on Frontiers in Handwriting Recognition (ICFHR)*, (IEEE, 2012).
[3] Walter G. Andrews, *Poetry voice, society song: Ottoman lyric poetry.* (Seattle and London: University of Washington Press, 1985).

whether a gap refers to an intra-word gap or an inter-word gap in Ottoman (see Figure 1 and Figure 2).[4]

Figure 1: Sample Ottoman documents with various writing styles and fonts. As can be seen, it is not easy to segment and recognize words.

Ottoman writing is a connected and cursive script that is actually a subset of the Arabic alphabet. Also, it has additional vocals and characters from the Persian and Turkish scripts.[5] Ottoman is very different from languages such as English in which there are explicit word boundaries. In Ottoman, a word may be composed of many individual sub-words and a space does not always correspond to a word boundary. A word can even be comprised of one, two or more sub-words, without an explicit indication of where a word ends and another begins. Another difficulty is that Ottoman characters may take different shapes according to their position in the sentence; being at the beginning, middle, and end as well as in the isolated form.[6] Most of the

---

[4] A. Ozturk, Silan Gunes and Y. Ozbay, "Multifont Ottoman character recognition," in *Proceedings of the 7th IEEE International Conference on Electronics Circuits and Systems (ICECS)* (IEEE, 2000), 945-949

[5] Niyazi Kılıc, Pelin Gorgel, Osman Nuri Ucan and Ahmet Kala, "Multifont Ottoman character recognition using support vector machine," in *Proceedings of the Third International Symposium on Control Communication and Signal Processing (ISCCSP'08)* (IEEE, 2008), 328-333.

[6] Arifoglu, Duygulu, Kalpakli, "Segmentation of Historical Documents using Cross Document Word Matching," 647–663.; Arifoglu, *Historical Document Analysis based on Word Matching Idea*; Arifoglu and Duygulu, "Word Retrieval in Ottoman Documents," 526-529.

characters are only distinguished by adding dots and zigzags (called diacritics), which makes the discrimination harder.

Figure 2: Examples of Ottoman words. As can be seen, Ottoman words are comprised of sub-words

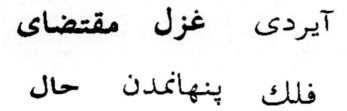

3. Related Work

In recent years, interest in preserving and accessing historical documents has increased. While indexing and retrieval of these documents are desired, applying ordinary optical character recognition (OCR) techniques on them is nearly impossible due to deformations caused by faded ink or stained paper and noise because of deterioration.[7] Word spotting techniques have been proposed as an alternative for easy access and navigation of historical documents.[8]

In word spotting literature, dynamic time warping (DTW) is one of the most commonly used methods to calculate the similarity of words.[9] DTW can tolerate spatial variations unlike other

---

[7] A. Marcolino, V. Ramos, M. Ramalho, J.C. Pinto, "Line and word matching in old documents," in *Proceedings of the 5th Iberoamerican Symposium on Pattern Recognition* (CIARP, 2000), 123–125

[8] R. Manmatha, C. Han, E. Riseman, "Word spotting: a new approach to indexing handwriting," in *Proceedings of IEEE Computer Society Conference on Computer Vision and Pattern Recognition* (IEEE, 1996), 631–63; R. Manmatha, Chengfeng Han, E. M. Riseman, W. B. Croft, "Indexing handwriting using word matching," in *Proceedings of the first ACM international conference on Digital libraries* (New York: ACM, 1996), pp. 151–159; T. M. Rath, R. Manmatha, V. Lavrenko, "A search engine for historical manuscript images," in *Proceedings of the 27th annual international ACM SIGIR conference on research and development in information retrieval* (New York: ACM, 2004), 369–376.

[9] Manmatha Han, Riseman, Croft, "Indexing handwriting using word matching," 151–159; Rath, Manmatha, Lavrenko "A search engine for historical manuscript images," 369–376; C. D. Brina, R. Niels, A. Overvelde, G. Levi, W. Hulstijn, "Dynamic time warping: a new method in the study of poor handwriting," *Human Movement Science* 27, no. 2(2008): 242–255; Alicia Fornes, Joseph Llados, Gemma Sanchez (2008) "Old handwritten musical symbol classification by a dynamic time warping based method," in *Graphics Recognition. Recent Advances and New Opportunities*, eds. W. Liu, J. Llados, J.M. Ogier (Berlin, Heidelberg: Springer, 2008), 51–60; Josep Lados, Marcal Rusinol, Alicia Fornes, David Fernandes, Anjan Dutta, "On the influence of word representations for handwritten word spotting in historical documents," *International Journal of Pattern Recognition and Artificial Intelligence* 26, no. 5 (2012); Ralph Niels, *Dynamic time warping: an intuitive way of handwriting recognition.* Master thesis (Radboud University Nijmegen, 2004).

methods such as XOR, Euclidean Distance Mapping, Sum of Squared Differences.[10] Alternative to the methods matching words based on whole images or profile-based features,[11] recently other features are also experimented, including word contours,[12] gradients,[13] shape context descriptors,[14] Harris corner detector outputs,[15] line segments,[16] and interest points.[17] In several works,[18] the problem of writing style variations in multi-writer datasets is tackled, but these studies generally require isolated words. In a recent study,[19] a method based on character HMMs is proposed as an alternative to template-based methods. These studies are inspired by the cognitive studies that have observed the human tendency to read a word as a whole[20] and generally use the image properties of a word to match it against other words.

In some studies[21] segmentation of Ottoman documents is studied by a word matching scheme and after column-based features are calculated, words are compared by using Dynamic Time Warping method. Matching is done in a cross-document word matching sense to segment

---

[10] T.M. Rath, S. Kane, A. Lehman, E. Partridge, R. Manmat, "Indexing for a digital library of George Washington's manuscripts: a study of word matching techniques," *Center for Intelligent Information Retrieval*, UMassAmherst, ciir.cs.umass.edu/pubfiles/mm-36.pdf, (accessed, January 24, 2020).
[11] T. Rath, R. Manmatha, "Word image matching using dynamic time warping", in *Proceedings of IEEE Conference on Computer Vision and Pattern Recognition* (IEEE: 2003), 521–527.
[12] T. N. Adamek, A. Smeaton, "Word matching using single closed contours for indexing handwritten historical documents," International Journal on Document Analysis and Recognition 9 (2007): 153–165.
[13] Y. Leydier, A. Ouji, F. LeBourgeois, H. Emptoz, "Towards an omnilingual word retrieval system for ancient manuscripts," *Pattern Recognition* 42, no. 9(2009): 2089–2105; J. A. Rodriguez-Serrano, F. Perronnin, "Handwritten word- spotting using hidden Markov models and universal vocabularies," *Pattern Recognition* 42, no. 9(2009): 2106–2116; S. N. Srihari, G. R. Ball, "Language independent word spotting in scanned documents," in *Digital Libraries: Universal and Ubiquitous Access to Information. Proceedings of the 11th International Conference on Asian Digital Libraries*, eds. George Buchanan, Masood Masoodian, Sally Jo Cunningham (Berlin, Heidelberg: Springer, 2008), 134–143; B. Zhang, S. N. Srihari, C. Huang, "Word image retrieval using binary features," *Document Recognition Retrieval* 9, no. 1(2003): 45–53.
[14] J. Llados, P. Pratim-Roy, J. A. Rodriguez, G. Sanchez, "Word spotting in archive documents using shape contexts," in *Proceedings of the 3rd Iberian conference on Pattern Recognition and Image Analysis*, Part II, eds. Joan Marti, Jose Miguel Benedi (Berlin, Heidelberg: Springer, 2007), 290–297.
[15] J. L. Rothfeder, S. Feng, T. M. Rath (2003) "Using corner feature correspondences to rank word images by similarity," *Computer Vision and Pattern Recognition Workshop (CVPRW3)* (IEEE, 2003), 30–36.
[16] Can, Duygulu, Can and Kalpakli, "Redif extraction in handwritten Ottoman literary texts"; Can and Duygulu, "A line-based representation for matching words in historical manuscripts," 1126–1138.
[17] Ataer and Duygulu, "Matching ottoman words: An image retrieval approach to historical document indexing," 341–347; Can, Duygulu, Can and Kalpakli, "Redif extraction in handwritten Ottoman literary texts."
[18] M. Bulacu, L. Schomaker, "Text-independent writer identification and verification using textural and allographic features," *IEEE Transactions on Pattern Analysis and Machine Intelligence* 29(2007): 701–717; N. R. Howe, T. M. Rath, R. Manmatha, "Boosted decision trees for wordrecognition in handwritten document retrieval," in *Proceedings of the 28th annual international ACM SIGIR conference on Research and development in information retrieval* (New York, ACM, 2005), 377–383; Rath, Manmatha, Lavrenko, "A search engine for historical manuscript images,"369–376; Adamek, Smeaton, "Word matching using single closed contours for indexing handwritten historical documents," 153–165.
[19] A. Fischer, A. Keller, V. Frinken, H. Bunke, "Lexicon-free handwritten word spotting using character HMMs," *Pattern Recognition Letters* 33(2012): 934–942.
[20] Srihari, Ball, "Language independent word spotting in scanned documents," 134–143.
[21] Arifoglu, Duygulu, Kalpakli, "Segmentation of Historical Documents using Cross Document Word Matching," 647–663.; Arifoglu, *Historical Document Analysis based on Word Matching Idea*.

documents into words. In a previous study by these authors (Arifoglu and Duygulu)[22], a word retrieval approach in a printed Ottoman document is presented by exploiting Dynamic Time Warping and Shape Context methods.

4. Proposed Method

Figure 3: Overview of proposed approach.

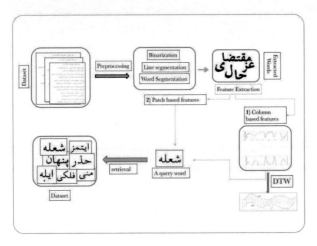

The proposed method consists of the following steps (see Figure 3). 1) After the dataset is constructed, pre-processing is done. 2) Lines and words are extracted. 3) Features are calculated for each word. 4) Word distances are calculated. 5) Query keywords are searched in the collection.

4. 1. Dataset

In this study, we choose to study two versions (10 pages) of Layla and Majnun divan, a famous work of Fuzuli, a poet who lived in the 16th century. The first version is a machine-printed book[23] which is in good quality and is not noisy or degraded. There is no deformation on the pages and is relatively easy to retrieve similar keywords in it. The second dataset is nearly 100 years older and is a lithograph version.[24] It is not of good quality as it has some deformations and noise. Datasets were obtained by scanning books with a resolution of 300x300 and they were manually

---

[22] Arifoglu and Duygulu, "Word Retrieval in Ottoman Documents," 526-529.
[23] Muhammed Nur Dogan, *Mecnun ve Leyla Dilinden Şiirler* (Istanbul: Enderun Kitabevi, 1997).
[24] Anonymous, *Külliyat-ı Divan-ı Fuzuli* (Hursid Matbaası, Istanbul, 1897).

labeled word by word to construct a ground truth version to test our method (see Figure 4). In the first dataset, there are 1379 words in total and 693 of them are unique. In the second dataset, there are 1175 words and 703 of them are unique.

Figure 4: Examples from our dataset. The first image is an example from the first dataset, the second one is an example from the second dataset and the third one is the second page's binarized version. As can be seen, in the second data set, matching words are relatively easier since it is a printed version and all words are in the same font, shape and size.

4.2. Preprocessing

The datasets used in the experiments are relatively clean, therefore we use simple methods for preprocessing. First, the original documents are converted into a gray scale, and they are binarized by Otsu's binarization method.[25] Small noises such as dots and other blobs are cleaned by removing connected components smaller than a predefined threshold (see Figure 4).

4.3. Feature Extraction

In this study, two different sets of features are used: **1)** Patch-based **2)** Column based. As the first feature, a given word is divided into patches and then a histogram of oriented gradients is calculated for each patch. As the second feature, many geometric features are extracted for each column of a given word image.

---

[25] N. Otsu, "A Threshold Grey Scale Histogram," *IEEE Transactions on System, Man and Cybernetics* 9(1979): 62-66.

4.3.1. Patch-based features

These features are extracted based on patches. Given a word image, it is divided into $n \times n$ patches and gradient orientations are calculated in each patch and quantized into k bins. In the end, for a word image, $n \times n \times k$ features are extracted.[26]

4.3.2. Column-based features

Firstly, 9 geometric features known as FKI features[27] are extracted as the following: These features are calculated for each column of a given word image.

- Number of black pixels in the column
- Center of gravity of the column
- Second order moment of the column
- Position of the upper contour in the column
- Position of the lower contour in the column
- Orientation of the upper contour in the column
- Orientation of the lower contour in the column
- Number of black-white transitions in the column
- Number of black pixels between upper and lower contour

Secondly, polar features are extracted in the following way. A sliding window circle is moved over columns of a word image and n circles are drawn with radii equally spaced up to the maximum radius r. Then equal m arcs are drawn on circles. In the end, the number of foreground pixels falling into each circle piece is counted.[28]

4.4. Retrieval

In the word retrieval task, given a query word, all other words are matched to it and a dissimilarity score is calculated. A distance threshold is empirically set and candidates that have a distance smaller than that threshold are retrieved.

---

[26] Dalal Navneet and Triggs Bill, "Histograms of Oriented Gradients for Human Detection," in *Proceedings of the 2005 IEEE Computer Society Conference on Computer Vision and Pattern Recognition (CVPR'05)* (IEEE, 2005).
[27] U. V. Marti and H. Bunke, "Using a statistical language model to improve the performance of an HMM-based cursive handwriting recognition system," *International Journal of Pattern Recognition and Artificial Intelligence* 15, no. 1 (2001): 65–90.
[28] F. Alvaro, J.A. Sánchez and J. M. Benedi, "Offline Features for Classifying Handwritten Math Symbols with Recurrent Neural Networks," in *22nd International Conference on Pattern Recognition (ICPR)* (IEEE, 2014), 2944-2949.

Figure 5: A given query keyword is searched in the set of extracted words and related words are retrieved.

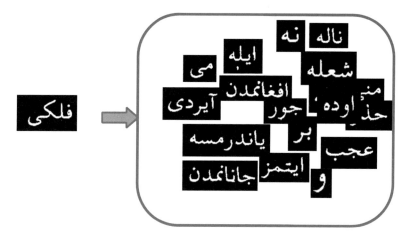

After features are extracted for words, their distance to each other is calculated. When column-based features and polar features are used, the distance is calculated by using the Dynamic Time Warping algorithm[29] (formula 1 and 2) and when the patch-based feature is used, their distance is calculated by Euclidean distance. And then words are retrieved if their distance is smaller than a predefined threshold. In formula 1, i and j are columns of two words and *d* is the distance of those columns, which is calculated by the Euclidean distance of those two column features as in Formula 2. Please refer to the work by Arifoglu, Duygulu. and Kalpakli[30], for more information on DTW matching of column-based features.

$$D(i,j) = min \begin{Bmatrix} D(i,j-1) \\ D(i-1,j) \\ D(i-1,j-1) \end{Bmatrix} + d(x_i, y_i) \quad (1)$$

$$d(A,B) = \sum_{k=1}^{n} d(a_k, b_k) \quad (2)$$

---

[29] Niels, *Dynamic time warping: an intuitive way of handwriting recognition.*
[30] Arifoglu, Duygulu, Kalpakli, "Segmentation of Historical Documents using Cross Document Word Matching," 647–663.; Arifoglu, *Historical Document Analysis based on Word Matching Idea.*

5. Results

Retrieval results are provided for both intra- and inter-documents. In intra-document retrieval, keywords are searched in the document it belongs, while in inter-/cross-document retrieval, keywords are searched in another document rather than the document it belongs. For example in intra-document retrieval, words of the first dataset are searched in the first dataset and words in the second dataset are searched in the second dataset, while in cross-document matching, query words extracted from the first dataset are searched in the second one. Intra-document keyword retrieval is relatively easier than cross-document retrieval since in a document, writing style, the font does not change and the shapes of words are more similar to each other. On the other hand, in cross-document retrieval, where writing styles and fonts differ, word shapes are different from each other, thus matching those words is more challenging. Additionally, this process is more difficult when one of the documents is very old since it will be degraded and noisy.

We use precision and recall values to measure the success of our method (see Formulas 3 and 4):

$$Precision = \frac{Number\ of\ relevant\ words\ that\ are\ retrieved}{Number\ of\ retrieved\ words} \quad (3)$$

$$Recall = \frac{Number\ of\ words\ that\ are\ relevant}{Number\ of\ relevant\ words} \quad (4)$$

Below, we present both intra- and cross-word matching results.

5.1. Intra-Document Retrieval

In this task, after a query keyword is entered, that word is searched in the document it is extracted from. In this experiment, all extracted words are treated as query keywords and matched to other words and the best candidates are retrieved. Given a query, after calculating the matching distance to all other words, strong candidates are retrieved based on a matching threshold. Retrieval results are reported in Table 1 when a patch-based feature is used for different threshold values and for different window and bin sizes. Highest precision is about 93% with a recall value of 70%. Also, in Table 2, results are reported when column-based features are used.

Table 1: word retrieval results on the first dataset with different thresholds when the HoG feature is used, results with different window and bin sizes are reported as well as, for example, 3x3x4 means, 3x3 patches with 4 bins are used, as it can be seen, when precision is increased, recall decreases.

Patch and bin size	TH	Precision	Recall
3x3x4	0.3	97.0149	53.7089
3x3x4	0.4	86.0438	65.1801
3x3x4	0.45	78.3145	70.3951
3x3x4	0.5	68.7580	76.7291
3x3x4	0.6	49.3491	85.1485
4x4x4	0.7	93.6416	70.3402
4x4x4	0.75	91.2630	73.0599
4x4x4	0.8	87.7455	75.1778

Table 2: word retrieval results on the first dataset with different thresholds when column-based results are used. The best result achieved has a precision value of 91.1 and a recall value of 80.83 with a threshold of 0.25.

TH	Precision	Recall
0.25	91.1	80.83
0.4	82.76	88.85
0.45	75.98	89.48
0.5	72.76	90.10

Table 3: Word retrieval results on the second dataset with a different threshold when the HoG features are used. The best result achieved has a precision value of 61.6308 and a recall value of 66.589 with 4x4x4 window and bin sizes.

Patch and bin size	TH	Precision	Recall
3x3x4	0.04	63.3948	60.3007
3x3x4	0.035	77.3269	53.2677
3x3x4	0.034	79.9638	51.6699
4x4x4	0.05	77.3126	59.379

4x4x4	0.08	61.6308	66.589
5x5x5	0.15	73	68

Table 4: Word retrieval results on the second dataset with different thresholds when column-based features are used. The best result achieved has a precision value of 90.74 and a recall value of 61.75 with a threshold 0.3.

TH	Precision	Recall
0.4	86.53	76.00
0.45	82.22	80.98
0.3	**90.74**	**61.75**

In Table 3, word retrieval results are reported when HoG features are used and in Table 4, word retrieval results are reported when column-based features are used. As it can be seen in Tables 1-4, word retrieval results are better on the first dataset since that dataset is a printed version and same words have same shapes and they are not deformed, but the second dataset is a lithography version and it is degraded, thus word matching is more challenging. Moreover, we see that column-based features are more helpful to retrieve the words since they can easily capture variances in the shapes of words.

5.2 Cross-Document Word Retrieval

In this experiment words extracted from the first dataset are searched in the second dataset. This matching procedure is more difficult compared to the first task since different documents have different writing styles and character fonts. Cross-document matching results are reported in Table 5. As can be seen, cross-document word retrieval results are not as good as intra-document word retrieval results. The reason for this is that matching two words with different shapes, fonts and styles in different documents is not easy and more robust features are needed to cover these kinds of variances.

Table 5: cross-document word retrieval results. Words extracted from the first dataset are used as queries and searched in the set of words extracted from the second dataset. The best result obtained has a precision value of 50% and a recall value of 46% with HoG features.

HoG Feature	TH	Precision	Recall
5x5x5	4.73	50.1127	46.068

4x4x4	4.5	35	35
6x6x5	5	59	38
Column-based features	1.2	23.65	25.16

6. Conclusion

In this study, we proposed a keyword search scheme in Ottoman documents. Word retrieval results are provided for inter-documents as well as intra-documents. Although cross-document keyword retrieval success rates are not as high as intra-document results, they are still promising. We showed that word retrieval between different versions of documents is possible.

7. Future work

In future work, we are planning to work with more robust features to match cross-document words which will make different writing styles matching possible. Moreover, we are planning to carry the word retrieval task to handwriting documents in which cross-document word matching is more challenging.

Notes on the Contributors

Himmet Murat Güvenç is a Professor at Kadir Has University in Istanbul and Director of Istanbul Studies Center. His research focuses on urbanism and Turkish urban history. He is the author of *Tracing Istanbul* (2009) and *Emlak Bankası: 1926-1998* (2000).

Mustafa Erdem Kabadayı is currently an Associate Professor at Koç University in Istanbul. His research interests include data analysis and the economic and social history of the late Ottoman Empire and the Republic of Turkey. He is the principal investigator within the ERC-project *Industrialisation and Urban Growth from the mid-nineteenth century Ottoman Empire to Contemporary Turkey in a Comparative Perspective, 1850-2000*, based at Koç University. He is the co-editor of *Popular Protest and Political Participation in the Ottoman Empire. Studies in Honor of Suraiya Faroqhi* (2011) and *Unfreie Arbeit. Ökonomische und kulturgeschichtliche Perspektiven* (2007).

Dr. Pınar Duygulu-Şahin is a member of faculty at Bilkent University in Ankara (Computer Engineering). She is co-director of RETINA Vision and Learning Group. Her research focuses on computer vision and multimedia data mining.

Dr. Elma Korić, (University of Sarajevo) is a senior researcher at the Oriental Institute (University of Sarajevo). Her research interests include Bosnian history under the Ottomans and historical GIS. She is the author of *Životni put prvog beglerbega Bosne: Ferhad-paša Sokolović (1530-1590)* (2015).

Dr. Dino Mujadžević is a researcher at the Humboldt University Berlin. His research focuses include the history of the Ottoman Balkans, Socialist Yugoslavia, contemporary Islam in Croatia and pro-Turkish discourses in Bosnia and Herzegovina. He is the author of *Bakarić* (2011) and *Asserting Turkey in Bosnia: Turkish Foreign Policy and Pro-Turkish Activism in Bosnia* (2017).

Dr. Siegfried Gruber is a researcher at the Department for History and Anthropology of the Southeast Europe of Graz University. His research interests include historical demography and data analysis. He is a co-author of *Historische Anthropologie im südöstlichen Europa. Eine Einführung* (2003).

Dr. Bülent Arıkan is an Assistant Professor at the Department of Ecology and Evolution, Eurasia Institute of Earth Sciences (Istanbul Technical University). His research interests include anthropological, cultural and environmental archaeology in combination with data-based researched methods.

Dr. Franz-Benjamin Mocnik is an Assistant Professor at the University of Twente and his interests include the application of GIS methods for social research.

Dr. Damla Arifoğlu is a research fellow at the University College of London with an interest in computer vision and machine learning.

Dr. Michael Połczyński is a lecturer at the history department of Georgetown University. His research concentrates on the application of the historical GIS for the history of Ottoman-Polish relations.

Dr. Sotirios Dimitriadis, received his Ph.D. from the School of Oriental and African Studies. He focuses on the application of GIS for the research of the history of Greece under Ottomans.

Lisa Maria Teichmann is a Ph.D. student at McGill University and her research concentrates on the computer-assisted analysis of modern Turkish literature.

Studies on Language and Culture in Central and Eastern Europe (SLCCEE)

Edited by Christian Voß

Band 1   DINKEL, Jürgen: Maximilian Braun als Südslavist. Eine akademische Biographie (1926-1961). 2009.

Band 2   VOSS, Christian; NAGÓRKO, Alicja (Hrsg.): Die Europäizität der Slawia oder die Slawizität Europas. Ein Beitrag der kultur- und sprachrelativistischen Linguistik. 2009.

Band 3   CHRISTIANS, Dagmar; STERN, Dieter; TOMELLERI, Vittorio S. (Hrsg.): Bibel, Liturgie und Frömmigkeit in der Slavia Byzantina. Festgabe für Hans Rothe zum 80. Geburtstag. 2009.

Band 4   IOANNIDOU, Alexandra; VOSS, Christian (eds.): Spotlights on Russian and Balkan Slavic Cultural History. 2009.

Band 5   TOLIMIR-HÖLZL, Nataša: Bosnien und Herzegowina. Sprachliche Divergenz auf dem Prüfstand. 2009.

Band 6   VOSS, Christian (Hrsg.): EU-Bulgaristik. Perspektiven und Potenziale. Festgabe für Norbert Randow zum 80. Geburtstag. 2009.

Band 7   VOSS, Christian; GOLUBOVIĆ, Biljana (Hrsg.): Srpska lingvistika / Serbische Linguistik. Eine Bestandsaufnahme. 2010.

Band 8   VOSS, Christian (ed.): Ottoman and Habsburg Legacies in the Balkans. Language and Religion to the North and to the South of the Danube River. 2010.

Band 9   VOSS, Christian; TELBIZOVA-SACK, Jordanka: Islam und Muslime in (Südost) Europa im Kontext von Transformation und EU-Erweiterung. 2010.

Band 10 KELLER, Susanne: Diminutiva im balkansprachlichen Übersetzungsvergleich. Eine Untersuchung am Beispiel des Romans „Buddenbrooks" von Thomas Mann. 2010.

Band 11 РУМЯНЦЕВ, Олег Є.: Питання національної ідентичності русинів і українців Югославії (1918-1991). 2010.

Band 12 RAJILIĆ, Simone; KERSTEN-PEJANIĆ, Roswitha: Theoretische und empirische Genderlinguistik in Bosnien, Kroatien und Serbien. 2010.

Band 13 ЛИПЧЕВА-ПРАНДЖЕВА, Любка: Битие в превода. Българска литература на немски език (XIX-XX в.). 2010.

Band 14 ČAPO ŽMEGAČ, Jasna; VOSS, Christian; ROTH, Klaus (eds.): Co-Ethnic Migrations Compared. Central and Eastern European Contexts. 2010.

Band 15 GIESEMANN, Gerhard; ROTHE, Hans (Hrsg.): Schulbildung und ihre Weiterbildung. Gedenkband zum 100. Geburtstag von Alfred Rammelmeyer. 2010.

Band 16 TOMELLERI, Vittorio S.; TOPADZE, Manana; LUKIANOWICZ, Anna (Hrsg.): Languages and Cultures in the Caucasus. Papers from the International Conference "Current Advances in Caucasian Studies" Macerata, January 21-23, 2010. 2011.

Band 17 MENZEL, Birgit; HAGEMEISTER, Michael; GLATZER ROSENTHAL, Bernice (Hg): The New Age of Russia. Occult and Esoteric Dimensions. 2012.

Band 18 SIKIMIĆ, Biljana; HRISTOV, Petko; GOLUBOVIĆ, Biljana (Hrsg.): Labour Migrations in the Balkans. 2012.

Band 19 STERN, Dieter: Tajmyr-Pidgin-Russisch. Kolonialer Sprachkontakt in Nordsibirien. 2012.

Band 20 KERSTEN-PEJANIĆ, Roswitha; RAJILIĆ, Simone; VOSS, Christian (Hrsg.): Doing Gender – Doing the Balkans. Dynamics and Persistence of Gender Relations in Yugoslavia and the Yugoslav successor states. 2012.

Band 21   BOBRIK, Marina (Hrsg.): Slavjanskij Apostol. Istorija teksta i jazyk. 2013.
Band 22   BESTERS-DILGER, Juliane (Hg.): Kommentierter Apostolos. Textedition und Kommentar zur Edition. (= Die großen Lesemenäen des Metropoliten Makarij Uspenskij Spisok.) Unter Mitarbeit von V. Halapats, N. Kindermann, E. Maier, A. Rabus. 2014.
Band 23   ILIĆ, Marija: Discourse and Ethnic Identity. The Case of the Serbs from Hungary. 2014.
Band 24   HLAVAC, Jim; FRIEDMANN, Victor (Hrsg.): On Macedonian Matters: from the Partition and Annexation of Macedonia in 1913 to the Present. A Collection of Essays on Language, Culture and History. 2015.
Band 25   HLAVAC, Jim: Three generations, two countries of origin, one speech community: Australian-Macedonians and their language(s). 2016.
Band 26   HEGEDŰS, Rita; GÖRBE, Tamás (eds.): Small Language, what now?. The Theory and Practice of Functional Linguistics in Teaching "Minor" Languages. 2016.
Band 27   TYRAN, Katharina Klara: Identitäre Verortungen entlang der Grenze. Verhandlungen von Sprache und Zugehörigkeit bei den Burgenländischen Kroaten. 2015.
Band 28   LORMES, Miriam: „Among good musicians there has never been an ethnical divide". Interkulturalität und politisches Engagement in Musikerdiskursen im postjugoslawischen Makedonien. 2013.
Band 29   GLANC, Tomáš und VOSS, Christian (Hrsg): Konzepte des Slawischen. 2016.
Band 30   GEHRKE, Stefan: Jedwabne und die Folgen. Eine semantische Analyse der Debatte über Juden in der polnischen Presse 2001–2008. 2018.
Band 31   STERN, Dieter; NOMACHI, Motoki; BELIĆ, Bojan (eds.): Linguistic regionalism in eastern europe and beyond. Minority, Regional and Literary Microlanguages. In memoriam Jiří Marvan. 2018.
Band 32   RAJILIĆ, Simone: Weiblichkeit im Serbischen. Weibliche Genderspezifizierungen zwischen Gewalt und Widerstand. 2019.
Band 33   SCHELLER-BOLTZ, Dennis: Grammatik und Ideologie. Feminisierungsstrategien im Russischen und Polnischen aus Sicht der Wissenschaft und Gesellschaft. 2020.
Band 34   FRIEDMAN, Victor A: Macedonia and its Questions. Origins, Margins, Ruptures and Continuity. 2020.
Band 35   MUJADŽEVIĆ, Dino (ed.): Digital Historical Research on Southeast Europe and the Ottoman Space. 2021.
Band 36   DANOVA, Tsvetomira: John of Damascus' Marian Homilies in Mediaeval South Slavic Literatures. 2020.

www.peterlang.com